SILVER SCREEN, HASIDIC JEWS

SILVER SCREEN, HASIDIC JEWS

The Story of an Image

SHAINA HAMMERMAN

INDIANA UNIVERSITY PRESS

This book is a publication of

Indiana University Press
Office of Scholarly Publishing
Herman B Wells Library 350
1320 East 10th Street
Bloomington, Indiana 47405 USA

iupress.indiana.edu

© 2018 by Shaina Hammerman
All rights reserved

No part of this book may be reproduced or utilized in any form or by any means, electronic or mechanical, including photocopying and recording, or by any information storage and retrieval system, without permission in writing from the publisher.

The paper used in this publication meets the minimum requirements of the American National Standard for Information Sciences—Permanence of Paper for Printed Library Materials, ANSI Z39.48–1992.

Manufactured in the
United States of America

Cataloging information is available from the Library of Congress.

ISBN 978-0-253-03168-6 (hdbk.)
ISBN 978-0-253-03169-3 (pbk.)
ISBN 978-0-253-03170-9 (e-bk.)

1 2 3 4 5   23 22 21 20 19 18

CONTENTS

Acknowledgments vii
Introduction: When Jews Are Like Jews xi

1. The Yarmulke beneath the Cowboy Hat: Signifying Jewishness in the Hasidic Western   1

2. The Jewish Type and "le juif typique": Typologies of Jewishness in *Les aventures de Rabbi Jacob*   26

3. Hard-Core Jews: Woody Allen's Religious Women and Men   53

4. *Cinéma judéité*: Projecting Jewish-Muslim Romance   77

5. What Lies beneath the Wig: *Hester Street* and Adaptation   104

   Epilogue: Hijab, Habit, and Hasid   132

   Filmography and Bibliography 139
   Index 149

ACKNOWLEDGMENTS

TRADITIONALLY, THIS IS THE PART of the book where the author offers thanks for the support of the various institutions and grants that funded her research. In my case, I can say that this book was reluctantly funded by my husband, Octavio, and no one else.

Fortunately, support comes in many forms that are not monetary. Octavio is first in line for recognition of that kind of sustenance as well. His affection and humor, as well as his challenges to many of this book's most basic premises, made this project better to write and better to read (I hope). I am fortunate to count among my closest supporters some brilliant writers and editors whose wisdom, sharp criticism, and friendship bolstered this project from the very beginning: Helene Wecker, Kara Levy, and Daniela Blei are constant inspirations for me as writers, mothers, and friends. Other close friends, within and outside academia, have provided assistance and most-needed distractions along the way. I thank my talented friend Becky Nelson for assembling the images for this book and designing its beautiful cover. Michelle Scheurich, Lilach Shafir, and Leah Glazer are part of my daily life, even though we don't speak daily. Rachel Rothstein offers me unparalleled camaraderie; even though our lives have taken different paths, I always have the feeling we're in this together. I cobbled together an amazing cohort of colleagues, and I'm grateful to Sarah Cramsey, Nicholas Baer, Erin Corber, and

Lynne Gerber for celebrating my successes with me and bolstering me during difficult moments.

Others in my life nourish me in ways that enable me to write: Coach Ethan Jefferson, Devin Farney, Shannon Lundling, and Claudia Kindler keep me healthy, take care of my family, and challenge me. I want to extend my gratitude to my various San Francisco communities: Little Bear School, the extended Splunk family, and my Shabbat Club friends (especially Deborah Sommers).

This book began as a doctoral dissertation, and I continue to be grateful for the guidance of my committee members. Your insights feature prominently in this book; rest assured, your time was not wasted. Anton Kaes gave me access to the discipline of film analysis, and Martin Jay inaugurated me into the world of European intellectual history. Deena Aranoff is a model of professionalism and showed me what it means to be an excellent teacher. Mitch Hart brought his sense of humor to this project and has done me the incredible honor of making me feel like an equal as his colleague.

I find great joy in writing about my advisor and mentor, Naomi Seidman. She has been a close friend and confidante, but I can find no better way to describe her than as my muse. Even as I sat down to write these acknowledgments, I first opened Naomi's books to see how she'd done it and let her prose inspire mine. Naomi is my favorite writer; she is the person I channel whenever I write. She is the reader I most want to challenge and surprise. I cherish our relationship, and I hope I have made her a little proud.

Speaking of people I hope to make proud, my family has always sustained me, even when they couldn't understand what it is I "do all day." My parents and siblings have challenged me to make my ideas clearer and my arguments more grounded. Along with my nieces and nephews, they keep me aware of what's most important in life. It has been my great fortune to count my sister, Jessica Hammerman, as a colleague and a best friend. Along the way, my brother, Eli, became a colleague, too. I thank my family for their support in this and in all things.

The questions this book poses about national identity and the power of Hasidic imagery originated in my own ambivalence about being Jewish while living in France in the early 2000s. Since then, those questions have gained some urgency, and they are no longer about me at all. Instead, I see the pernicious powers of racism, xenophobia, and sexism bubbling at the surface of both French and American national discourses. This book is meant to expose, in its small way, how the benign world of popular filmmaking and the whims of those with great intentions can come together to reveal exclusionary and potentially dangerous impulses. I am very grateful to Dee Mortensen and the whole team at Indiana University Press for giving me a forum to voice these concerns in what feels like an ominous time in our social and political history.

This book is dedicated to Max and Ariana. Truthfully, an idea became a dissertation and a dissertation became a book because I wanted to model perseverance for you. I wanted to show you that only you define the terms of your success. You don't have to read this book to know that I have found my greatest success in life in being your mom.

INTRODUCTION

WHEN JEWS ARE LIKE JEWS

> Science, history and art have something in common: they all depend on metaphor, on the recognition of patterns, on the realization that something is "like" something else.
>
> —John Lewis Gaddis, *The Landscape of History*

A "SPECIAL REPORT" ON JON STEWART's satirical news program, *The Daily Show*, from March 23, 2011, covered a controversy that was taking place among Jews in Long Island. The conflict and eventual lawsuit revolved around the Orthodox community's attempts to erect an *eruv*, a ritual boundary that enables observant Jews to carry objects in public spaces on the Sabbath. The eruv, as the report explains, is a barely visible line often made of fishing wire and usually suspended near power lines. Once in place, the eruv alters the legal characteristics, but not the aesthetics, of a space. Interviews with Westhampton Beach's Jewish residents, both for and against the eruv, brought to light the conflict's irony and thereby its comic utility for Stewart's show. "It will totally transform the look of this town which I enjoy," pronounces business owner Charles Gottesman. But when comedian-reporter Wyatt Cenac asks what an eruv looks like—with the faux naïveté made famous by *Daily Show* investigative reporters—Gottesman, apparently missing the irony, explains that "it really is almost invisible."

The group who filed suit, Jewish People Opposed to the Eruv, grounds its opposition on the notion of religious infringement on public spaces. But members like Gottesman are candid about their feelings: they are not concerned that the eruv in itself will transform the town's look; instead, they worry that by its barely visible presence, it will turn the seaside village into a Jewish ghetto.[1] As Cenac jokes in his report, Jews like Gottesman fear less the

Figure Intro.1 *The Daily Show* imagines what Westhampton Beach would look like if the eruv legislation passes (screen grab).

"almost invisible" string around the town and more the potential invasion of religious Jewish masses that such a measure invites (fig. Intro.1).

Gottesman and Jews like him fear the hypothetical altering of the town's social aesthetics; but their fears are undermined by the religious Jews featured in Cenac's report. Jeff Weisenfeld, interviewee and member of the Hampton Orthodox Synagogue, does not look like the Jews in *The Daily Show* graphic (fig. Intro.1). Without a beard, hat, or yarmulke, his difference from the other Jews in the segment is indiscernible, marked only by the silver menorah strategically displayed behind him during the interview. Weisenfeld calmly acknowledges that for those not invested in its legal-symbolic powers the eruv is basically imaginary. The eruv is often described as a legal fiction. But the controversial power of the "imaginary" boundary rests in the imaginary Jews it evokes in the minds of its opponents.

The absence of actual Jews who look like the men in *The Daily Show* graphic—from the lawsuit, the town of Westhampton Beach, and *The Daily Show* interviews—gives way to their haunting presence in the minds of those invested in the story either as concerned citizens of the seaside town or as television viewers looking to laugh. Their dark beards, large hats, *peyos* (sidelocks), and black caftans animate intra-Jewish conflicts in the United States, even when the real Jews who wear this clothing are far removed from such debates. In the example of *The Daily Show*, the religious Jewish figure motivates both the lawsuit and the comedian's punch line. Once the garb is emptied of any individual or historical substance, Hasidic attire becomes a site where Jews and non-Jews can experiment with what it means to be Jewish in America or, more broadly, what it means to be American. Cenac, black and not Jewish, concludes his report by sporting a large black hat with a miniature version of an eruv built on it while eating a bacon sandwich. His "eruv hat" pokes fun at both sides of the debate: the Orthodox Jews whose ritual he describes as a "loophole" that allows them to break their own rules; and members of the opposition who fear an aggressive Jewish takeover of their town, marked by ostentatious garments.

The Daily Show's punch line is not only fleeting but wordless, just an image of a crowd of Hasidic Jews. That a black comedian can make this joke operate successfully for an audience of nearly two million nightly viewers speaks to the pervasive power of this type of imagery.[2] Yet, scholars have avoided asking *why* such a gag works and what it means. This scholarly reticence may owe to the image's signifying immediacy: Hasidic garb reads quickly and simply as "Jewish." However, I found in the imagery not transparency but opaqueness—a history of complex and compound meanings that, like the eruv, invite viewers to consider who is in and who is out. This is about Jews and non-Jews, religious Jews and secular Jews, men and women, belonging and alienation.

Identity politics drive *The Daily Show* segment in ways spoken and silent. Jon Stewart's Jewishness and Cenac's blackness, the show's satirical interview style and political skepticism, combine seamlessly with an established history of Hasidic-garbed comedy to produce laughter. But the garb and Cenac's parodic reporting conceal unspoken assumptions that prompt a number of questions: Is this comic device restricted to Hasidic-looking men, or would the joke work if the image foregrounded religious Jewish women? Is the imagery restricted to the comedic realm, or would it also operate in dramatic settings? And does the Hasidic joke work in the same way outside the United States, in other nations with significant Jewish populations? As I compiled Hasidic-looking images from film, television, theater, and photography to consider these questions, trends in multiculturalism that began in the 1970s and were expressed through film emerged as a launching pad for answers.

When I expanded my research outside of the United States, France came to the fore as an equal partner in deploying this imagery during the same period, in spite of the country's divergent relationship with the United States regarding the politics of identity.

This book demonstrates how ethnic imagery in popular film can operate as both a reflection of and a tool for constructing national identities. But this is also a book about how and why specifically Hasidic-garbed Jews appear again and again in these construction projects. These questions were propelled by a curious phenomenon I observed in representations of Jews that located Hasidic-looking men at the top of a hierarchy of Jewish authenticity. But as I worked through that problem, the films laid bare for me—through their manipulation of Jewish imagery—the much larger question of how Arabs, Muslims, black Americans, Native Americans, and women of any color or religious affiliation fit into the more malevolent ethnic hierarchies in France and America.

In these pages, I identify the aesthetic power of imaginary "Hasidic" Jews in film and explore the anxieties and fetishes about the religious Jew that have given rise to this imagery in America and France. *The Daily Show* joke is evocative on its own, but it is by no means novel. Instead, it is a by-product of decades of representation of imagined Hasidic Jews in film, television, theater, and photography. Analyzing popular films from the 1970s through the turn of the century, I unravel the various implications of a shared visual vocabulary in which meaningful questions of Jewish identity and authenticity are played out in what might be easily brushed off as inconsequential slapstick comedies and sexy dramas about forbidden relationships. When Cenac plays inventively with Jewish dress-up by donning an "eruv hat," he is but one recent iteration of a global cinematic tradition in which actors and characters take off and put on Hasidic garb.

Cinema scholar Nathan Abrams laments the potential negative effects of such "one-dimensional portraits" of religious Jews on the uninformed viewer.[3] While the twofold dangers of nostalgia and contempt lurk behind every portrayal of Hasidim on-screen, my task is not to undercut such readings but to understand the contexts from which they emerge. Hasidic imagery does more than pose and respond to questions about Jewishness. When on-screen religious Jews are reduced (or stretched!) to fluid, often empty signifiers within disparate national contexts, the imagery also serves as a vehicle through which to explore broader questions about ethnic belonging, gender, and national identities writ large. In the chapters that follow, I make a claim for why these questions about Hasidic imagery are meaningful and for whom (everyone, as it turns out).

TWO NATIONS, FIVE FILMS

The archive of Hasidic imagery in film continues to grow, but this particular study offers close readings of five discrete films that span thirty years and two continents: *The Frisco Kid* (1979), *Les aventures de Rabbi Jacob* (1973), *Deconstructing Harry* (1997), *La petite Jérusalem* (2005), and *Hester Street* (1975). Each of these films betrays its particular context in ways I find compelling and revelatory. The films' popularity and critical reception, as well as their longevity decades after production, commanded my attention and careful analysis. Countless other films feature Hasidic-looking imagery, such as *The Chosen* (1981) and *L'homme est une femme comme les autres* (1998); but I believe that their themes and outcomes for viewers can be understood in terms of the films I've selected. It is my hope that this book will spark conversations about the role and function of Hasidic garb in those films and in the many that are sure to hit theaters in the future. Beyond such conversations, I hope this transnational analysis and interdisciplinary approach to "reading" film will translate for scholars invested in uncovering how other ethnic, religious, or racial imagery operates on screens.

My choice to interrogate film in France and America, as opposed to, say, literature in Germany and Israel, certainly relates to a long-standing personal interest in the cultures of filmmaking in Paris and Hollywood. But the choice has much more to do with the indisputably central role that cinema plays in popular French and American cultures: as art, entertainment, and capitalist enterprise. Vanessa Schwartz details the interconnected development of "cosmopolitan film culture" between Paris and Hollywood that emerged during the 1950s and 1960s, just before my story of Hasidic representation begins. She explains that scholars continually debate whether the two countries should be examined in light of "mutual exchange" as "sister republics" (terms that easily apply to these nations' revolutionary origins) or whether they ought to be considered in terms of an ongoing cultural rivalry (of the "freedom fries" variety, among other manifestations).⁴ In either case, the United States and France are embroiled in a superpower sibling rivalry, regularly imagining themselves in relation to their overseas adversary/friend.

While the two nations are similar in their use of cinema to disseminate cultural ideas, they differ in their relationships to multiculturalist ideology. Beginning in the 1970s, American popular culture placed a premium on drawing out ethnocultural differences as ethnic pride movements emerged. France, on the other hand, aside from some brief and isolated dabbling with diversity efforts, instituted legal and social regulations that continue to enforce the suppression of multiculturalism in favor of national unity. The fact that indistinguishably similar iterations of the on-screen Jew can promote the American multiculturalist ideal in one film and the French *anti*multiculturalist ideal in another supports my claim for Jewish, especially Hasidic-garbed Jews', symbolic fluidity in film. Other nations with significant Jewish populations (e.g., Germany, Israel, the U.K., and Argentina) produce related outcomes but are fodder for a different study.

Film, unlike the written word, provides a visual (and aural) language for the various conflicts and anxieties experienced by Jews. Unlike stage performances, film has the unique quality of endurance. For example, Jewish-Americans may once have looked to an immigrant film like *Hester Street* as a way to lay claim to their (imagined) Jewish past. Now, the film itself, in addition to the world it represents, is a site for nostalgia. *Les aventures de Rabbi Jacob*, a megahit when it came out in 1973, has been revisited by new generations of French viewers as it is aired on television, explored in documentaries, and remade as a stage musical. The Hasidic garb featured in this film is a site for expressing longings about French identity; revisiting the film forty years later, new audiences create a space to reflect on their station in French society. These same longings are reexamined in a new and dramatic context via the fragile romance between a religious Jewish woman and a Muslim man in *La petite Jérusalem* (2005). *Rabbi Jacob* was also recalled more explicitly when a new ethnic comedy, *Qu'est-ce qu'on a fait au bon Dieu?* (2014), not only reopened themes from the now classic film but also directly sampled music from *Rabbi Jacob*'s famous soundtrack. Rewatching early Woody Allen films or Gene Wilder's *The Frisco Kid* has a similar effect, as the practice of nostalgia for "old" movies becomes a venue for viewers to perform their Jewishness and their Americanness. I found that a thick description of brief filmic moments—a handshake, a sight gag, a close-up—can illuminate a host of national concerns, speaking to the power of film to reflect, comment on, and influence attitudes about national identity. The abundant meanings I find in the details of these films and the Hasidic-looking Jews they feature provide a map for understanding how Jews and non-Jews in France and America conceive of, react to, and perform their identities.

Certainly, secular Jews are represented on-screen with far greater frequency than religious Jews, and very few feature films directly treat the insular world of Hasidim. When Hasidic-like images do appear, it is most often as part of the backdrop of ethnically or racially marked figures that make up the urban landscape of New York, Los Angeles, or Paris. These backdrop Hasidim, Jewish "extras," appear on-screen to indicate Jewishness or Jews-in-general, even when the vast majority of Jews do not look Hasidic at all. Such Hasidic performances require no explanation. The easily identifiable costume and set of associations invite instant recognition (if not an instant chuckle) from the viewer. Conversely, as scholarship on "coding Jewish" demonstrates, secular Jewish characters present the viewer with some assortment of complicated markers or codes for Jewishness, enabling these figures to offer a full, nuanced set of characteristics that may or may not be related to their Jewishness.[5]

But Hasidim on-screen are important precisely because of their presumed decipherability, obviousness, or lack of nuance. These imaginary Jews are *categorically* Jewish: they signify an absolute, indisputable Jewishness as they, like the eruv, delimit the boundaries of what belongs within the category "Jewish." The invisible work performed by the eruv that serves to contain and define the legal bounds of Jewishness appears to be the mirror opposite of the Hasidic garb, which seeks to contain and define Jewish identity in the most visually assertive manner.

WHAT I TALK ABOUT WHEN I TALK ABOUT HASIDIM

A pietistic movement with roots in eighteenth-century eastern Europe, Hasidism gave rise to opposition from at least two sides: the traditional rabbinic legal structures that revolved around organized Torah study and the "enlightened" Jews intent on both escaping the oppressive framework of the traditional Jewish family and integrating into European society. The Haskalah, or Jewish enlightenment, and its proponents (*maskilim*) advocated a

Jewish variation on the European Enlightenment, a belated and often inward-looking critique of Jewish practices. This maskilic (enlightened) critique often came from artists and thinkers raised in Hasidic homes and comprised a variety of sentiments toward Hasidism, including nostalgia, resentment, contempt, and veneration. Hasidic dress is the gateway for playing out these varying attitudes. The origins of the garb are widely disputed and entrenched in myths constructed by secular or non-Hasidic Jews (e.g., the widespread notion that Hasidim dress like Polish nobility) and by actual Hasidim (e.g., the religious basis for the garb). In addition to the mythic origins of Hasidic dress, a variety of styles reflects the diversity of Hasidic sects. A multiplicity of head coverings, coats, and caftans; different lengths and positions for peyos and beards; and even different types of socks distinguish groups that have discrete geographical origins and ideological or religious positions.

The films discussed here fail to capture either the complex history of the Hasidim or their internal diversity, even though I describe the garb the characters wear as "Hasidic." In fact, none of the films I analyze use the label "Hasid" to describe the characters, although various visual and narrative cues point to at least an imagined variety of Hasid. The figures might just as easily be labeled *haredim*, the preferred term used in Israel that encompasses all ultrareligious Jews, including those who are decidedly not Hasidic. To the uninitiated, a non-Hasidic haredi man will be indistinguishable from a Hasid; they will both wear beards, a black suit or caftan, and a hat (e.g., a fedora, a round fur hat called a *shtreimel*, a homburg). The visible difference is even subtler between Hasidic and non-Hasidic haredi women, whose sectarian distinctions are often undetectable. Some of the characters described in these chapters, especially some of the central women figures, might also be described as Orthodox or by the less polite "ultra-Orthodox." These terms, like Hasidic and haredi, capture fervid religious observance, distinct dress codes, and resistance to modern secular culture.

While I occasionally append more generic descriptors like "religious" to the characters in question (such as the Jewish women featured in *Deconstructing Harry*, chapter 3), my choice to frame this book in terms of "the Hasid" is a deliberate—if slippery—one. In fact, there are inaccuracies not just in my language but in the very depictions of these filmic Jews. These slippages, whether intended or not by filmmakers, preserve the Jews portrayed in the films as fantasy figures, fantastic Hasidim. But the "Hasid" label is no mere shortcut.

Instead, it places the Jewish imagery from these late twentieth-century films within the historical network of Hasidic representation. The signifiers of Hasidism in these films—the beards, hats, peyos, and caftans—are remarkably similar to early theatrical portrayals of the "Hasid."

In fact, modern Jewish performance begins with a critique of Hasidism. Abraham Goldfaden, the "father" of modern Jewish theater, describes the birth of the Yiddish stage in Romania in his autobiography.[6] A poem he composed, "The Jolly Hasid," intended as a dramatic critique of Hasidism, took on a vaudevillian air when performed by one of Goldfaden's leading actors, Israel Grodner.[7] According to the autobiography, Grodner decided on the spot to perform the poem—presumably to be delivered in the reserved "German" style with top hat and tails—in Hasidic garb: "Lightning fast, he threw himself into a long caftan, socks and shoes, and a shtreimel, with a pair of long peyos (he only forgot to put on a beard, which didn't make a difference), and, light as air, he leapt onto the stage. . . . He acted crazy, dancing with exaggerated gestures, wildly casting his legs about."[8] This performance was revelatory for Goldfaden, who saw in the audience's delight at Grodner's act a desire to laugh at the Hasid and not just deride him.

Both Grodner's performance and Goldfaden's description of it suggest that not only the garb but also the transformative act of putting it on make the performance resonate. In Grodner's case, as in the films explored in detail here, dressing (and undressing) enables the enlightened or secular Jew to perform his secularity alongside, behind, beneath, or within the Hasid. In the chapters that follow, I argue that the Hasidic garb's signifying power depends upon the simultaneous presence of the non-Hasidic or secular actor who dons it. Grodner's performance, which places the Hasid on the outside (the garb) and the secular Jew on the inside (the actor), is the inverse of the Haskalah's rallying cry, "Be a man in the streets and a Jew at home." The motto, culled from the 1863 Hebrew poem "Awake, My People!" by Russian Jewish poet Yehudah Leib Gordon, implores Jews to synthesize their national identities with their Jewishness, becoming, according to Moses Mendelssohn's legacy, "a loyal Jew, true to one's nation and one's faith."[9]

Regardless of the poem's authorial intent, the phrasing gives way to the kind of identity doubling at the heart of this book. Whether or not it is possible to integrate "one's nation and one's faith," to "be a man [and] a Jew," both Gordon and Mendelssohn before him envisioned these as distinct categories.

In Gordon's biblically inflected Hebrew metaphor, the two categories are divided by the external "streets" (literally, "your goings out") and the internal "home" (literally, "your tent"). When the actor Grodner put on Hasidic garb in 1876, he embodied the failure of the maskilic injunction toward synthesis in his ostentatious performance—in Yiddish—of Jewishness. On the other hand, this mockery of the Hasid was enacted (at least according to Goldfaden's account) in a "Western" style and environment that until then was alien to the Yiddish-speaking world: the theatrical stage.[10] In performing the Hasidic fantasy in a "European" manner, Grodner places himself, Goldfaden, and the cheering audience well outside the realm of the type of Jew Grodner depicts, intimating the success of both integration projects: Jews integrating into European society (via the "European" theatrical mode) and Jews integrating their national identities with their Jewish identities (via the "Jewish" performance).

Only six years after Y. L. Gordon published his epic poem, another maskil, Mikhl Gordon (Yehudah Leib's brother-in-law), published his own version of "Awake, My People!" in Yiddish.[11] Mikhl saw Hasidism as the great inhibitor to the kind of integration his brother-in-law and other maskilim sought. Like Goldfaden's poem "The Jolly Hasid," Mikhl's poem was a scathing satire of Hasidism, but it is easy to imagine a light, parodic performance of the type Grodner gave in full Hasidic garb, especially when we consider the verse about Hasidic dress:

> Start wearing clothes like everyone else wears—
> What do you need with your old granddad's garments?
> No, don't go out on the street in a long robe [*khalat*].
> People shouldn't say, "There goes an Asian [*asiat*]."

The verse that follows continues the poem's appeal for aesthetic change: "Don't speak a language that no one understands. / Your tongue is strange, scrambled, stymied." Writing in Yiddish, he goes on to implore his readers to speak and write in the "state language" (Russian). Just as the effectiveness and pleasure derived from Goldfaden's critique of Hasidism depended on the actor performing it in Hasidic garb, Mikhl Gordon's critique of Hasidism—its outdated manners, clothing, and speech—depended on it being dressed in the very garment it condemns: the Yiddish language.

FROM HASKALAH TO HOLLYWOOD

In these instances from the nineteenth century, a critique of Hasidism is clothed in its embrace. Or the opposite may be true instead (or at the same time): a nostalgic embrace of the Hasid is clothed in a critique of this figure. One hundred years later, when audiences warmly received the films explored here, this cycle of critique and nostalgic appropriation surfaced in a new context and with new motivations. In 1970s Hollywood and Paris, critiquing the imagined Hasid was less urgent. The figure no longer posed a threat to the already successful project of Jewish emancipation from the European ghetto or to the less explicit demands for Protestant conformity in the United States and secular integration in France. Instead, such demands in America had been met with the competing appeal of the so-called ethnic revival. Matthew Frye Jacobson writes of the 1970s that "a wholly new syntax of nationality and belonging" emerged as white ethnics—a term that here applies to American Jews, Irish, Italians, Poles, Greeks, and others—laid claim to a space within an ethnic collectivity. Group solidarity and shared heritage became the norm among working-class whites. Jacobson argues that such involvement in particularistic concerns was the way that these groups "recast American nationality" and redefined what qualifies as American.[12] While mainstream French culture tended to reject multiculturalism in favor of national cohesion, that country was not immune to multiculturalist trends. As I explain in chapter 4, French ideas of diversity, which ultimately placed the highest value on the individual, were exclusionary in ways different from American ones. In both nations, the 1970s inaugurated a period of seeking to explain the value of difference and the ethic of tolerance in relation to national identity. In France, this sometimes meant identifying through protest with victimized populations. In the United States, assimilation took on new meaning during this period. Rather than rendering ethnic specificity invisible, becoming American meant asserting specificity, creating homogeny through difference. Here as before, Jews worked through their anxieties about difference and conformity through performance.

The American films explored here are artifacts of this great multicultural project that began in the 1970s, a project that placed value on (white) ethnic difference. The French films stem from related urges that set out to embolden the high ideal of French individualism by raising up minorities to the level of the white Catholic in France. These undertakings would seem to "rescue" the Hasid for secular Jews while helping them assert their national belonging. But as the films shuffle through minorities, Jewishness (along with blackness, Arabness, Indianness, etc.) becomes trapped by the limiting options presented by the Hasidic garb.

For American Jews, the familiar image of the Hasid featured prominently in their contribution to 1970s ethnocentrism. Laying claim to the figure through film, however, incites many of the same anxieties and contradictions present in earlier theatrical and poetic iterations of the image. In popular film, characters cloaked in Hasidic garb, gestures, and speech patterns—the very substance of the critiques by Y. L. Gordon, M. Gordon, Goldfaden, and Grodner—revisit long-standing questions about the Jew's place in the modern world using a new medium. Finding a place within the multiculture through this limiting and ambivalent imagery enabled Jews to participate in a new form of American nationalism, as Jacobson explains. In fact, according to the requirements of "Ellis Island whiteness," asserting this type of difference was precisely what made Jews into Americans.[13] But if the Hasidic fantasy answers the question, Can you be a Jew *and* an American? A Jew *and* a Frenchman? in the affirmative, it also poses a new question: Can you be a Jew without being *that* kind of Jew? The early twentieth-century work Jews did to shed their visible specificity and blend into the majority Christian populations of France and America deprived Jews of Jewish visibility at the very moment when American nationalism required it and French identity politics finally tolerated it.[14] Beginning in the 1970s and continuing through the turn of the twenty-first century, being American meant laying claim to ethnic "minority" status, cherishing the hyphen that blended various national ancestries with patriotic ideals (e.g., Polish-American, Italian-American, Irish-American, Jewish-American). France's more restricted approach to multiculturalism made space for a charming vision of Jewishness in the guise of the Hasid—so long as this figure remained visibly detectable and geographically constrained.

Rather than being a Jew at home and a man on the street, Jews are obliged by multiculturalism to be Jews everywhere. The response to this obligation was not *becoming* Hasidic but *performing* Hasidic. In certain ways, these options are equal in their extremity. The two-faced imagery that locates the secular and Hasidic Jew on a single body also restricts Jewishness to two types: secular and Hasidic, "man" and "Jew." When the secular Jew performs in Hasidic garb, the two categories are presented as both overlapping and mutually exclusive.

One of the most famous depictions of Jews on-screen is also one of the most important for cinematic history: 1927's *The Jazz Singer*, a technological pioneer for its use of synchronized sound. The film is about a man torn between his predetermined path as a cantor in his father's synagogue and his dream of singing jazz on Broadway. He ultimately chooses the stage but is able to do so unambivalently only after his father passes away. If a film like *The Jazz Singer* is about the fantasy of Jewish integration, then *The Frisco Kid*, along with the other films discussed here, participates in signaling the death of that fantasy and its replacement with its polar opposite: the fantastic Hasid. This figure's Jewishness is plainly, permanently, and proudly marked. His external visibility signifies his incontestable internal Jewishness.

In France, the public contended with their complicity in the Nazi genocide on-screen through haunting, controversial documentary and by embracing the charming Hasidic figure as a comic device. Reifying the Hasidic fantasy in France, especially in *Rabbi Jacob*, in which the Hasidic garb is worn by a confirmed antisemite, distances postwar French men and women from their crimes of complicity as the antisemite becomes a harmless joke of a character and a person capable of redemption from his racist sins. Abrogating France's guilt through cinematic depictions of charming Hasidim has the additional outcome of breeding Jewish ethnocentrism, not so distant from the brand observed at this time in the United States (and often inspired by a love for American film). Comic confessions of antisemitism both cleanse and shape part of a subliminal struggle to suppress French responsibility in the ongoing travails of its ever-growing postcolonial populations.

American Jews latched on to immigrant stories such as the one told in the 1975 film *Hester Street* as a way to connect and lay claim to their roots both as Jews and as Americans. But their urge to represent their difference visually depended upon imagining an Ellis Island and a Lower East Side occupied by pious men in beards, black hats, and peyos. Many Jewish immigrants, of the more than two million who made the trek between 1880 and 1924, reached American shores already secularized. Laura Levitt explains that in order "to assimilate into the dominant Protestant culture of the United States, Jews were required to identify their Jewishness as a form of religious faith to remain visible as Jews."[15] In other words, maintaining Jewish difference for the descendants of these secularized immigrants meant "remembering" ancestors whose Jewishness was visibly discernible. The Hasidic garb as it functions in French and American films beginning in the 1970s offers a way in to these distorted versions of the past to assert their veracity or test their significance. The films addressed in this book approach this "way in" by having nonreligious Jews and sometimes gentiles experiment with the garb.

Between the maskilic performances of the 1860s and the multicultural costume play beginning in the 1970s, Hasidic imagery was sometimes revisited on American and European stages and screens. Significantly, the Nazi propaganda machine relied on religious markers like beards, hats, and caftans to stress Jewish difference. Recalling Grodner's "lightning fast" costume change, the famous Nazi "documentary" *Der ewige Jude* (The eternal Jew, 1940) employed the same strategy of dressing/undressing to showcase Jewish trickery. In one scene, a line of religious Jewish men magically transform as their beards, peyos, caps, and caftans fade from view. As the narrator ominously claims, without the Jewish garb, "only sharp-eyed people can spot [their] racial origins."

In some ways, the figures that take the stage (or screen) beginning in the 1970s are nothing new: the vaudevillian styles and variations on minstrelsy of films like *The Frisco Kid* and *Les aventures de Rabbi Jacob* hark back to the origins of modern Yiddish theater. However, the Nazi cataclysm and the multicultural movement append new descriptors to the Hasidic figure's already complicated taxonomy. The fantastic Hasid, as I call him here, signifies Jewish racial difference *and* whiteness, Jewish particularism *and* universal belonging, Jewish authenticity *and* Jewish performativity. The five films that make up this analysis are part of Goldfaden's maskilic legacy, and they are the forebears of future representations of religious Jews in the twenty-first century such as *A Serious Man* (2009), *Holy Rollers* (2010), and *The Daily Show*'s eruv sketch. Comedy and drama act as subversive responses to the Nazi construction of Jewishness even as the films' sight gags seem to mimic the bogus tactics of the propaganda film.

Hasidic imagery's multiple and contradictory meanings are possible partly due to the complex classification "Jewish," which challenges notions of nationhood, race, ethnicity, and gender, exposing the permeability and instability of these categories. Significant and often tragic consequences befall Jews and others, due partly to a collective failure to fit Jews within these modern classifications. Aamir Mufti articulates the riddle of Jews and modernity and the way this riddle leads to representational confusion: "The 'Jew' of modern Western imagination is both the threat of particularism confronting the secularizing and universalizing state and the figure of universal exchange that serves as a marker for the uprootedness and abstraction of bourgeois culture."[16] The films I pursue here take measures to test Jews' attempts to either cohere to or resist categorization. Comedy and predictable genre conventions end up being sites for exploring Mufti's Jewish paradox. Through acts of dressing and undressing, the Hasidic garb tests the limits and desirability of both Jewish particularism and Jewish universalism. While the films feature black people, Muslims, Arabs, women, and Native Americans as an indirect means to explain Jewishness and the Jewish place within the national landscape, they also employ the Hasidic fantasy as a means to explain Jewishness. In other words, while races, ethnicities, and genders are employed as analogies for "the Jew," the Jew becomes an analogy for himself (almost always a "he"). Jews are *like* black people, women, and Indians, but mostly, Jews are like Jews—an analogy that carries the implicit message that all Jews at their core adhere to the visibly religious type. This symbolic gesture assigns a visible specificity to what it means to be Jewish while emptying the Hasidic figure and the real Jews who look like him of their specificity either as particular varieties of Jews or as individuals. The imagery also consigns Jewish women to the realm of invisibility—or at the very least to a place where expressing themselves visibly via a set of visual codes becomes nearly impossible. The ease and supposed obviousness with which this image is employed to point to the broader category "Jewish" has implications for the secular or non-Hasidic Jewish men and women who rely on it as a mirror.

Hasidic performances materialize as crucial components for understanding unspoken anxieties about the Jewish position on the national landscape. While the films I survey may sometimes feel silly or inconsequential, deciphering the Hasidic code scene by scene introduces a host of serious questions about how boundaries may be drawn: between Jewishness and Americanness or Frenchness and among Jews. Like *The Daily Show*'s eruv conflict, these cinematic boundaries are points of contention replete with ironies and self-contradictions. Jewish women, it turns out, are a major disrupting force for debates about Jewish authenticity. Peeling off layers of Hasidic garb stops short of the Jewish woman's body, where legs, breasts, and hair become their own kind of garb in film. Religious Jewish dress emerges as an arena for testing more than what it means to be Jewish. The garb illuminates what it means to be French, American, a man, or a woman.

PLAN OF THE BOOK

Given the popular appeal of the sources I have selected and the types of analyses I undertake, this book will by necessity present itself as a mélange of history, cinema studies, and cultural criticism. When asking how national and Jewish identities are formed and expressed, detours seemingly unrelated to the films in question animate the discussion. These indirect and sometimes noncinematic frames—including political protests, Talmudic dicta, jury trials, foreign wars, urban billboards, and social media trends—establish the theoretical and historical contexts for the film discussions. At the same time, because this book is about more than just an analysis of the films, the framing devices I use are meant to stretch the reader beyond the screen and toward larger questions of identity and authenticity. In light of this, the films are not discussed in chronological order but according to the types of questions that arise from them.

I begin with the Gene Wilder western *The Frisco Kid* (1979), which, through its costume play with cowboys, Indians, and one comically disharmonious Hasidic rabbi, gets to the heart of the question of whether Jewishness and Americanness are compatible. This film, in a rigorous test of identity types, stars a secular Jewish actor (Wilder) who plays a Polish rabbi who disguises himself as a goyish (gentile) cowboy. Next, I closely examine the popular French farce *Les aventures de Rabbi Jacob* (1973). This film poses the same types of identity-category questions we see in *The Frisco Kid* but via the opposite maneuver, as a first-generation French actor (Louis de Funès) plays an antisemitic Catholic Frenchman with pure French ancestry who disguises himself as a Hasidic rabbi.

Both of these films rely on the signifying power of the Hasidic image to pose questions and assert anxieties about the Jew's place within the architecture of national identity. But in focusing solely on Hasidic men, *Frisco Kid* and *Rabbi Jacob* leave open the problem of how Jewish women may be signified on-screen. In chapter 3 I draw Woody Allen into the conversation, a pivotal crossover figure for understanding how the Hasidic fantasy operates in both France and America, as his films are widely celebrated in both contexts. Notoriously derided as a self-hating Jew and misogynist—at least in America—Allen provides an unexpected voice for religious Jewish women in his 1997 film *Deconstructing Harry*. Not only are these women characters subtle and interesting, they also contrast with images of the Hasidic man, whose signifying immediacy often forecloses the possibility for more nuanced renderings of characters.

In chapter 4 I return to French film, pushing beyond the singular fantasy of the Hasidic man and the more nuanced representations of religious Jewish women and toward the fantasy of romance between religious Jews and Muslims. Focusing on 2005's existentialist drama *La petite Jérusalem*, I return to the question of religious Jewish women's modesty and sexuality, this time in terms of French sexual norms. I argue that depicting a Jew and Muslim engaging in French standards of heterosexual sex resolves, in the minds of its viewers, the historic divide between Jews and Muslims and between these groups and the hegemonic ideal of French Catholic whiteness. The romance at the film's center also underscores the distinct but related social positions of Jews and Muslims in a post–*Rabbi Jacob* France as religious imagery continues to be a tool in popular explorations of national identity.

Finally, I argue for exploring the 1975 immigrant drama *Hester Street* as an adaptation in two senses: as the translation of Abraham Cahan's 1896 immigrant novel *Yekl* into film and as the Americanization of its Jewish immigrant characters. The questions of authenticity that emerge when examining adaptations and their presumed originals shed light on how religious garb may serve both to demonstrate and to mask a figure's authenticity. Not only are religious Jewish women more complex figures on-screen, but their religious garb, specifically the wig, gives the lie to the myth of authenticity that Hasidic male garb proclaims.

The Hasidic fantasy may not have altered the cinematic universe, but in each filmic instance, the fantasy reflects how non-Hasidic and often non-Jewish filmmakers and audiences imagine themselves and their positions within their respective national landscapes. If the idea of the Jew, as Mufti made clear, reflects ambivalence about what he calls "the projects of modernity," then the *image* of the Jew—refracted through beards, hats, caftans, and peyos, deeply gendered, both comic and tragic—gives voice to that ambivalence and, like the eruv, provides it with clear boundaries. In turn, new ambivalences emerge, and with them new imagery, as the gag Grodner made on the nineteenth-century stage appears again and again on twenty-first-century screens.

NOTES

All translations are my own unless otherwise noted.

1. Michael Helfand, "An *Eruv* in the Hamptons? Why Not? The Fight over a Proposed *Eruv* in Westhampton Beach, N.Y., Is about Much More Than String and Telephone Lines," *Los Angeles Times*, August 12, 2012.
2. On average nightly viewers, see Michael Starr, "Jon's Got Game," *New York Post*, September 25, 2008.
3. Nathan Abrams, *The New Jew in Film: Exploring Judaism and Jewishness in Contemporary Cinema* (New Brunswick, NJ: Rutgers University Press, 2012), 140.
4. Vanessa Schwartz, *It's So French: Hollywood, Paris, and the Making of Cosmopolitan Film Culture* (Chicago: University of Chicago Press, 2007), 2–4.
5. Notably, Henry Bial, *Acting Jewish: Negotiating Ethnicity on the American Stage and Screen* (Ann Arbor: University of Michigan Press, 2005); Andrea Most, *Making Americans: Jews and the Broadway Musical* (Cambridge, MA: Harvard University Press, 2004); Vincent Brook, *Something Ain't Kosher Here: The Rise of the "Jewish" Sitcom* (Piscataway, NJ: Rutgers University Press, 2003); Harley Erdman, *Staging the Jew: The Performance of an American Ethnicity, 1860–1920* (Piscataway, NJ: Rutgers University Press, 1995).
6. Abraham Goldfaden, *Goldfaden-bukh* (New York: Idishn Teater Muzee, 1926), 54–58.
7. Abraham Goldfaden, "Dos Freilekhe Hosidl," in *Dos Yidele: Yiddishe lider af prost Yiddisher shprakh* (1886; Warsaw: Yaakov Lidsky Book Handler, 1903), 94–100. For an analysis of how this moment led to the "birth" of Yiddish theater and a complete history of Goldfaden as poet and businessman, see Donny Inbar, "A Closeted Jester: Abraham Goldfaden between Haskalah Ideology and Jewish Show Business" (PhD dissertation, Graduate Theological Union, 2007).
8. Goldfaden, *Goldfaden-bukh*, 55.
9. Gordon was a frequent contributor and eventual editor of the Hebrew maskilic daily *Ha-Meliẓ*, from which this quotation is taken. Gordon, "'Arba'ah ḥarashim ke-ve-maḥazeh," *Ha-Melitz*, December 23, 1885, 1603–1606. See also Michael Stanislawski, *For Whom Do I Toil? Judah Leib Gordon and the Crisis of Russian Jewry* (Oxford: Oxford University Press, 1988), 217. Gordon's poem "Hakitẓah 'Ami" was first published in *Hakarmel* 6, no. 1 (Iyyar 5626 [1866]): 1.
10. See Joel Berkowitz and Barbara Henry, introduction to *Inventing the Modern Yiddish Stage*, ed. Joel Berkowitz and Barbara Henry (Detroit: Wayne State University Press, 2012), 1–4. The authors debunk the myths surrounding Yiddish theater's origins, explaining its long history dating back to the medieval period.
11. Mikhl Gordon, "Shtey af mayn folk," in *Shirei M. Gordon: Yidishe lider fun Mikhl Gordon* (Warsaw, 1889), 29–35. See also Inbar, "A Closeted Jester," 101–103.
12. Matthew Frye Jacobson, *Roots Too: White Ethnic Revival in Post–Civil Rights America* (Cambridge, MA: Harvard University Press, 2006), 6–7.
13. Ibid., 7.

14. This "melting pot" project also found a home in cinema. Films from the first half of the twentieth century like *The Jazz Singer* (1927), *To Be or Not to Be* (1942), and *Gentleman's Agreement* (1947), show the modern Jew to be (almost) entirely indistinguishable from non-Jews.

15. Laura Levitt, "Impossible Assimilations, American Liberalism, and Jewish Difference: Revisiting Jewish Secularism," *American Quarterly* 59, no. 3 (2007): 822.

16. Aamir Mufti, *Enlightenment in the Colony: The Jewish Question and the Crisis of Postcolonial Culture* (Princeton, NJ: Princeton University Press, 2007), 38–39.

SILVER SCREEN, HASIDIC JEWS

1

THE YARMULKE BENEATH THE COWBOY HAT

Signifying Jewishness in the Hasidic Western

> The apparel oft proclaims the man. . . . [T]o thine own self be true.
> —Polonius's advice to Laertes in *Hamlet*

> Now look, you go up and change. . . . If I'm who
> I am, how come you ain't what you are?
> —Tommy's advice to Avram in *The Frisco Kid*

IN 1977 HISTORIAN JAMES CLIFFORD spent several weeks observing and analyzing members of a Wampanoag Indian community in Mashpee, Massachusetts, whose authenticity was quite literally on trial. Before they could legally sue the state for lost lands, these individuals were asked to prove their authenticity as an Indian tribe: biologically, linguistically, by virtue of dress or costume, knowledge of tribal history and tradition, belief in Wampanoag religion, and so on.[1] As he observed anthropologists and historians testify for or against the community's validity, Clifford wondered who has the right and the authority to speak for cultural authenticity. Of course, his book explores this question as a rhetorical one—not only because lawyers, judges, and juries lack the tools to prove or disprove a community's authenticity but because authenticity itself is a myth, albeit a powerful and persuasive one. Courts of law depend on these myths in cases like the Mashpee trial, so Clifford's project to debunk essentialist notions such as authenticity unravels in the courtroom.

Clifford wrote about cultural relativity in the late 1970s and 1980s—the very same period when assertions about Jewish authenticity, usually rendered in Hasidic garb, featured prominently or as a recurring punch line in American movie theaters. *Fiddler on the Roof* (1971), *Hester Street* (1975), *Annie Hall*

(1977) and other Woody Allen films, *The Chosen* (1981), *History of the World: Part I* (1981), *Yentl* (1983), *An American Tail* (1986), *Crossing Delancey* (1988), and *A Stranger Among Us* (1992) are just a handful of representative films that hit screens during that era. It is no coincidence that there was an upsurge in films grappling with the imagery of Jewish authenticity just as Clifford was investigating how culture operates. During this historical moment, "white ethnics," to use Matthew Frye Jacobson's term, were seeking to establish their immigrant (European) roots and demonstrate their prideful ethnic pasts. On the heels of black liberation movements (and at the expense of all people of color), white Americans romanticized imagined histories in Ireland, Greece, Italy, and, for Jews, eastern Europe. "Real" Americans became defined by their nostalgic assertion of an ambitious immigrant past. This "ethnic revival" project demanded essentialist notions like authenticity.

Even as Clifford challenges the notion of cultural authenticity, he cannot escape it. In his account of the "predicament of culture," he sometimes relies on clearly defined cultural categories to organize his argument. In his words, "culture is a deeply compromised idea I cannot yet do without."[2] This chapter takes on Clifford's predicament in the context of a film from that same era, *The Frisco Kid* (1979), a Wild West comedy about a Polish rabbi's journey to San Francisco. *The Frisco Kid* showcases themes from all of the above-listed movies—from the nostalgia of *Fiddler*, to the place of faith in a changing world in *The Chosen*, to the enigmatic sexualization of the Hasid in *Stranger*. As a participant in the 1970s white ethnic revival, *The Frisco Kid* offered American Jews the opportunity to embrace a charming version of the Hasidic figure on-screen, an essentializing model of Jewishness. But the film may also be read as a commentary on the "predicament of culture." Through the act of dressing and undressing from Hasidic garb, it emphasizes the relativity of the categories it seeks to define: Jewish, American, cowboy, and Indian.

Clifford explains that the Mashpee trial was not about land rights but about rights to claim certain identities. "Looked at one way," he asserts, "they were Indian; seen another way, they were not. Powerful *ways of looking* thus became inescapably problematic. The trial was less a search for the facts of Mashpee Indian culture and history than it was an experiment in translation, part of a long historical conflict and negotiation of 'Indian' and 'American' identities."[3] Clifford's observations led him to argue that authenticity is not a component of some fundamental, demonstrable aspect of group identity but a fluid notion that changes depending upon who is being asked to speak for it. Authenticity is always dependent on and considered in relation to the *in*authentic.

The Mashpee trial, during which issues of race, intermarriage, and, most interestingly for this book, dress codes took the stand, serves as a reminder of the central role of visibility in determining belonging. Film demands that spectators, like jurors, scrutinize the performer's believability. *The Frisco Kid* revolves around the ways that Jewish visibility and aurality may be used as flash points for defining Jewishness. The main character, a Hasidic rabbi, removes his garb and masks his Yiddish accent in order to recuse himself of his Jewish identity and survive in the Wild West. *Ways of looking* Jewish, to adopt Clifford's language, and *ways of looking at* Jews frame this film's major conflicts just as ways of looking Indian framed the trial. Furthermore, the film's use of Native Americans (among other groups) as an analogy for Jewishness raises the question of tribal identity as a potential classifier for American Jews. It thereby poses challenges to the other ways of categorizing Jewishness discussed in these chapters: as a race, religion, or nationality.

For the real Indians of Mashpee, as for the fictional ones represented in *The Frisco Kid*, tribal identities are inflected with notions of oppression and homelessness. Rachel Rubinstein writes, "Jews certainly do not hold a monopoly on experiences of exile and dispossession in the twentieth century even if they developed some of the most elaborate aesthetic responses to them."[4] Her book underscores how both Jews and non-Jews have historically looked to Native Americans as a way to negotiate and construct Jewishness, first in Europe and later in the United States. She points to a common "typographical slippage" from the early modern period (e.g., in versions of Shakespeare's *Othello*) between Iudean/*iudio* (Jew) and Indian/*indio* (Indian).[5] This orthographic confusion mirrors the underlying ethnographic confusion between the two groups. Centuries later, a deliberate, modern variation of the Shakespearean phenomenon appears in the form of a Yiddish-speaking Indian chief in Mel Brooks's outrageous western spoof *Blazing Saddles* (1974). Preceding *The Frisco Kid* by five years, *Blazing Saddles* also starred Gene Wilder as a cowboy, although in a role not explicitly marked as Jewish. Between Shakespeare and *Blazing Saddles* are copious vaudevillian manifestations of Yiddish cowboys and Jewish Indians, magnifying the *indio/iudio* confusion, as the identities of both the actor and the character are simultaneously on display. The disorienting quality of this doubling (or tripling, as in Shakespeare's play-within-a-play) also enables one group to use the other as a substitute or metaphor in order to explicate its identity, as Indians do for Jews in *The Frisco Kid*.

Like the Shakespearean orthographic mistakes and the Mashpee courtroom centuries later, *The Frisco Kid* reopens questions of ethnic identity and authenticity, this time in a late 1970s Hollywood context. The Mashpee trial implicates real individuals whose lives, livelihoods, and identities depended heavily on the outcome of the case. I do not wish to create a parallel between a mostly comic film and the much graver outcomes of a Native land rights trial. But the trial brings to light how fictional identity issues, even ones seemingly exaggerated for comic or melodramatic effect, are not limited to a "merely" fictional realm. Printed on paper, testifying in court, or performing on-screen, it is what spectators *see*—visibility—that so often determines ethnic belonging and even which kinds of performances are permissible, obligatory, or transgressive.

THE "KOSHER COWBOY"

Set in 1850, *The Frisco Kid* tells the story of a clumsy Hasidic rabbi (Gene Wilder) whose disappointed colleagues decide to send him from his shtetl in Poland to San Francisco, where he will serve as a rabbi for a gold rush era congregation. Upon docking in Philadelphia, the rabbi, Avram Belinski, misses his ship to California, is robbed on the stagecoach he hires as alternate transportation, and narrowly avoids a second robbery on a train. Belinski works on the railroad and manages to earn enough to purchase a horse. But soon after, he inadvertently participates in a third robbery, this time of a bank, committed by a young bandit, Tommy Lillard (Harrison Ford).

Inexplicably captivated by Belinski's innocence and integrity, Lillard agrees to help him make his way to San Francisco. On the way, they are pursued by the sheriff of the town where they robbed the bank, captured by Indians, rescued by a mission of silent monks, assaulted at a saloon—in a moment of cinematic uncanny—by the same men who initially robbed Avram on the stagecoach, and nearly die of frostbite as they journey across the West's unforgiving landscape. Once they finally reach the Pacific, they must defend

Figure 1.1 The Jewish American friendship is sealed at Belinski's wedding (screen grab).

themselves against the same men from the stagecoach and saloon, resulting in Avram fatally shooting one of the men.

Arriving at last in San Francisco, Avram decides that since he has taken a life (among other reasons), he no longer deserves to be called rabbi. Lillard persuades him against this choice, so Avram eventually accepts his position as rabbi and marries the chaste daughter of the wealthy synagogue president. The film's end—Belinski's wedding celebration, where Lillard serves as best man—seemingly resolves every tension set out by the film: the rabbi-immigrant finally finds a home in America, the unlikely friendship between Belinski and Lillard is symbolically sealed with a wedding (requiring the presence of a Jewish woman), and the lone bandit Lillard appears to be reformed through his friendship with the rabbi.

Beyond these resolutions, Rabbi Belinski learns the true meaning of being a rabbi (or Jew): human relationships take precedence over the Torah (in both its literal and figurative sense). Part of Avram's reason for wanting to abandon his title is that when the thugs attack on the beach, he first acts to save the Torah scroll he has carried with him from Poland and only then reaches out to his friend Lillard, who has been shot. Although Lillard later claims that he understands Avram's impulse to protect the Torah, Avram feels he has betrayed a fundamental ethic. Rabbi Belinski never, however, expresses regret over risking his own life to save the Torah scroll when Indians capture the two men earlier in the film. In this way, the film's ambivalence about observant Judaism is settled with an unresolved compromise: we learn that good religious Jews must place the Torah above all else but that good men must place other men above all else. Outside of Hollywood, good religious Jews must of course be good men (and women!). Jewish law explicitly places human life above all other precepts. However, throughout the film, "Judaism" and "humanism" are presented as incompatible categories, as incongruous as the notion of a "kosher cowboy," the film's tagline.

The "kosher cowboy" premise is funny because it feels like an oxymoron. The eastern European Jewish male, the soft study-house Jew, seems entirely incompatible with the rugged, chiseled, risk-taking image of the American cowboy, embodied by Harrison Ford's Tommy Lillard. *New York Times* reviewer Vincent Canby argues that "the gimmick is exhausted in the telling of it."[6] As if the audience could forget the silliness of these incompatible categories, we are reminded of their incommensurability in nearly every scene, including when Lillard shouts an awkward "Oy vey!" as his horse dives into a river. From a strictly comedic point of view, then, Canby is right. The film tests the oxymoron relentlessly, relying on every type of comic approach, as critic Roger Ebert describes, from slapstick to dialect humor to costume jokes to puns and double entendres.[7] But I would argue that the "gimmick," when taken seriously, can never be exhausted.

The gimmick's contrasting categories have implications for how the viewer is made to understand both Jewishness and the Wild West. *The Frisco Kid* frequently uses wide panoramic shots of the American West to locate the characters and welcome the spectators into a dream version of the 1850s. But in imagining a Hasidic rabbi occupying a western landscape, the film also reaffirms the purity of the Wild West in part by disrupting it. Jewish settlers came to California in the mid-nineteenth century, so it is not ahistorical to imagine a Jew in the West. The distortion here is Belinski's improbable position as a lone rabbi-bandit in his (pseudo)-Hasidic garb. Early Jewish settlers generally came from Germany and were not Hasidic.[8] Belinski's awkward presence on the rugged western terrain, the way he appears out of place, reinforces the fixity and authenticity of the film's backdrop. Furthermore, Avram's Hasidic

Figure 1.2 The Hasid in the Wild West landscape (screen grab).

dress behaves as its own kind of landscape, signifying a certain version of the Jewish past in the dark garb. Like his alien presence in the Wild West, when Belinski replaces parts of his garb for cowboy clothing, the act reaffirms the appropriateness and believability of the Jewish garb as a genuine historical "landscape."

THE ROMANCE

Unlike other Jewish-themed dramas and comedies, *The Frisco Kid* does not rely on the sexual taboo that pairs a Jewish man and a gentile woman—a pervasive dramatic device in American films about Jews.[9] Instead, a less forbidden relationship, the Jewish-gentile friendship, drives the film, and not without its fair share of homoerotic subtext. Polar opposites in everything but gender, Belinski and Lillard's budding friendship actually becomes a story entirely about gender as the film compares two varieties of masculinity. In what can only be described as a love affair, their relationship follows the course of a typical Hollywood romance: they meet in improbable circumstances, find each other irresistible in spite of their major differences, fight to the point of nearly destroying their relationship, face danger and loss together, and finally seal their union ceremoniously. What makes the romance conceivable (by Hollywood standards) is the pairing of Lillard's rugged masculinity with Belinski's feminized Jewish man. The visible Jewish-gentile divide conveyed in the film through costume thereby signals a most fundamental difference about what it means to be a man.[10] The film, then, is part buddy picture, part romantic comedy.

Understanding this film as a romantic comedy, one that introduces the possibility for enduring love between rabbis and cowboys (or Jews and Americans in general), clarifies its lesson to audiences. Love between Jews and Americans is possible as long as they remain distinct as Jews and Americans. Belinski's journey does not result in the expected outcome of assimilation or even secularization. In fact, Jewish-American harmony is possible in *The Frisco Kid* only when he resists those outcomes and accepts his Jewish difference (with slight modifications). Likewise, whenever the film appears to comply with genre expectations—those of the buddy picture, road film, or western—it takes a different turn when Jewish identity politics enter the frame. As Ebert writes, the film lacks "consistent comic logic," and Canby accuses the film of resulting in "harmless chaos."[11] The film betrays every genre for the sake of the Jewish narrative it tells. This Jewish narrative poses challenges to Belinski's Jewishness at every turn: he must betray his Jewish ideals for the sake of his friendship (and his survival). Genre norms break down in the face of the Jewish-gentile friendship/romance, which itself breaks gender norms. But the film is rescued from its illegibility, from the "chaos" its reviewers describe, by virtue of the love story that drives the narrative. The fact that the film does not know what it is—or pretends that it can be everything—deviates from the central message conveyed by its protagonist: that we can only be who we are, or, more precisely, that a Jew must always be a Jew.

This conflict between form and message in *The Frisco Kid* resists the seamless metaphorical reading that Michael Rogin offers of *The Jazz Singer* (1927). For Rogin, the conversion from Jewish to American in that film is mirrored by the conversion from silent cinema to sound and from white skin to blackface. Whether intended or not by its creators, *The Jazz Singer* is both narrative and history lesson: it tells one immigrant family's story, including the death of the patriarch, as it announces the migration of cinema from silence to sound, heralding the death of the tradition of the silent drama. Despite the similar journey Gene Wilder's Hasidic character takes in *The Frisco Kid*—from Old World to New World, East to West, Jewish to American—*The*

Frisco Kid's messages are much murkier. This film is not about conversion but resistance to it. If *The Jazz Singer* looks forward to the future of "talking" Hollywood cinema and the future of assimilated Jews as entertainers, *The Frisco Kid* tells a related story, but one that looks nostalgically backward, both to cinematic history (in the form of the western) and Jewish history (in the shape of the Hasidic fantasy).

The Frisco Kid's near constant reiteration of the incommensurability of apparently opposing categories takes hold as early as the opening credits and continues throughout the film without much development, other than the developing friendship between Lillard and Belinski. However, the two components that make up the unlikely pairing of Hasidic and western fantasies, of kosher and cowboy, may share more than meets the eye. Rogin's discussion of blackface illuminates the potential for synthesis among incompatible categories. Comparing what he calls "the myth of the west" to blackface, Rogin cites a relevant passage from Frederick Jackson Turner's famous frontier thesis, which I present at length here:

> The wilderness masters the colonist. It finds him a European in dress.... It strips off the garments of civilization and arrays him in the hunting shirt and the moccasin.... Before long ... he shouts the war cry ... in orthodox Indian fashion. ... Little by little he transforms the wilderness, but the outcome is not the old Europe.... The fact is, that here is a new product that is American. At first, the frontier was the Atlantic coast. It was the frontier of Europe in a very real sense. Moving westward, the frontier became more and more American.... [T]he advance of the frontier has meant a steady movement away from the influence of Europe, a steady growth of independence on American lines.[12]

Turner's thesis, for Rogin, is an analogy he employs to argue that blackface, like "the myth of the west," is "a form of racial cross-dressing."[13] As the European takes on the Indian garb or the white man puts on a black face, a "new product" appears. Gene Wilder's performance as a Hasidic rabbi, his "Jewface," has similar characteristics. Rabbi Avram Belinski makes the harrowing journey first from Poland to the Atlantic frontier (Philadelphia) and then to the next frontier, the Pacific coast, in *The Frisco Kid*. Like blackface, the Wild West drag both enables white Europeans to assert their European civility and aids them in becoming a "new product that is American." Becoming American depends upon disciplining the wilderness—in the way the imagined natives had done but also in disciplining the natives themselves.

Turner's *The Frontier in American History*, first delivered as a lecture in 1893, investigates the historical significance of the frontier, its institutions, and its social structures; he does not make use of terms like "culture" and "identity." But for our purposes we should notice how Turner's description of the way the European becomes American pivots around adopting the dress and language of an oppressed group. Turner presents a dialectic where "European" meets an appropriation of Native American attire and skills to produce the "American." Rogin's model—where Jews become white by becoming black (temporarily, through blackface)—depends less on hybridization than on posing as one thing in order to reject it. Nevertheless, Turner and Rogin share the basic premise that asserting a desired identity requires disguising oneself in its presumed opposite: Europeans become American by putting on Native garments and shouting the war cry—the same tools used by Jews in blackface (burnt cork and jazz) and Jews in Jewface (Hasidic garb and Yiddish). Ironically, borrowing the look and sound of other Others enables secular Jews to distance themselves from these figures.

JEWFACE AND OTHER DISGUISES

Turner's European (embodied by Lillard in the film) puts on "Nativeface" in order to produce an American. Likewise, Wilder's Jewface highlights his comfortable familiarity as a white, American, secular actor. The audience is invited to laugh at Jewishness in this form, partly because the Jewish actor, Wilder, gives them permission to do so. (This invitation is not so different from the one Grodner offered audiences in 1870s Romania when dancing to the "The Jolly Hasid.") The potentially threatening, uncomfortable, dissonant quality of being Jewish and American is eliminated through Wilder's exaggerated performance of Jewishness. In watching a Jew like Belinski, the audience knows that Jews are not like Belinski, they are like Wilder.

The scene in which Lillard and Belinski encounter a tribe of Indians is rich with ambivalence about Belinski's Americanization process. Even as the scene (and the film in general) appropriates Native American symbols and deals in stereotypes, it also critiques American barbarism toward Indians—a staple of 1970s westerns (and of one of *Frisco Kid* director Robert Aldrich's earlier films, *Ulzana's Raid*, from 1972). Upon first seeing a group of Indians on the horizon, Lillard convinces Belinski that they must run away as fast as they can. When Belinski innocently asks why the Indians would want to harm them, Lillard answers, "They've been shit on by the white man so long they don't ask questions no more." Here, we see elements of the revisionist western, the subgenre of classic western film that portrays Native Americans sympathetically and challenges traditional authority structures.[14] The film's compassion for Native Americans nevertheless confines them to a marginal position and prevents them from being American in the way Lillard is.

Belinski quickly realizes that in their haste to escape the approaching Indians, the Torah he had so carefully carried with him all the way from Poland had fallen out of its sack. He insists, despite Lillard's pleas to the contrary, on returning to find it. In the following scene, the two men have been captured by the Indians and tied to T-shaped wooden posts (unmistakably conjuring the crucifix). Here, visible difference, especially clothing, is once again central to explaining cultural boundaries. The Indians' garb is comically overdetermined: feathers, black wigs in braids, face paint, and ponchos serve to mark their exoticism. They immediately begin stripping Lillard, taking his cowboy hat and jacket. Curious about Belinski's fur hat, one Indian removes it (leaving Belinski's yarmulke), tries it on, and tosses it to the crowd. When the Indian chief (played by famed "ethnic" character actor Val Bisoglio) emerges from his teepee, he also wears a black hat, calling attention to both the similarities and the differences between the men present at the arrest.

The chief glares at Belinski and asks, "Who the hell are you?" to which Belinski responds, "Me rabbi. Jewish rabbi. Come from far away. Across big ocean! I read much books about Indians." "You don't speak English very well," the chief replies. Belinski, of course, was adjusting his English to meet some expectation he had of how Indians speak/comprehend, an expectation he shares with filmgoers. His English is much better than this first impression implies. On the other hand, the chief is right: Belinski's Yiddish accent is quite strong, and his syntax is frequently off the mark. In his enactment of "Indian"-speak, Belinski's Nativeface, like blackface, at once whitewashes him (he is white, unlike the Indians) *and* draws attention to his foreignness (his accent renders him more "colored" than white).

After quizzing Belinski about the Torah he has come to retrieve, the chief asks, "If I give you back Torah, will you purify your soul through fire?" reminding viewers of stereotypes about Native Americans: they are spiritually

Figure 1.3 Crucifying Belinski (screen grab).

sophisticated but primitive in meting out justice. Belinski reluctantly agrees. Several men then proceed to lower Belinski—still on the T-shaped wooden post—onto a fire pit. The post and the camera's angle temporarily render Belinski into a Wild West Jesus on the cross, sacrificing himself not for others' sins but for his precious Torah scroll. If Belinski and his Torah conjure up Jesus and salvation, then the hooting Indians around him in this scene stand in for the murderous Jews of the traditional Passion play, savagely delighting in killing the savior. The scene redeems the Jew by transforming him into an acceptable—indeed, the ideal—white Christian as it transforms the Indians into Jews. These mixed metaphors have a single consequence for Native Americans: they reiterate Indian savagery. But the message this scene puts forth about Jews is more muddled. Jews have the potential to be Messiah-like (like the Jewish Jesus), but they have equal potential to be barbaric, like the Indian-Pharisees who delight in violence.

It turns out that Belinski's display of bravery and martyrdom in this scene was a kind of test by the Indian chief, one that Belinski passed in putting the scroll before his own safety. The next scene shows the tribe communing inside a tent. Some Indians play drums, while others dance, praying for rain. The chief and the rabbi conduct a theological debate about the power of their respective gods to bring rain. Just as Belinski insists that the Jewish God (who is everyone's God, he explains, as there is only one God) can make rain if he wants to but apparently does not at that moment want to make rain, we hear the crack of thunder, and a great downpour ensues.

The Jew's power to call on his God for rain—even as he denies that this is what his God does—and his spiritual integrity in general clearly impress the Indian chief. While part of the revisionist western stereotype about Native Americans is their heightened spirituality and connection with nature, Belinski's presence alone is more successful at bringing the tribe what they require than their hours of prayer and dance. Belinski's bravery in the face of danger makes him a better cowboy than Lillard the actual cowboy; Belinski was not afraid to return to the Indians to retrieve his belongings. Belinski's faith and spirituality, his connection with the planet, and his ability to bring rain also make him a better Indian than the Indians. *The Frisco Kid* relies on other ethnic, religious, racial, and national identities as analogies for the complicated category of Jewishness. The audience experiences a play on the old adage, "Jews are just like everyone else, only more so."

However, for all of the ways the film relies on other Others to explicate Jewishness, a subtler analogy is created when the Hasidic garb is used to signify Jewishness in general. The movie thus cycles between Other as Jew (e.g., Indians) and Hasidic Jew as Jew. When Aamir Mufti writes that the "Jew" in modern imagination represents "the threat of particularism" and is "the figure of universal exchange," he is pointing to the kind of representational slipperiness that we see here.[15] Both maneuvers alienate secular Jewish filmgoers from themselves: as Americans and as Jews. In comparing Jews with Indians, Jews remain on the margins of America's social landscape, distant from the "real" American embodied by Lillard. But in comparing Jews with "Jews," the film establishes a false equation between Jews and Hasidim. Secular Jewish filmgoers, taught by this film that Jews are not the same thing as Americans, are left without options when Jews are limited to a single type.

It is interesting that a film that uses Indians as an analogy for Jews, presenting tribal identity as a possible way to classify Jewishness, centers on a single Jewish individual, rather than on a group, as the word "tribe" implies. While we see a group of Jews in the opening shtetl scene and another group of Jews in the final San Francisco scenes, most of the time the story is about a lone Jew. The notion of a "lone Jew," a tribe of one, is at least as oxymoronic as the idea of a "kosher cowboy." These two concepts share connotations: cowboys are loners, rugged individualists, but Jews cannot be. Jews must be part of a larger communal or tribal structure. The film challenges this notion by insisting that it is the clothes, accents, and mannerisms that make the Jew, not other Jews.

Delighted by the rain, the Indians shift from rain dance to celebration dance. "What do Jewish people do to express joy?" asks the chief. "Just like de Indians, dey dance, just like dis!" responds Belinski. "Dance with my people," the chief insists. Belinski then leads the tribe in a hora. Although Jews in eastern Europe adopted the hora from their neighbors in the Balkans, by the late nineteenth century (when the film is set) and certainly by the 1970s (when the film was made), the dance was a powerful symbol of Zionist longings and eventually the national dance of Israel. Of a particularly adept hora-dancing Indian, Belinski cries, "I tink dat lady's a Jewish Indian!" As incongruous or ridiculous as this statement seems—just like the "kosher cowboy" tagline—the bringing together of incompatible identity categories serves in this moment to define and contain each identity. Jews are one thing (they look and sound like Belinski), whereas Indians look and sound like the dancing woman. On the other hand, as the film sets out to delineate and regulate identities (Jew, cowboy, Indian), it confuses what it seeks to define by having a nineteenth-century Polish rabbi teach a group of Native Americans the national dance of Israel. While the Indians' exoticism undoubtedly makes the exotic Hasid appear more white and more American, when Belinski highlights the two groups' similarities, he also helps deexoticize Indians by making them more like "white" Jews. He then reexoticizes Jewishness by equating Jews with Indians. This semiotic tug-of-war—where Jews adopt the middle position between white and black (or Indian), between primitive and enlightened, between savages and saviors—fuels the engine of representations of religious Jews in American film.

It is not just collective memories of the imagined Wild West—its savage bandits, savage Indians, and savage landscapes—that provide a mirror through which to explore collective memories of the imagined Jew. Cinema, specifically the western genre, also provides an opportunity for nostalgia (both Jewish and cinematic). Ben Furnish describes how the western and Hasidic fantasies may be associated in *The Frisco Kid*:

Both Belinski and Lillard are walking representations of the idealized, mythic pasts of Americans and Jews: the Wild West and the shtetl. The incongruity of that juxtaposition is accented by its taking place in a satirical form of the conventional studio Western film. (By the late 1970s, the Wild West had already long been an object of nostalgia long celebrated in film. But the Western film genre itself was becoming an object of nostalgia; almost none were then being made any longer. Hence there is an intertextual nostalgia for the Western, albeit a humorous one, present in *The Frisco Kid*.)[16]

The Wild West and the Hasid are representative of the two ideals of American and Jew, but they later become venues for nostalgic reflection about what Americanness, Jewishness, and Hollywood once were but no longer can be. The Indians, too, no longer inhabit the open plains, threatening pioneers. The urge to move forward (from East to West, Old to New, Jewish to American) once again meets the impulse to look backward: toward Poland and a simple, authentic Jewishness, toward a Wild West riddled with violent or enlightening encounters between cowboys and Indians, toward the classic western film, toward an imagined, dreamlike past when identity categories were more clearly defined.

In good Hollywood fashion, Avram learns at the end to balance his apparently conflicting priorities/identities as he aligns himself with Jewishness and Americanness. He achieves the first in taking the job as the synagogue's rabbi and marrying the president's daughter. He accomplishes the latter in making the non-Jewish Lillard a best man and brother, someone for whom Belinski would risk not only his life but also his Torah (the same Torah he was willing to die for in the scene with the Indians). The implicit critique of religious Judaism that comes to the fore at the film's end is matched only by the film's steady romanticizing of the Hasidic figure. Both of these tropes are apparent in the Indian scene when the Jew's superior integrity and spirituality are manifested by his foolish willingness to die for a scroll.

YOU ARE WHAT YOU WEAR

The film works hard to assert that Belinski has no choice but to be Rabbi Belinski, based at least in part on his Jewish visibility: the Hasidic garb and the Yiddish accent. These inherently superficial markers are meant to signify Belinski's inalienable Jewishness, a quality he cannot shed even when he tries his best to reject it (including attempting to adopt the bandit identity by taking on a "cowboy" appearance/accent at one point in the film). But the film's climax, where the audience learns that religious Jews are afflicted with the (near) fatal flaw of putting Torah before friendship, seems to undermine the content of the inalienable Jewish quality. The viewer is led to believe that Belinski's religiosity—for example, his refusal to ride a train or horse on the Sabbath—demonstrates his Jewishness. But as the film gradually chips away at the value of such practices, we are left to wonder why Lillard insists so forcefully that Belinski is and must always be a rabbi.

Attacked on the beach, Belinski reaches first to protect his holy Torah scroll before leaping to save his friend, who has been shot. Deciding his behavior was unethical and because he took a life during the fight, Avram concludes he is unfit to be a rabbi. When the pair arrives in San Francisco, Belinski masquerades as a cowboy, taking Lillard's clothing and adopting his accent in a scene where Wilder's acting skill truly shines. Belinski as cowboy wishes to leave the Torah scroll for which he has risked his and Lillard's lives with the synagogue president, Mr. Bender. Placing the scroll on the doorstep and leaning in to give it a kiss, Belinski tumbles over when Bender's daughter opens the door. Introducing himself, he says, "Well! gall dang it, ma'am, my name is Tommy Lillard and I come from de Texas!" Wilder masterfully masks Belinski's Yiddish accent with a cowboy one, just enough so that the audience believes Bender's daughter might be fooled, but not enough that we ever forget who he really is beneath the cowboy mask (and we cannot forget the third layer of this masquerade, the Jewish-American celebrity Gene Wilder beneath both veneers).

Explaining that his "friend de rabbi" asked him to leave "dis ting" with Mr. Bender, the daughter asks, "What is it?" to which Belinski replies, "I dunno! I tink it's some kinda Torah!" When the woman asks where the rabbi is, Belinski fibs, saying, "De rabbi! Well, I don't rightly know, ma'am."

In the following scene, Belinski, still dressed as a cowboy, is eating dinner with Lillard at a saloon. Tommy beseeches Avram, "Now look, you go up and change and we'll go together and we'll tell your people that the new rabbi's arrived." Significant here is Lillard's insistence that Avram must look the part in order to play it. If he is to return to Mr. Bender's house, he must wear *tzitzit* (ritual fringes) and fur black hat, not the bandana around his neck and the sand-colored cowboy hat. Lillard believes that Belinski must be a rabbi, that he can be nothing but a rabbi, because that's who he is deep down. Still, it is

THE YARMULKE BENEATH THE COWBOY HAT   17

Figure 1.4 "Now you go up and change" (screen grab).

only appropriate that he *looks* like a rabbi and represents his identity on the surface.

When Belinski refuses, Lillard is outraged. After all, he had guided Belinski across the Wild West, risking his life time and again in order for Belinski to assume his post. This is when Belinski confesses that the reason he cannot be a rabbi is that in the heat of the fight he went to save the Torah, even though Lillard was injured: Belinski "cared more about a book than [his] best friend." Lillard is ready to forgive Belinski for this: "You're a man of God," Lillard he says. "I can understand that." But Belinski insists it was not about God, it was about "a book": "I chose a piece of paper instead of you!" Here, Belinski twice says, "I'm not a rabbi," indicating that being a rabbi (or even a Jew) may not depend upon loyalty to "a book" but on loyalty to friends.

While Belinski decides that his behavior was unethical during the fight and minimizes the significance of the Torah scroll as "a piece of paper," his choice to reach for the scroll rather than for his gentile friend falls in line with Talmudic directives. The Talmudic tractate *Shabbat* explains that saving a Torah scroll from a fire, similar to saving the life of a fellow Jew, is permissible on the Sabbath even though this act violates certain Sabbath prohibitions.[17] A gentile's life does not supersede the Sabbath, however. While one is permitted to save a gentile's life during the week, on the Sabbath, "only for our own, who keep the Sabbath, may we waive [the Sabbath]."[18] Therefore, the "life" of a Torah scroll supersedes the Sabbath, whereas the Sabbath supersedes the life of a gentile. In reaching for the scroll, Belinski acted out one interpretation of Jewish law.

Of course, these Talmudic dictates are far from cut-and-dried. The discussion surrounding saving a Torah scroll includes arguments concerning whether holy texts in translation (e.g., Greek, Aramaic) qualify as sacred enough for a Sabbath violation.[19] The disputed sanctity of a translated Torah—regardless of the rabbinic position about whether it may be saved—pulls into focus the unquestionable purity and sanctity of the original Hebrew. Any change to the textual body—the form of the letters (not their content), the *way the text looks*—calls into question its purity and authenticity.

Lillard, as if taking the more conservative rabbinic position, bears no ill will toward Belinski for prioritizing his scroll and even expresses deep frustration at Belinski's attempts to alter his own appearance and thereby forgo his status as rabbi. At their dinner, Lillard launches into a dramatic monologue: "You are a rabbi. I'm a bank robber. I'm a card player and a whoremonger. That's what I am. *You* are a rabbi. You can fall in the mud, you can slip on your ass, you can travel in the wrong direction. But even on your ass, even in the mud, even if you go the wrong direction for a little while, you're *still* a rabbi. *That's what you are.* Right? If I'm who I am, how come you ain't what you are?" Lillard demands an answer from Belinski, who appears in close-up speechless, a single tear running down his cheek.

Before he has the chance to answer, a throng of Jews enters the saloon. Mr. Bender's daughter, suspicious about the cowboy who left the Torah on her doorstep, points out Belinski and Lillard to her father. Mr. Bender at first assumes that the clean-shaven, tie-and-jacket-wearing Lillard is the rabbi. He addresses him at length in Yiddish. Lillard pleads with Belinski to tell the Jews the truth. Avram stands up, still in cowboy garb, and says, *"I'm* de rabbi." "You're de rabbi?" asks a bewildered Mr. Bender, looking Belinski up and down. "Funny, you don't *look* like a rabbi." After a beat, Avram responds. "I just traveled tree-tousand miles across dis country," he says as he removes the bandana from around his neck. "And I was tanking my best friend for gettin' me here alive." He removes Lillard's beige overcoat, revealing a white shirt and black vest. "My name is Avram Belinski," he insists as he puts on his black jacket. "I come from a small village in Poland, and don't you judge people by their appearance!" He punctuates the monologue by removing Lillard's cowboy hat and throwing it down on the table, exposing the large black yarmulke underneath. The on-screen costume change has transformed the funny-looking pseudocowboy into the perfect rabbinic specimen. "We have a rabbi!" the congregants cry out, elated.

Once again, the viewer is met with conflicting messages. On the one hand, the film tells us that you are what you are, regardless of how far off the path you travel. What you wear on the outside has no bearing on who you truly are, on the inexorable qualities of your identity. It is futile to attempt to hide or escape from this identity. On the other hand, your identity is always in question unless your external appearance matches who you are on the inside. Belinski's unresolved internal conflict at the end of *The Frisco Kid* originates in the Talmud, where both positions—the one that values aesthetic change and the one that dismisses it—sit side by side in the foundational text of Jewish religion.

Belinski's exhortation to the Jewish throng that one shouldn't judge based on appearances is immediately undermined by the action he takes to strip off the "false" layer of the cowboy uniform and return to his native state as rabbi. His Jewish authenticity, as Clifford argues of authentic identities in general, is entirely dependent on his initial performance of inauthenticity. Belinski's disclosure in this scene is complicated because his stripping down is met with a dressing up. He takes off one jacket as he puts on another; he removes one head covering to reveal a second head covering beneath it. There is no blank slate, no pure state of Belinski. "Rabbi" is revealed to demand as much of a performance as "cowboy."[20] After all, the congregants are only satisfied with their new rabbi when he looks like one.

This scene, the film's denouement, replicates in Jewish form the description Roland Barthes provides of a French striptease in his critical deconstruction of popular mythologies. In striptease, Barthes explains,

> a whole series of coverings [are] placed upon the body of the woman . . . as she pretends to strip it bare. Exoticism is the first of these barriers . . . which transports the body into the world of legend or romance . . . aim[ing] at establishing the woman *right from the start* as an object in disguise. The end of the striptease

is then no longer to drag into the light a hidden depth, but to signify, through the shedding of an incongruous and artificial clothing, nakedness as a *natural vesture of woman*, which amounts in the end to regaining a perfectly chaste state of flesh.[21]

In Belinski's case, the exotic disguise he strips off is his cowboy gear, and the nakedness he exposes is the Jewish garb. As with the woman Barthes describes, the act of stripping away clothing establishes the naturalness of what lies beneath. Belinski's natural state as a Jew is as inextricable from his body as a naked woman's flesh, although for Barthes, even nudity is "vesture." Removing Lillard's cowboy gear does not "drag into light a hidden depth" about Belinski's character but instead exposes his natural state as a rabbi. The maskilic architecture of the Jewish male, as articulated by Y. L. Gordon—a Jew at home (inside) and a man in the streets (outside)—is undermined by Belinski's reveal, as it was by the multicultural movement in general. The scene and multiculturalism demand that Jewishness is kept on the "outside" *because* Jewishness is what's on the inside.

The on-screen costume change at the end of *The Frisco Kid* is not the first scene in which Belinski strips and dresses up again. In one of the film's earliest scenes, Belinski is robbed on his rented stagecoach. The robbers take his money and throw all of the objects they deem worthless into the road behind them. Belinski is stripped down to his (comical) long underwear and thrown out of the coach. Lacking even a yarmulke, the stripped-down Belinski stands up and begins to collect his clothing as the opening credits roll. First he puts on his boots. Then he appears in his black pants and unbuttoned white shirt, revealing his tzitzit underneath. He wears his hat and clutches his jacket and socks. Contrary to the scene at the end of the film where the Jewish garb stands in for Belinski's nakedness, here, the exotic barrier, to use Barthes's language, is the Jewish garb, and the long underwear takes the place of his natural, naked state. Seen this way, Belinski's Jewish attire is both the exotic disguise masking his natural body and his body. On the one hand, both scenes demonstrate that Jewishness is a performance, requiring an ostentatious costume that begins with special undergarments. On the other hand, the scenes reinforce Belinski's Jewish authenticity, verifying that he is a Jew all the way down to his underwear. As Clifford explains of the Mashpee Indians, the question of Belinski's Jewish authenticity pivots around *ways of looking*.

Ethnic drag, like blackface, is about the incongruity between the mask and the face behind it.[22] Burnt cork on a white face or a man in woman's dress have the same effect of drawing out the performer's two faces, male and female, black and white. On the other hand, as the major queer and feminist theorists have contended, gender on its own is performative: a woman acting feminine is a performance but not a drag act, she is simply meeting some societal expectations, demonstrating in her behavior who she truly is.[23] Jewface, like the example we see in *The Frisco Kid*, participates in elements of both types of performance. The Hasidic garb is a false veneer. Like drag or blackface, it gives the effect of seeing double. But like the woman acting feminine, the Jew in Jewface is meeting expectations rather than betraying them. Jewface is at once a masking and an unmasking. The Jew "belongs" in the garb the way a woman "belongs" in a dress. Jewface creates a unified picture of Jewishness. But Jewface remains a costume act like drag or blackface, demanding that the audience see two faces at once, the secular Jewish performer and the Hasid he pretends to be.

Although Belinski (temporarily) fools Bender's daughter, their encounter as he delivers the Torah dressed as a cowboy is a romantic one. He comments on her eyes, and she takes a great interest in him and his unlikely story. Returning to the saloon to straighten the story out, Bender's daughter allows herself to fall for Belinski only once he wears the appropriate rabbinic garb. She even proposes to him, and they dance at the saloon. Their final wedding scene presents an unquestionably happy ending but not a resolution to the contradictions the film puts forward. If Belinski and Lillard's friendship answers the question of how to be Jewish and American, the film's ending does not show the viewer what this friendship looks like after the wedding. Belinski finds his community, but how does Lillard fit in? Despite *The Frisco Kid*'s happy ending and a few key moments when the rabbi and cowboy identities seem to coexist, the question of how to be a rabbi (Jew) and a cowboy (American) persists into the credits. This is arguably a question posed one way or another by almost every "Jewish" film, story, or novel about the American-Jewish experience. What makes *The Frisco Kid* and the other films treated in this book so compelling is how their creators consistently turn to Hasidic imagery in externalizing this problem.[24]

Ambivalence about Judaism in America drives the film—the same ambivalence that appeared five decades earlier in *The Jazz Singer*. In that film,

Jack Robin stands in for his father in the penultimate scene, chanting the powerful Kol Nidre prayer in his father's stead. Jack's prayer serves as a kind of funeral dirge, a eulogy for the immigrant Jewishness he ultimately abandons for the Broadway stage. In *The Frisco Kid*, there is no eulogy, no final goodbye to one identity in favor of another, because as Lillard explains to Avram over dinner, he has no choice but to be a rabbi. If anything, the film sends up an unspoken tribute to the possibility of Jewish assimilation in America, laying the potential for passing—and the desire for it—to rest at long last.

THE VERDICT

Clifford closes his discussion of the Mashpee trial with a transcribed dialogue that took place between an Indian teenager and the trial judge. The teenager wears jewelry and a red bandana, and the judge calls into question whether the bandana is "an Indian headband" or whether it is "an ordinary red bandana." The question is misleading because the bandana is both. It is an Indian headband because an Indian is wearing it, and the way he wears it cultivates images of a "typical" Indian look. It is an "ordinary" bandana because as the judge suggests, it is no different from any bandana "you buy in the store and fold up in that manner."[25] The teenager's Indian authenticity thus depends both on how he looks (he attends court in a headband and jewelry) and how the judge and jury look at him: Do they see an Indian headband or an ordinary bandana? Is the bandana the boy's "natural" naked state, or is it the Barthesian exotic barrier?

Just as *The Frisco Kid* establishes Jewish visibility—notably, of the Hasidic type—as the prerequisite for laying claim to Jewish identity, it is precisely the Mashpee Indians' inability to prove consistent Indian visibility that caused them to lose the lawsuit. Assimilation in these contexts is undesirable, not because it disrupts relationships with the past, as in *The Jazz Singer*, and not because antisemites are able to see through the assimilatory masquerade, as in the Easter dinner scene in *Annie Hall* when the character briefly transforms into a Hasid (see chapter 3). Instead, assimilation is undesirable because it is both inauthentic and futile. The Mashpee Indians lost their lawsuit because the jury found that the testimonial and written evidence were not sufficient to prove the Indians' continued existence as a tribe since the nineteenth century (the requirement set forth by the judge). Their lawyer claimed that the Mashpee had consistently been a tribe from that period until the time of the lawsuit, while the opposing lawyer argued that although there had been Indians in Mashpee since that time, they never constituted the legal definition of a tribe. The jurors found a third path, arguing that at some points in history the Indians had constituted a tribe and at other points had not. Jurors did not side with the Indians because they could not retrieve a history of tribal continuity—not because there never was a tribe.

Continuity and discontinuity are the axes upon which authentic claims to identity may be made in the trial. These themes reappear in *The Frisco Kid* on virtually every level. Along the Jew's journey from shtetl to San Francisco, he loses and regains the garb multiple times, signaling discontinuity; but Avram's Jewish look in the opening scene is no different from his Jewish look at the close of the film (although he sports a special embroidered white yarmulke for the wedding scene), signaling continuity. The film adopts the generic conventions of the classic western—continuity—but disrupts the genre by placing a Hasid in the midst of the rugged landscape—discontinuity. Avram emerges from his adventures with his Jewish religiosity (and Torah scroll) intact, prepared to serve as rabbi of his congregation—continuity. But the compromises he makes along the way, as well as the unconventional marriage proposal and gentile best man, demonstrate the changes he has made since coming to America—discontinuity.

Continuity is thus always already a flawed litmus test for a group's authenticity. However, like the tribal institutions discussed at the Mashpee trial, "claims to purity are . . . always subverted by the need to stage authenticity *in opposition* to . . . alternatives."[26] For all its comic and "gimmicky" conceit, the "kosher cowboy" conundrum provides a fictional, visual manifestation of the issues at play in the Mashpee's real-life courtroom drama. Avram's moments of dressing and undressing, his striptease, indicate how authenticity is relative and dependent on performances of the inauthentic. His Jewishness is performed in opposition to the cowboy, to the Indian, and, furtively, to the secular Jewish actor beneath the garb. In spite of its happy resolution, the film leaves open the question its tagline puts forth: how to be authentically Jewish and authentically American, and whether it's worth the effort to attempt to be both.

NOTES

1. James Clifford, introduction to *The Predicament of Culture: Twentieth Century Ethnography, Literature, and Art* (Cambridge, MA: Harvard University Press, 1988), 1–17; Clifford, "Identity in Mashpee," in ibid., 277–346.
2. Clifford, introduction, 10. See also Richard Handler, review of *The Predicament of Culture* by James Clifford, *American Ethnologist* 16, no. 3 (August 1989): 600–601.
3. Clifford, "Identity in Mashpee," 289, emphasis in original.
4. Rachel Rubinstein, *Members of the Tribe: Native America in the Jewish Imagination* (Detroit: Wayne State University Press, 2010), 182.
5. Ibid., 9–10.
6. Vincent Canby, "Movie Review: *The Frisco Kid* (1979), Screen: Gene Wilder in Aldrich's 'The Frisco Kid': Polish Rabbi Out West," *New York Times*, July 6, 1979.
7. Roger Ebert, "*The Frisco Kid*," *Chicago Sun Times*, January 1, 1979.
8. For a thorough history of Jews in California, see Ava Kahn and Marc Dollinger, eds., *California Jews* (Lebanon, NH: Brandeis University Press, 2003).
9. See, for example, Michael Rogin, *Blackface, White Noise: Jewish Immigrants in the Hollywood Melting Pot* (Berkeley: University of California Press, 1998), 103–104. During the sequence on the train, a buxom woman distracts the chaste Rabbi Belinski. His efforts and inability to avert his eyes from the woman's body affirm his status both as a pious Jew and as an agent of sexual desire.
10. Foundational texts on the history of Jewish masculinity include Daniel Boyarin, *Unheroic Conduct* (Berkeley: University of California Press, 1997); and Paul Breines, *Tough Jews: Political Fantasies and the Moral Dilemma of American Jewry* (New York: Basic Books, 1990).
11. Ebert, "*The Frisco Kid*"; Canby, "Movie Review."
12. Frederick Jackson Turner, *The Frontier in American History* (New York: Henry Holt and Company, 1920), 4. See also Rogin, *Blackface, White Noise*, 12.
13. Rogin, *Blackface, White Noise*, 12.
14. For example, Leslie A. Fiedler, "The Demon of the Continent," in *The Pretend Indians: Images of Native Americans in the Movies*, ed. Gretchen M. Bataille and Charles L. P. Silet (Ames: Iowa State University Press, 1980); see also the essays in *Hollywood's Indian: The Portrayal of Native Americans in Film*, ed. Peter Rollins and John O'Connor (Lexington: University Press of Kentucky, 1998).
15. Aamir Mufti, *Enlightenment in the Colony: The Jewish Question and the Crisis of Postcolonial Culture* (Princeton, NJ: Princeton University Press, 2007), 38–39.
16. Ben Furnish, *Nostalgia in Jewish-American Theatre and Film, 1979–2004* (New York: Peter Lang, 2005), 59.
17. See *b. Shabbat* 115a.
18. See *b. Avodah Zarah* 26a. The English passage is taken from the Soncino Edition of the Babylonian Talmud (London: Soncino Press, 1935–1948).
19. See *b. Shabbat* 115a.
20. This insight about Jewishness is inspired by Judith Butler's discussion of the performative nature of gender. See chapter 2 for more on Butler and performativity.
21. Roland Barthes, "Striptease," in *Mythologies*, trans. Annette Lavers (New York: Hill and Wang, 1972), 84–85, emphasis in original.
22. See, for example, Katrin Sieg, *Ethnic Drag: Performing Race, Nation, Sexuality in West Germany* (Ann Arbor: University of Michigan Press, 2002), especially her discussion about Nazi-era performances of the famous play about a fictional Indian hero that emphasized the actor's whiteness (255–60).

23. See, for example, Esther Newton, *Mother Camp: Female Impersonators in America* (Chicago: University of Chicago Press, 1972); Marjorie Garber, *Vested Interests: Cross-Dressing and Cultural Anxiety* (New York: Routledge, 1992); Judith Butler, *Gender Trouble* (New York: Routledge, 1999), especially 163–170.

24. If Hasidic visibility/aurality serves in this film as a metonym for Jewishness, then Lillard's cowboy visibility serves as a metonym for Americanness. The category "American" is no less problematic than the category "Jewish." But in this case, the tough loner cowboy represents a kind of American Protestantism that appears to be universal.

25. Clifford, "Identity in Mashpee," 346.

26. Clifford, introduction, 12, emphasis in original.

2

THE JEWISH TYPE AND "LE JUIF TYPIQUE"

Typologies of Jewishness in Les aventures de Rabbi Jacob

> Now this Jew talked the same way as I heard thousands of others talk before. . . . His face seemed familiar—he was typical.
>
> —Sigmund Freud, "Some Early Unpublished Letters"

> It did me a lot of good because . . . I don't want to confess here, but I used to have a few little ideas that were a bit anti . . . uh . . . well, some of them might still be with me! But as I said to Gérard Oury, it cleansed my soul.
>
> —Louis de Funès on playing the antisemitic Victor Pivert in *Les aventures de Rabbi Jacob*

DURING THE NAZI OCCUPATION OF FRANCE (1940–1944), propaganda photos were posted on Paris street corners featuring a man's face with the caption "le juif typique" (the typical Jew). The man was Marcel Dalio, one of the most sought-after French actors of the 1930s, best known for his roles in Jean Renoir's *La grande illusion* (*Grand Illusion*, 1937) and *La règle du jeu* (*The Rules of the Game*, 1939).[1] In both films, Dalio played assimilated aristocratic Jewish characters. The Nazi propagandists enlarged frames from these films for their posters. It remains unclear, however, what exactly is so "typically Jewish" about these images. In fact, it is likely the *invisibility* of Dalio's Jewishness—he was an assimilated middle-class Jewish actor playing assimilated Jewish aristocrats—that positioned him as the quintessential Jewish "menace."

Dalio (1900–1983), born Israel Mosche Blauschild in Paris, had by the time of the occupation safely fled to Hollywood to be cast as various French characters in American films, most famously, *Casablanca* (1942). Dalio's

Figure 2.1 Marcel Dalio as the Jewish Robert, marquis de La Chesnaye in *La règle du jeu*, 1939 (screen grab).

transformation from "typical Jew" in Nazi-occupied France to typical Frenchman in Jewish-occupied Hollywood is not unique to him. German-Jewish actors in exile were similarly cast in the late 1930s, 1940s, and 1950s as Nazis.[2] But Dalio's trajectory ultimately took him back to French cinema after the war, and he was later *re*cast as "the typical Jew," this time by Jewish filmmakers in *Les aventures de Rabbi Jacob* (1973), as the eponymous Rabbi. In full Hasidic garb, Dalio's conversion on-screen from one kind of typical Jew in the 1930s (the wealthy, invisible aristocrat) to another kind of typical Jew in the 1970s (the Hasidic rabbi) indicates how French constructions of Jewishness radically changed over the course of thirty years.

Rabbi Jacob was the fourth feature film for the comedy team of actor Louis de Funès and director Gérard Oury, but it was the first film that served as a star vehicle for de Funès. His face was the prominent feature on the ad posters as the character Victor Pivert in comic disguise as Rabbi Jacob. The two posters of Dalio and de Funès span three decades. One features a Jew who "looks like" a non-Jewish Frenchman and who is therefore perceived as a serious threat; the other features a non-Jew who is dressed as a Jew and who thereby renders Jewishness comically nonthreatening. In Dalio's case, the costume is the supposedly false veneer of assimilation that masks his belonging to the Jewish race: that costume is difficult to remove because it is difficult to detect. For the character Pivert, Jewishness is the costume in its extreme: it is a comic and comfortably removable manifestation.

The story these posters tell seems at first glance to indicate significant progress away from the kind of antisemitism promoted by Nazism and toward an embrace of Jewishness as a welcome part of the French landscape. But as I argue here, what looks like a major ideological advance actually reinscribes deeply conservative myths about Jews and Frenchness. Just as Rabbi Belinski's drag act as a (non-Jewish) cowboy calls into question the value and feasibility of assimilation in *The Frisco Kid*, *Les aventures de Rabbi Jacob* arrives at similar conclusions employing the opposite maneuver, when a gentile dresses up as a rabbi. In *The Frisco Kid*, the viewer follows a rabbi's journey from East to West—Poland to San Francisco. In *Rabbi Jacob*, we follow a rabbi's journey from West to East—New York to Paris. If *The Frisco Kid* invited both Jewish and cinematic nostalgia (in the forms of the Hasid and the western), *Rabbi Jacob* also invites a look backward—once again, to the Hasidic fantasy and also to an imagined French past where religious difference was geographically contained and bigotry was a charming but by no means dangerous quality of some French men.

The 1970s manifestation of typical Jewishness as represented in the wildly popular film *Les aventures de Rabbi Jacob* and the events surrounding the film's release work to resolve "the Jewish Question" for post-1968 French audiences. By "the Jewish Question" I intentionally adopt both the language of Nazi ideology and the question that predates the Nazis, particularly in revolutionary France, when Jewish status in the Republic was repeatedly called into question.[3] But "the Jewish Question" is likewise a Jewish concern about what it means to be Jewish and whether, or in what ways, Jewish difference is desirable. The idea of the Jew in France has long been symbolically salient vis-à-vis other Others in a manner that far outweighs their actual numbers in France.[4] From revolutionary times through the late twentieth century, the Jew has served as a contested site for the meaning of citizenship and national belonging. The Jews' status as familiar yet foreign posed a problem at the time

Figure 2.2 The movie poster: Louis de Funès as Victor Pivert disguised as Rabbi Jacob (Facets Multimedia).

of their emancipation in the eighteenth century, through their integration in the nineteenth century, and during their deportation in the mid-twentieth century. Finally, in the late twentieth century, the idea of the Jew was an emblem for issues of Zionism, decolonization, immigration, and multiculturalism. The particular representation, or resolution, of Jewishness offered by *Les aventures de Rabbi Jacob* was so powerful and successful that it has endured through the first decades of the twenty-first century.[5]

Despite its immense and enduring popularity, *Rabbi Jacob* has been ignored in the scholarly literature (both French and English). This is likely due to its release at the tail end of the Nouvelle Vague, or New Wave, in French cinema, the experimental trend in French filmmaking from the 1950s and 1960s. Unlike the Nouvelle Vague films, *Rabbi Jacob* does not experiment with form; instead, it traffics in stereotype and convention. Although seemingly derivative, its status in French popular culture indicates that it participated in the (re-)creation of some of these conventions, including the convention of how to represent Jews on-screen. The film's backstory, which includes a terrorist attack protesting the film on the day of its release, and its afterlife, which includes a stage musical and rap video homage, attest to the film's resonance with a large audience. This resonance is due in part to the ways its plot and the events surrounding the film come together to offer an audience both inclusionary and exclusionary responses to the Jewish Question.

Les aventures de Rabbi Jacob is a misleading name for the film, as the story does not center on Dalio's Rabbi Jacob but rather on the character played by the actor Louis de Funès: the antisemitic, racist Victor Pivert. On the way from Normandy to his daughter's wedding in Paris, Pivert, a wealthy industrialist, and his chauffeur, Salomon (Henri Guybet), get into a messy car accident. After assisting an erratic Pivert throughout the day, the Jewish Salomon refuses to help once the Sabbath approaches, a move that gets him fired by Pivert. On top of that, Salomon departs because his uncle, the famous Rabbi Jacob, is coming to Paris from New York for a visit. Seeking help at a nearby factory, Pivert accidentally witnesses the murders of two Arab revolutionaries by a team of counterrevolutionary policemen. He is then kidnapped by the surviving leader of the revolutionary party, Mohamed Larbi Slimane (Claude Giraud), who forces Pivert to accompany him as a hostage to the Paris airport in order to return to his home country. Along the way, the two must avoid the

Figure 2.3 Pivert and Slimane disguised as Jews at the airport (screen grab).

pursuing murderers and the French police, who take Pivert to be responsible for the deaths at the factory.

At the airport, Slimane and Pivert decide to disguise themselves as Hasidic rabbis to fool both sets of pursuing policemen. In an unexplained behind-the-scenes maneuver, the pair "steal" the beards, peyos, hats, and caftans from two unsuspecting Hasidim at the airport. Pivert and Slimane are then mistaken for Rabbi Jacob and his traveling companion by Jacob's family (who hasn't seen him in thirty years). Playing along with their mistaken identities, Pivert and Slimane arrive in the Jewish neighborhood of Paris to a grand welcome by the community. Pivert's chauffeur, Salomon, recognizes him immediately but agrees to protect both men.

After almost getting caught several times by the Jews who believe them to be rabbis, the Arab militants, and the French police, Pivert and Slimane, still in Hasidic garb, finally arrive at the church for Pivert's daughter's wedding. Before the ceremony begins, Pivert's daughter decides on a whim to leave her fiancé for the handsome Slimane, now president of his country after a successful coup d'état. Pivert gives his blessing to this unlikely union and announces his friendship with Salomon and his extended family, now finally

Figure 2.4 Pivert, no longer in Hasidic garb, greets the real Rabbi Jacob, played by Dalio (screen grab).

reunited with the real Rabbi Jacob (Dalio) just outside the church. The film's end offers a multicultural message about the value of diversity and the acceptance of Jews and Arabs into French society. The French-Arab intermarriage receives the happy approval of Jew, Arab, and white Catholic Frenchman.

The film's key joke repertoire relies on Pivert's trying-on of various skins. A puff of exhaust fumes from his car sprays him with ash, and he is mistaken for black. His famous slide into a giant vat of chewing gum at the warehouse where he witnesses the murders covers him in a surreal, sticky, bright-green second skin. Finally, the beard and peyos that he steals from a Hasid at the Paris airport provide him with his most important "skin," Jewish garb. Unlike his blackface and "greenface" performances, when Pivert dons Jewface, he adopts not only the garb but also a Yiddish accent, Jewish gestures, an uncanny aptitude for Hasidic dance, and a Jewish conversational style as the Arab Slimane teaches him to answer all questions with another question. Losing his beard, peyos, and shtreimel by the film's end, Pivert reembodies his given role as a Frenchman and publicly pronounces his friendship with the real Rabbi Jacob and his family. Each of the categories—French, Jewish, and Arab—occupies a clearly defined, happy, safe, contained space at the end of the film. The film's experiment with Jewish drag, as Judith Butler has argued

Figure 2.5 Pivert's skins (screen grab).

of other drag performances, can have a liberating, deessentializing effect.[6] Multiple layers of performativity resist the kind of typological reading that forced Dalio into exile during the occupation and draw attention to the variability of the categories of Jewishness, Arabness, and Frenchness.

MULTICULTURAL POSSIBILITIES FROM 1968 TO 1973

On October 6, 1973, Israel was invaded by Egypt and Syria. Two weeks into the fighting, a coalition of Arab states, OPEC, instituted an oil embargo against states supporting Israel, including France. Gérard Oury, *Rabbi Jacob*'s writer and director, aptly describes the moment in his memoirs: "It was in this climate that *Rabbi Jacob* peeked out over the tip of his beard on the walls of Paris."[7] This idiomatic phrase, a play on "pointer le bout de son nez" (peeking out over the tip of one's nose), implies the timidity Oury felt at the audacity of de Funès's Jewish image plastered on posters across Paris at this sensitive moment. The movie poster featured de Funès as Pivert as Rabbi Jacob, with beard, peyos, and black hat. Surrounding his image are smaller pictures of the character in blackface and greenface, as well as some other sight gags from the film. Oury and the film's producers agonized over what to do about the film's scheduled release on October 18: "Would the poster of Funès as a rabbi, even the [film's] title come across as a provocation? Would there be protests at the movie theaters? Or worse?"[8]

Oury and his team decided to go ahead with the film's release, and audiences were delighted, even moved, by the film. In one memorable scene, Salomon aids Pivert and Slimane in making their escape from the Jewish rue des Rosiers toward the church for Pivert's daughter's wedding, saving Slimane's life along the way. Here, Pivert observes, "Salomon, Slimane, Slimane, Salomon, could you two be some kind of cousins?" "Cousins?" asks Salomon, raising an eyebrow at Slimane. "Distant," responds Slimane soberly, "thank you." Then Jew and Arab share an extended handshake, and the camera zooms to a close-up of their hands. What might have been, during filming, a lighthearted jab at the tension surrounding Jewish-Arab relations took on epic, dramatic meaning at the film's release during wartime. According to Oury, the scene received "nourishing applause" in theaters across France.[9]

This celebrated handshake, along with the images of Pivert and Slimane as Hasidic rabbis dancing with other Hasidim on the rue des Rosiers to a jolly klezmer melody, and the happy intermarriage between Pivert's daughter and Slimane, became famous cinematic moments. These moments created a liberal vision of French multiculturalism in response to the Nazi antisemitism of the 1940s and to the resurgence of French nationalism in the 1970s. Audiences and critics embraced *Rabbi Jacob* at its debut in 1973, and the film, along with its multicultural message, continues to be popular with new generations of French audiences. However, the film's positive, multicultural surface is both dependent upon and contradictory to its deeper assumptions about French national identity and the roles of Jews and Arabs in that system.

Rabbi Jacob's great show of multiculturalism is complicated by unspoken, elided issues. What is elided is the real political, historical difference between the parties in front of the church, even as this difference is smoothed over to produce a marriage. Multiculturalism depends on the production of exotic difference, like the museum exhibition *The Great Family of Man*, which included photos of people from around the world and which is described in an essay by Roland Barthes. At the exhibit, "the diversity in skins, skulls and customs are made manifest.... [F]rom this pluralism, a type of unity is magically produced: man is born, works, laughs and dies everywhere in the same way."[10] In other words, multiculturalism depends on both the creation of difference and the suggested equivalence of differences: all peoples experience life, work, death (to which I would add marriage). This equivalence, or paring down, removes history from different populations by naturalizing and thereby neutralizing the human experience. The film's attempt at an inclusionary multicultural morality lesson is disrupted by the way it reifies specific kinds of difference. Both of these projects are products of and reinforced by the film's historical context.

Beginning in May 1968, massive general strikes led by an unprecedented mix of students and workers swept across France and nearly brought the nation's entire economy to a screeching halt. These revolutionary events signaled the beginning of the end of the Trente Glorieuses, the thirty years of economic success during the postwar period. The violent eruption of sexual, ethnic, age, and class categories that captured the nation during the strikes initiated a period of reevaluation, in which Charles de Gaulle managed to maintain his power and popularity after he was credited with stemming the tide of what could have been a civil war. Georges Pompidou's Gaullist presidency continued the economic growth until the oil embargo of October 1973—the same month *Rabbi Jacob* came out in theaters to a record 7.3 million moviegoers.[11]

But even before the oil embargo—which developed into a full fledged economic disaster—the seeds of far right racism, caricatured by de Funès in *Rabbi Jacob*, were already in place. Despite de Gaulle's success with "centrist" humanist politics, the events of May 1968 initiated what may be termed a "category crisis" that exposed the gulf between a center-right nationalist population and a leftist movement born after World War II. It was, as Kristin Ross explains, a "shattering of social identity" that left no one in French society unaffected.[12] In fact, Ross's argument about how May 1968 has been conceived in French memory hinges on the notion of category crisis. In her words, the events "swept away categorical territories and social definitions, and achieved unforeseen alliances and synchronicities *between* social sectors and between very diverse people working together to conduct their affairs collectively. . . . The event of 1968 was above all else a massive refusal on the part of thousands, even millions, of people to see in the social what we usually see: nothing more than the narrowest of sociological categories."[13] Ross describes here how traditional identity category divisions were broken and new alliances were formed. These new alliances could only take effect at the expense of a functioning society. French men and women eventually had to return to work, school, and family life. In order to do so, they also had to return to the clearly defined social architecture they had successfully resisted during the strikes.

Les aventures de Rabbi Jacob resolves the category crises of May 1968 by offering a part Gaullist (French unity) and part American (multiculti) answer to divisions of race, ethnicity, nationality, class, and gender. The new alliances created during the strikes are re-created as a French Catholic marries an Arab, a Jew and an Arab (in Hasidic garb) share a meaningful handshake, and a working-class Jewish chauffeur saves the life of his bourgeois industrialist Catholic boss. The social boundaries that were broken by the 1968 strikes are comically rebroken as Pivert tries on various faces—blackface, greenface, Jewface. The historical inequities between these faces are "effaced" once all categories return to their "separate but equal" realms in the French social order, so violently disrupted that May.

Jewish identity took on a curious role at the height of the May '68 events. An unwitting leader of the student movement, a German-born Jew named Daniel Cohn-Bendit, became a lightning rod for both the French government's aims to control the mass protests and the activists who saw him as a symbol of their struggles. For both parties, Cohn-Bendit's status as a foreign-born Jew contributed to his symbolic political clout. After a trip to his native Germany, Cohn-Bendit was refused reentry into France by the Council of Ministers. This act invigorated the protesters, who saw in the ministers' prohibition a reminder of the Vichy regime's restrictions on Jewish freedoms, beginning with the banishment of foreign-born Jews. Objecting to Cohn-Bendit's expulsion and seeing themselves similarly as victims of the French bureaucracy, French students and other protesters adopted a new slogan, "Nous sommes tous des juifs allemands" (We are all German Jews). Sarah Hammerschlag contrasts this powerful slogan with the types of outcries made by the French public during the Dreyfus affair more than a century earlier:

> Those who rallied for Dreyfus's cause did so in the name of the Enlightenment ideal of humanity, an ideal uniting men above and beyond their differences. They protested the suspicion directed at Dreyfus *as a Jew* and established their solidarity with him as a man and as a French citizen. . . . The student protesters of May '68, in contrast, allied themselves with Cohn-Bendit by adopting his Jewish identity. They protested, not in the name of an idea of humanity, but in the name of "the Jew"; they claimed the status of exception, of Jewish particularity, for themselves.[14]

These protesters harnessed the peculiar power of victimization that emerged alongside multiculturalism by adopting the victim's position—in this case, both Cohn-Bendit's position and the shadow of Vichy's Jews. At the same time, they disassociated themselves from the French identities they linked to the unsavory actions of French police and military. As Ross explains, the proclamation of "we" in the slogan is less about actual identification with Jews and more about "disidentification or declassification" from a certain variety of French identity.[15]

Pivoting around characters who cross-dress as Jews, *Rabbi Jacob* reenacts and resolves the challenge set forth by the 1968 slogan "We are all German Jews." As the protesters had, Pivert and Slimane adopt the position of Jewish particularity with the aim of disassociating themselves from other identity types: for Pivert, the antisemitic Frenchman; for Slimane, the violent, radical Arab. Jews are the vehicle for the peaceful category resolution in *Rabbi Jacob*. The riddle they present to ethnic, racial, and national categorization is solved for a French audience as Jews are abbreviated to a certain ethnoracial type, separated from "real" French men and women via a strong Yiddish accent, relegated to a single Parisian street, and made into a quaint, folkloric, and nonthreatening idiosyncrasy of French society. Blackness and Arabness also take the stage as equal players in the great French family of man, as garb/skin switching permits Pivert to journey through French diversity.

Rabbi Jacob is one kind of response to May 1968, but other radical or violent responses were born from these events as marginal groups forcefully asserted their position on the French social landscape. The *Front National*, a Far Right xenophobic political party headed by Jean-Marie Le Pen, was founded in 1972, more than a year before the oil crisis. The party's slogan, "La France aux Français" (France for the French), indicates its anti-immigrant position but also implies a particular white Catholic definition for French national identity.[16] *Rabbi Jacob* confronts this right-wing definition of Frenchness. The film also defies the new Pan-Arab movement. Closely aligned with the Palestinian cause, Pan-Arabism was taking hold at the time, initiating a transnational Arab nationalism. Especially violent examples include the hijacking of four planes by Arab nationalists in 1970 and the massacre of eleven Israelis at the Munich Olympic Games in 1972. This second form of radical nationalism, as well as moderate Pan-Arabism and anti-Zionism, had a significant effect on France, as it had the largest populations of Muslim Arabs and Jews in all of Europe.[17]

Pivert's flexibility in wearing various ethnic, racial, and religious masks depends on the fixedness of these types. The main Arab character, Slimane, joins Pivert in wearing the Jewish mask but notably returns to his country at the end of the film. *Rabbi Jacob* consigns the Jews to a single street, the historically Jewish rue des Rosiers in central Paris, as fascinating artifacts of European folklore; and it "returns" the Arabs to their countries of origin. In so doing, *Rabbi Jacob* performs the conservative work of reserving Jewishness for Ashkenazic Hasidic Jews and France for the French, "La France aux Français." Out of his Jewish garb at the end of the film, Pivert has redeemed French identity in the manner of the '68ers by aligning himself with the Jews. But as each character reembodies his native self, the ethnic categories and their attendant hierarchies are reinforced, even if the now beardless Pivert has become the face of goodness instead of evil.

Certainly, the Jewish filmmakers, Gérard Oury and his daughter Danièle Thompson, would reject such a harsh critique of the film, because the nationalist slogan "La France aux Français" seems so incompatible with the family of man message that the film also suggests. But by relegating nonwhite ethnicities to "ghettos," the film retains a version of French national identity (white, Catholic, bourgeois) that harmonizes with the nationalist ideal. Despite the film's many celebrated feel-good moments, the film itself constructs multiculturalism by reinscribing a limiting variety of Jewish difference.

MIMICRY, MOCKERY, MULTICULTURALISM

The combination of the film's comedic treatment of a serious subject and its public release less than two weeks after the outbreak of the Yom Kippur War enabled *Rabbi Jacob* to inaugurate a new aesthetic for representing Jews in France, one that offered a creative solution to the ongoing Jewish Question. The hats, beards, peyos, caftans, accents, and neighborhood—in other words, the semiotics—of the Hasidic world as presented in *Rabbi Jacob* became monuments that served to signify and explain "Jewishness" for a French audience, both Jewish and gentile.

These Jewish and gentile viewers are internally diverse and often overlapping, but utilizing these categories may nevertheless contribute to understanding the film's enduring popularity. The film reminds non-Jewish French viewers of their successful historical resistance to antisemitism (a history that suppresses Nazi collaboration) by mocking the antisemite. Such mockery allows the French audience to distance itself from Vichy collaboration by making antisemitism both laughable and nonviolent (and more about class than race). Jewishness in the film is friendly and welcoming, superstitious but jovial, and comfortably confined to clearly identifiable visual codes and easily detectable Hasidic garb.

For Jewish audiences, on the other hand, the film protects their specificity as Jews by insisting on Jewish difference—again, through the garb. The provincial eastern Jew, or *Ostjude*, is firmly and safely positioned within the Parisian landscape, and the Jewish audience can imagine a French past that includes and embraces Jewishness. But this Jewishness is limited to a certain type, the most visibly different Jew. Laura Levitt explores a similar phenomenon in the American context. In her essay "Impossible Assimilations," Levitt argues that religious difference became the only kind of acceptable difference for American Jews in the mid-twentieth century, suppressing the rich history of Jewish political and cultural difference, as well as the possibility for other varieties of Jewish difference.[18] In *Rabbi Jacob*, Jewish difference in France also becomes a strictly religious difference, specifically the visible, Hasidic variety.

In the film's opening sequence, set in a Hasidic enclave on Manhattan's Lower East Side, a group of Jews waves good-bye to Rabbi Jacob, who is returning to France for his nephew's bar mitzvah. Jacob (Dalio) emerges from his residence in full Hasidic garb, ceremoniously kisses the mezuzah, and in a series of goofball sight gags makes his way to the airport. Jacob, the viewer is told more than once during the film, hasn't been to Paris for thirty years. His good-bye scene in Manhattan reminds the viewer of his status as a Jew in exile returning (temporarily) to his homeland. Neither Dalio nor his family was Hasidic, but Jacob's comic return to France is a restaging of Dalio's own return to French cinema, which, without ever explicitly saying so, acknowledges France's dark history for Jews.

In the taxi on the way to the airport, Jacob literally sings the praises of France. In an exaggerated Yiddish accent, Jacob croons the French folksong "Ma Normandie."[19] Jacob's traveling companion, a young beardless American Hasid, improvises a Hasidic *niggun* (melody) to accompany Jacob's folksong. Jacob cuts off his companion, rejecting his "dai dai dai" Hasidic ad-lib.

"Non non non . . . pas daidaidai," Jacob insists, "c'ist françis!" (No no no . . . not dy dy dy [Hasidic singing] . . . eez Frrraynch!). Like the film's other famous scenes, this one may be read for its multicultural embrace of Jews as Frenchmen. Jacob loves France in spite of his years of exile. When he rejects the Hasidic melody, it is because he wishes to preserve the glory and purity of the folksong. Jacob might have been in America for thirty years, and he may be a Hasidic rabbi, but he knows what it means to be French, pointing to the potential compatibility of these categories. At the same time, by rejecting the Jewish melody, Jacob erects a clear boundary between Jewish and French. The film succeeds at one level in resolving this opposition, but the film's true resolution—and its wild success—lies in its reiteration of Jacob's boundary.

Further evidence of the dissonance between the two categories of French and Jewish becomes apparent in this opening exchange. Rabbi Jacob's insistence that Hasidic *niggunim* (read: Jewish) must be kept separate from French folksongs is undermined as his own chanting of the folksong is Judaized, and therefore rendered "grotesque," by way of his strong Yiddish accent. As postcolonial theorist Homi Bhabha has suggested, the colonized subject must reform himself, become a mimic, in order to show that he willingly accepts the power dynamic in place. Jacob's accent (not to mention his garb) prevents him from being French, and his only option is to imitate Frenchness. The colonizing power demands mimicry as "the desire for a reformed, recognizable Other, *as a subject of difference that is almost the same, but not quite.*"[20] In Bhabha's system of colonial power, mimicry demonstrates the shared value held among colonizer and colonized that the ways of the colonizer are superior. On the other hand, if the colonizer were to enable the colonized to transform entirely, to erase the difference, then the hierarchical system collapses, as there is no longer a power class. Therefore, "in order to be effective, mimicry must continually produce its slippage, its excess, its difference."[21] The slippage in this opening scene is produced through Jacob's visual and aural difference. His Frenchness is imitative and thus retains the power dynamic and separation between French and Jewish. Jacob's Yiddish-accented French folksong establishes both the character's "Frenchness" and his Jewish difference. To paraphrase Bhabha, Jacob is *almost* French, but not quite.

The "pure" French figure is entirely absent from this opening scene in a New York taxi, but Jacob's reproduction of the colonial power structure outside the realm of the colonial gaze reveals his willing submission to the system. Describing France as a colonial power and the Jew as a willingly submissive colonial subject in this context is historically as well as theoretically problematic. But this framework points to the various discourses at play in *Les aventures de Rabbi Jacob*: French colonialism and the ongoing decolonization project beginning in the 1950s, the historic Jewish middle space between Frenchman and colonized Arab, and French Jewry's double (and thus always incomplete) emancipation as internally colonized subjects first in 1789 and again in 1945. By the end of the film, Victor Pivert's experience hiding within the Hasidic community as Rabbi Jacob has enabled him to rise above his racism: he has befriended both the Jews and the Arabs. However, while Pivert overcomes his racism and antisemitism, Rabbi Jacob and his friends do not overcome their Jewish difference.

Like *The Great Family of Man* museum exhibition, *Rabbi Jacob* levels out difference, endorsing universal humanism by literally placing one kind of man (the white Frenchman) into another man's shoes (the Hasidic Jew). While this "leveling out" might promote a certain kind of human equality between Jew, Arab, and white Frenchman, there are consequences to this type of universalism. As Cynthia Ozick provocatively argued of Shakespeare's Shylock in 1970, "Shakespeare, even at his moral pinnacle, does not see the Jew as *a man*, but only as Mankind."[22] The Jewish role as a member of the "family of man" elides not only the particularities of the Jewish experience but also the particularities of each Jewish individual. Jewish difference vis-à-vis gentiles is maintained in such displays, while Jewish difference vis-à-vis other Jews disappears. Lacking any reference to the North African, non-Ashkenazic Jewish population that constituted the vast majority of French Jewry in 1973, relegating all Jews to a Hasidic type and then localizing them to a single Paris neighborhood, *Rabbi Jacob*, like a photograph in Barthes's museum exhibition, works to show its audience the Jewish type as an equal member in the family of man; instead, the film does the reductive work of presenting its audience with a new "juif typique."

The film's slapstick comedy smooths the way for conceiving of Jewish difference in part by taking conflict and resolving it into a costume, an accent, and a set of mannerisms. This immediately recognizable representation of Jewishness is an example of what Barthes understood as myth. Myth "points out and it notifies, it makes us understand something and it imposes it on us."[23] Hasidic garb in *Rabbi Jacob* behaves for French viewers like Barthes's conception of the Eiffel Tower as a monument myth. Following this analogy, the enduring iconography of "the Jew" introduced by the film is, like the tower, "a riddle; to enter it is to solve [it], to possess it."[24] Like the literally and symbolically empty Eiffel Tower, Hasidic garb (and its representation in *Rabbi Jacob*) is "the pure signifier . . . in which men unceasingly put *meaning* . . . without this meaning . . . ever being finite and fixed."[25]

Contrary to Bhabha's view of mimicry as a reiteration of power structures, Judith Butler addresses in *Gender Trouble* the liberatory potential of imitation when applied to drag. She puts forth an illuminating analysis of the slippery relationship between the presumably coherent categories of sex, gender, and performance: "As much as drag creates a unified picture of 'woman' . . . it also reveals the distinctness of those aspects of gendered experience which are falsely naturalized as a unity through the regulatory fiction of heterosexual coherence. *In imitating gender, drag implicitly reveals the imitative structure of gender itself.*"[26] The liberatory reading of *Rabbi Jacob* is bolstered by this analysis and recognizes the bigoted Pivert's experiment with Jewish drag as teaching him an important lesson about tolerance in a multiethnic France. Jewish drag, as in Butler's system, may be subversive, as it reveals the performative "fiction" of the racist version of French national identity and deessentializes the categories of Jew, Catholic, Arab, black, white, and French. Nevertheless, Butler's idea of drag assumes that the man in women's clothing "feels" like a woman, whereas Pivert puts on Jewish drag out of convenience and desperation. But drag's enduring power continues to affect Pivert, the Catholic beneath the Jew, the longer he wears the disguise. Not only does he master the elaborate performance of Jewishness in order to convince the Jews on the rue de Rosiers that he really is Rabbi Jacob, but he also sustains his Jewish performance even for those in the know, like Slimane. In fact, as long as Pivert is in the Jewish costume, he maintains his Yiddish accent. The only time he ceases to use the accent occurs when he makes a phone call to his wife, who, significantly, cannot see him. Pivert's Jewish drag in *Les aventures de Rabbi Jacob* saves lives and spreads tolerance. This double power of Jewish visibility stands in sharp contrast to the powerlessness of Jewish invisibility in occupied France for Jewish men like Dalio and *Rabbi Jacob*'s writer/director, Gérard Oury, who was also forced to flee France to avoid deportation.

But the other reading of the film, the one I argue for here, challenges the subversive potential of drag argued for by Butler. Pivert's performance as a

Jew *reestablishes* distinct identity categories in the wake of May 1968 and *reifies* essentialist notions of Jewishness. In the final scene outside the church, when all groups "return" to their native types, the "fiction of coherence" is asserted as natural fact as Jew, Arab, and Frenchman take their separate places on the national stage.

Even the seemingly subversive intermarriage between Pivert's daughter and Slimane resists a liberatory reading. It is only Slimane's status as president of his nation that qualifies him as an acceptable object of exotic sexual desire, and even this couple must be removed from the national "stage" as they fly off to his country in a helicopter. Pivert's wife, Germaine, attempts to protest the union ("But he's . . . he's . . ."), but before she can insert the controversial predicate, her husband interrupts with, "He's president of his country!" Germaine's ellipses, her silent inability to pronounce the word "Arab," keys into the unspoken politics of the film. Her husband's blessing at the end of the adventurous masquerade cuts off the underlying voice of racial superiority still latent in at least one of the characters. That same latent racism was also present in the actor de Funès, who in the interview cited in the chapter epigraph could not pronounce the word "antisemite" even as he confessed to being one.

RABBI JACOB'S IMAGINARY JEWS

In his memoirs, filmmaker Oury describes his experience as a child under Vichy. In June 1941 all Jews were required to declare their Jewishness to the police. According to Oury, his mother tortured herself over this declaration, eventually concluding that it was necessary to follow the law. In composing her official letter to the police, Oury's mother declared that she was, "mère juive d'un fils qui ne l'est pas" (Jewish mother to a son who is not).[27] In making *Rabbi Jacob*, Oury reclaims the Jewishness that his mother is responsible for both imparting to and denying him. Oury's reclamation comes at the expense of his secular Jewish identity and a more inclusive notion of which Jews matter in filmic representations and storytelling. He uses Jewishness in the guise (or disguise) of the Hasid as a foil for mocking the antisemite.

Devoid of imagery of North African or secular Ashkenazic Jews in France, the Jewish filmmakers locate themselves safely outside the provincial category "Jewish," all the while preserving Jewish difference—this notion of difference becoming the defining characteristic of French Jewish identity. Alain Finkielkraut wrote about the questionable content of Jewish difference when recounting the secular, atheist Jewishness of his childhood, which he associated only with his parents' suffering during the Holocaust.[28] Finkielkraut felt different from other French children as a Jew, although his book is a critique of this kind of contentless difference. He writes, "My gestures, language, habits, appearance, and way of life have been washed clean of every particularity.... I am identical to non-Jews, an impeccable likeness."[29] Interestingly, *Rabbi Jacob*'s response to this kind of contentless Jewishness is similar to Finkielkraut's personal solution: religious observance.

Oury's Jewishness, then, like Finkielkraut's "juif imaginaire" (imaginary Jew), is defined by the antisemite and located in someone else's memory. In Finkielkraut's case, this memory was provided by his parents' story of survival. In Oury's case, his "memory" was triggered by a series of eastern European Jewish images that he re-created as a film via the casting (e.g., Dalio as Jacob), the costumes, the accents, and the mannerisms of the Hasidic characters and by the setting of these characters on the historic rue des Rosiers. Oury's "juif imaginaire" is therefore dislocated from the vibrant, active, growing Jewish communities in France when the film was being made. His filmic representation of Jewishness also seems to reveal nostalgia for the Ashkenazic French community, which was being eclipsed by the growing visibility of Jews from the Maghreb.

Oury explains in his memoirs that a photo book of destroyed synagogues from eastern Europe inspired the set design for the synagogue scene in *Rabbi Jacob*. He then describes the destruction of the film's faux synagogue in terms that might just as easily be applied to the images he saw of burned-down synagogues in Poland and Russia. "Our temple [was] superb," he writes, "but condemned to disappear like all film sets."[30] The temple Oury had built and dedicated to *Rabbi Jacob* and then destroyed follows a parallel narrative to the Polish synagogues destroyed by an antisemitic war; beyond that, it mirrors the story of the original Holy Temple in Jerusalem, built according to God's command and destroyed by an anti-Jewish empire. Oury's story about the set thereby echoes the historic loss of European Jewry at the hands of the Cossacks and the Nazis, as well as the cosmic loss of the Jewish homeland. Positioning his experience metaphorically, if unwittingly, along this sacred timeline calls attention to how Oury worked to construct both French Jewishness through the film as limited to the Hasidic variety and the literal constructedness of the Jewishness represented in the film through faux sets.

While the crew had originally planned to film on the real rue des Rosiers in Paris, they were prohibited from doing so because their presence might have disrupted traffic flow. Instead, Oury seized upon a small block of houses destined to be demolished in the northern Parisian suburb of Saint-Denis. It was there that the iconic film version of the rue des Rosiers was built, including a kosher butcher and small shops with "typical names" like Rosenburg and Rosenfeld. Saint-Denis at the time was inhabited mostly by working-class Maghrebin immigrants, who, according to Oury, did not hesitate to call out "Shalom Rabbi Jacob!" to a Hasidic-costumed de Funès during filming. Despite these warm exchanges between North African factory workers and the film crew, the final erasure of actual working-class immigrant life in Paris came when Oury replaced the neighborhood's couscous stand, El Djézaïr (Arabic for Algeria or Algiers) with the fictional Jewish delicatessen, À l'étoile de Kiev (The star of Kiev).[31] Oury's construction of an authentic Jewish aesthetics appears at the expense of both other Jewish types and certain non-Jewish types.

Three years after publishing *Gender Trouble*, Butler revised and clarified her position on the liberatory potential of drag in *Bodies That Matter*: "I want to underscore that there is no necessary relation between drag and subversion, and that drag may well be used in the service of both the denaturalization and reidealization of hyperbolic heterosexual gender norms. At best, it seems, drag is a site of certain ambivalence, one which reflects the more general situation of being implicated in the regimes of power by which one is constituted and, hence, of being implicated in the very regimes of power that one opposes."[32] Pivert's Jewface likewise denaturalizes the ethnic norms and power structures prevalent in 1970s France through acts of slipping in and out of garbs and skins. But it also "reidealizes" these norms, particularly in its assertion of the ideal, natural Jewish type. Butler introduces popular drag films like *Tootsie* (1982) and *Some Like It Hot* (1959) as sites where drag is not a subversive act. (The meeting of drag and Jewishness in these films is a question for a separate project.) Labeling these films "high het entertainment," Butler argues that "such films are functional in providing a ritualistic release for a heterosexual economy that must constantly police its own boundaries against the invasion of queerness."[33] This analysis rings true of *Rabbi Jacob* as well, where ethnic, racial, religious, and national boundaries are policed via Jewish and other forms of drag. But while films like *Rabbi Jacob* seem to reify a hegemonic, normative, privileged state, they do not lose their potential for subversive readings. Pivert's drag *also and at the same time*, to paraphrase Butler, disputes the white, bourgeois, Catholic Frenchman's "claim on naturalness and originality."[34]

Henry Bial describes the effect of two contradictory meanings present in a single film as "double coding."[35] But for him, two distinct readings depend on two distinct (if imagined and idealized) audiences, a Jewish one and a gentile one. The dynamics of Jewish cross-dressing, particularly as they take place in *Rabbi Jacob*, invite *both* readings—the liberatory, subversive one and the hegemonic, naturalizing one—from all viewers. Pivert in *Rabbi Jacob*, like Avram Belinski in *The Frisco Kid*, spends the film in a liminal state between identities, always cementing as he challenges myths about Jewish, Arab, and French national identity.

RABBI JACOB'S AFTERLIVES: TERROR AND TRIBUTE

In the midst of war and international economic crisis, a more personal crisis reached those involved in the making of *Rabbi Jacob*. Danielle Cravenne, the wife of the film's publicist and Oury's friend, Georges Cravenne, hijacked an Air France flight. She was protesting the film's release, which she saw as anti-Palestinian (despite never having seen the film). This was an extreme political response to a film so easily dismissed as a simple comedy when removed from its historical context at the onset of the Yom Kippur War. Having released her hostages, Cravenne demanded food be brought to her. Dressed as flight attendants and mechanics, a group of police entered the plane. When Cravenne made a "suspicious move," she was fatally shot in the head. Her widower husband, Georges, would later tell Oury that had he actually shown Danielle *Rabbi Jacob*, her violent death would have been avoided.[36] The reconciliatory potential of the film is thus produced on both the national and the personal levels. Filmmakers and audiences pronounce the gravity of this comedy, an unintentional gravity that was shaped by external events.

This constellation of violence and popular comedy, in addition to the film's resolution of the category crises of post-1968 France, contributed to the film's enduring presence in French popular culture. In 1993 the French television network France 2 solicited Oury for a journalistic voyage to Israel in order to celebrate the twentieth anniversary of *Rabbi Jacob*.[37] In that film, Oury recounts his dismay at how very distant the metaphorical "Salomon-Slimane" cousins had become, but he maintains his hope for a future "inevitable" reconciliation. Oury even describes the remarkable image of a uniformed Israeli soldier at a checkpoint imitating for him Louis de Funès's famous grimaces as Pivert.[38] (This anecdote is an inversion of the scene in the film when Pivert, stopped at a gas station to be interrogated by police, makes a series of famous funny faces in order to hint to the authorities that Slimane was kidnapping him.) The reach of Oury's film twenty years after its theatrical release and thousands of miles from Paris is impressive.

The greatest evidence of *Rabbi Jacob*'s enduring legacy, however, came in the form of a musical adaptation of the film for the French stage in 2008. With the participation of Danièle Thompson (Oury's daughter and the film's coauthor) and Vladimir Cosma, who wrote the original score for the film, the musical featured a large cast of dancers and singers, fourteen original songs, and thirteen dance numbers, including a step-by-step reproduction of the iconic Hasidic dance scene from the film.[39] The production received mixed reviews and was called a "complete failure" by the popular French daily *Le Figaro*.[40] Regardless of critical reviews, the production was mostly about fulfilling the audience's expectations of reliving the now classic film—including the wordplay, bubblegum factory scenes, and famous handshake. The musical, although it had little success, introduced the iconic film and its imagery—including its representations of Jews—to a new generation of French audiences.

Popular French rapper MC Solaar contributed a song for the show called "Le Rabbi Muffin," a play on the name for an electronic subgenre of reggae music called Raggamuffin. The song is about the rabbi's journey from New York to Paris, and it samples Vladimir Cosma's original musical theme from the film. In the widely viewed music video that accompanied the song's release, a multiethnic group of Hasidic-garbed hip-hoppers adds contemporary moves to the choreography from the film. The spectacle of black and Arab yeshiva students dancing Hasidic style to the words of a black hip-hop artist who raps about *beyt-din*s and bar mitzvahs highlights the seamlessness with which category switching may happen in the wake of *Rabbi Jacob*. It also indicates the widespread desire to adopt the identity of "the Other," to participate in what Alain Finkielkraut called "the regime of equivalence."[41] *Rabbi Jacob*'s "family of man" message enables MC Solaar to exclaim that he feels he fits in with the Jews, since his dreadlocks mirror their sidelocks.[42] Jews, represented by the Hasidic break-dancers in the video, evoke one likeable face of the rich "urban jungle" referred to in the rap. Replicating *Rabbi Jacob*'s aesthetic, Jewishness continues to be relegated to a single type, albeit a relatable, celebrated one.

Category switching in twenty-first-century France certainly has historical implications different from the ones it had in 1973. For example, the popular and critically acclaimed comedy *La vérité si je mens!* (*Would I Lie to You?*, 1997) is another story of a non-Jewish Frenchman disguised in Jewish drag, although this time as a Sephardic Jew in the Jewish garment district of Paris, Sentier. *L'homme est une femme comme les autres* (*Man Is a Woman*, 1998) draws even more attention to the performative quality of both gender and Jewishness through Hasidic garb. In that film, a secular Jewish gay man masquerades as straight in order to wed a Hasidic woman and receive his promised inheritance. At the same time, the woman's brother is also masquerading as both straight and Hasidic, going so far as to glue peyos to the sides of his head whenever his authoritarian father is near. These films and others like them fall in the shadow of *Rabbi Jacob*'s lasting legacy, as artists and audiences continually turn to the imagery of *Rabbi Jacob* to provide a format for understanding French national identity and celebrating specific yet limited varieties of ethnic difference.

Oury's second memoir describes a real-life example of the kind of French-Jewish difference his film valorizes. He relates the story of the late Lubavitcher Rebbe Menachem Mendel Schneerson, whose life was spared from genocide in southern France. The Rebbe's commitment to the France that protected him inspired him to honor the French national anthem, "La Marseillaise." To this day, Lubavitch Hasidim chant various psalms and prayers to the tune of "La Marseillaise."[43] In this example, real-life Hasidim render Jewish texts French, a mirror image of the film's first scene, in which Rabbi Jacob's assistant renders a French folksong Hasidic. But the Lubavitchers' homage does not necessarily imply the reconciliation of Jewishness and Frenchness. As with *The Frisco Kid*, it also leaves open the question of what such a reconciliation would ultimately look like: Jewish identification as French? Complete annihilation of Jewishness? Or the dissolution of the category of Frenchness? While Dalio's Rabbi Jacob put up a clear barrier between the two categories by resisting his companion's Hasidic "daidaidai," this example from the Lubavitch case seems to point to a more fluid reality than the film suggests. Lubavitch Hasidim embrace exactly the kind of visible difference that the film attributes to Jews.⁴⁴ Their use of the French national anthem is more a tribute to France than colonial mimicry, because its aim is not integration. Unlike Rabbi Jacob's "Ma Normandie" or Dalio's own assimilated image as used by the Nazis, these Hasidim are Judaizing Frenchness more than they are attempting to displace or cover over Jewishness by becoming French. As *Rabbi Jacob* reasserts, their visible difference prevents the Hasidim from being seen as a threat to French national identity.

Bhabha explains that mimicry is what maintains the colonial order, but it is also the source of a potential threat. Mimicry weakens the structure it seeks to support: when the colonizer recognizes his mirrored self in his subject and ostensibly identifies with him, he is revolted, and the myth of his power collapses.⁴⁵ Dalio's image on the Nazi propaganda posters embodies this threat, as there is nothing obviously Jewish about his photograph. "Le juif typique," according to Nazi ideology, is the Jew who passes for French (or Aryan). The Nazi desire to expose the Jews who "look French" is corrected by *Rabbi Jacob*: its multicultural message presents a Jew who looks markedly different and yet whose difference is cause for celebration. But in correcting the Nazi message, the Jew who "looks French" is left outside the narrative. Oury disavows who he is (a secular Jew) by making a claim for who the Jew is (a visible Hasid). He never addresses the reality or possibility for secular Jewish identity, in part, I believe, because he lacks a clear semiotic language for the "invisible" Jew. The poster of de Funès in Hasidic garb on the walls of Paris in the 1970s does not negate the poster of Dalio as "le juif typique" in the 1940s. The celebration of Jewish visibility maintains (as it erases) the frightening prospect of Jewish invisibility.

In a television documentary about *Les aventures de Rabbi Jacob* made in 2009, Danièle Thompson describes the reluctance she, her father, and the producers felt about the release of the film so close to the outbreak of war in the Middle East. Worried that the ad posters would be seen as a provocation, Thompson and Oury went around Paris ripping them down. The Jewish face on the walls of Paris—whether it was Dalio's in the early 1940s or Rabbi Jacob's in the early 1970s—becomes a source of anxiety and suspicion for Jew and gentile alike, a visual incarnation of the Jewish Question. But Oury's and Thompson's attempt to reduce the Jewish face to a Hasidic one in order to celebrate its status as different but equal is subverted by the very posters they feared were so provocative. After all, the face in these photos was not the "real" Rabbi Jacob, played by the Jewish Dalio; it was Louis de Funès as Victor Pivert *disguised* as Jacob. These layers of performativity and disguise may, at one level, resist the reading I have argued for here, the one that says all Jews are the same because all Jews are different. There is something comic about arguing that all Jews are the same when this claim is obviously and immediately undermined by putting a non-Jew in Jewish clothes and calling him "Rabbi." De Funès as Pivert as Rabbi Jacob demands that the viewer look through the costume and at the individual.

The film offers several ongoing symbolic cycles between Jewishness and Frenchness: Thompson and Oury removed the posters, but their action was nevertheless followed by the release of the film as scheduled; Dalio made a historic turn from an invisible Jewish Frenchman to an immediately visible French Jew; and the openly reformed antisemite Louis de Funès starred as a non-Jewish-Jewish antisemite Hasidic rabbi. Such cycles ultimately point to the fact that the two categories of French and Jewish are, as Amos Funkenstein has argued of Jews and Germans, coconstitutive and inseparable.[46] Both readings are made available by the poster and the film itself—the inclusionary liberatory one and the exclusionary limiting one. In fact, these contradictory meanings are constantly at play in reinforcing one another.

If *Les adventures de Rabbi Jacob* puts forth a possible solution to the Jewish Question, the events that surround the film reveal this question to be circular, even self-contradictory. The Jewish Question—for Jews and gentiles—is always subject to a cyclical, unending discourse about the meaning of Jewishness, its historic specificity, and its potential universalism.

NOTES

1. For Dalio's biography, see, for example, Jacques Mazeau and Didier Thouart, *Les grands seconds rôles du cinéma français* (Paris: Editions Pac, 1984), 19–29.
2. See, for example, Reinhold Schünzel and Lionel Royce.
3. On "the Jewish Question" in revolutionary France, see Jay R. Berkovitz, *Rites and Passages: The Beginnings of Modern Jewish Culture in France, 1650–1860* (Philadelphia: University of Pennsylvania Press, 2007), 89–161.
4. For example, see Ron Schechter, *Obstinate Hebrews: Representations of Jews in France, 1715–1815* (Berkeley: University of California Press, 2003).
5. Examples of the film's many reincarnations in the twenty-first century include an homage to director Oury at the 2007 César Awards, when actress Valérie Lemercier performed the famous Hasidic dance scene with a troupe of dancers in Hasidic garb; a stage musical adaptation in 2008; a rap music video called *Le Rabbi Muffin* by MC Solaar in 2008; and a television documentary about the film in 2009. The film *Qu'est-ce qu'on a fait au bon dieu?*

(*Serial [Bad] Weddings*, 2014) references *Rabbi Jacob* visually, musically, through dialogue, and in its plot.

6. Judith Butler, *Gender Trouble* (New York: Routledge, 1999), 174–175.
7. Gérard Oury, *Ma grande vadrouille* (Paris: Plon, 2001), 94: "C'est dans ce climat que Rabbi Jacob pointe le bout de sa barbe sur les murs de Paris."
8. Gérard Oury, *Mémoires d'éléphant* (Paris: Olivier Orban, 1988), 265.
9. Oury, *Ma grande vadrouille*, 42.
10. Roland Barthes, "The Great Family of Man," in *Mythologies*, trans. Annette Lavers (1957; New York: Hill and Wang, 1972), 100.
11. Oury, *Mémoires*, 266.
12. Kristin Ross, *May '68 and Its Afterlives* (Chicago: University of Chicago Press, 2002), 3–4.
13. Ibid., 6.
14. Sarah Hammerschlag, *The Figural Jew: Politics and Identity in Postwar Jewish Thought* (Chicago: University of Chicago Press, 2010), 3–4.
15. Ross, *May '68*, 56–58.
16. For example, see Pierre Birnbaum, *"La France aux Français": Histoire des haines nationalistes* (Paris: Seuil, 1993).
17. These events and their link to the film are addressed in Auberi Edler's television documentary about the film for France 5, *Il était une fois . . . Les aventures de Rabbi Jacob*.
18. Laura Levitt, "Impossible Assimilations, American Liberalism, and Jewish Difference: Revisiting Jewish Secularism," *American Quarterly* 59, no. 3 (2007): 471–493.
19. The folksong, along with alluding to Pivert and Salomon's car accident in Normandy, also references another film where Dalio's character sings the song, Georges Lautner's *Le monocle rit jaune* (1964).
20. Homi K. Bhabha, *The Location of Culture* (1994; London: Routledge, 2005), especially 121–131.
21. Ibid.
22. Cynthia Ozick, "Toward Yavneh," in *What Is Jewish Literature?*, ed. Hana Wirth-Nesher (New York: Jewish Publication Society, 1994), 27.
23. Barthes, "Myth Today," in *Mythologies*, 117.
24. Roland Barthes, *The Eiffel Tower and Other Mythologies*, trans. Richard Howard (New York: Hill and Wang, 1979), 14.
25. Ibid., 5.
26. Butler, *Gender Trouble*, 175.
27. Oury claims that his mother, regretting what she wrote in the letter, waited for the postman to unlock the mailbox, removed the letter, and ripped it to pieces (*Mémoires*, 102). See also the television interview with Oury featured in Edler's documentary.
28. Alain Finkielkraut, *Le juif imaginaire* (Paris: Seuil, 1980). Translated as *The Imaginary Jew* by Kevin O'Neill and David Suchoff (Lincoln: University of Nebraska Press, 1994).
29. Finkielkraut, *Imaginary Jew*, 37.
30. Oury, *Mémoires*, 259.
31. Ibid., 259–260.
32. Butler, *Bodies That Matter: On the Discursive Limits of Sex* (New York: Routledge, 1993), 85.
33. Ibid., 86.
34. "Drag is subversive to the extent that it reflects on the imitative structure by which hegemonic gender is itself produced and disputes heterosexuality's claim on naturalness and originality" (ibid., 85).

35. Henry Bial, *Acting Jewish: Negotiating Ethnicity on the American Stage and Screen* (Ann Arbor: University of Michigan Press, 2005), 16–21.

36. Oury, *Mémoires*, 265.

37. Oury, *Ma grande vadrouille*, 41–54.

38. Ibid., 50.

39. Laurence Haloche, "Le retour de Rabbi Jacob," *Le Figaro*, August 29, 2008.

40. Anthony Palou, "'Rabbi Jacob,' un vrai ratage," *Le Figaro*, September 26, 2008.

41. Alain Finkielkraut, *Au nom de l'autre: Réflexions sur l'antisémitisme qui vient* (Paris: Gallimard, 2003).

42. The French lyrics: "Je me sens comme tout le monde avec mon paquet de dredlocks. Ils portent des tefilines des papillotes" (I feel like everyone else with my packet of dreadlocks. They wear tefilin and sidelocks). Various blogs contain full lyrics to "Le Rabbi Muffin."

43. Oury, *Ma grande vadrouille*, 45–46.

44. On the particularities of Lubavitch Hasidic garb, see Samuel Heilman and Menachem Friedman, *The Rebbe: The Life and Afterlife of Menachem Mendel Schneerson* (Princeton, NJ: Princeton University Press, 2010), 52.

45. Bhabha, *The Location of Culture*, 121–131.

46. Amos Funkenstein, "The Dialectics of Assimilation," *Jewish Social Studies* 1 (Winter 1995): 1–14.

3

HARD-CORE JEWS

Woody Allen's Religious Women and Men

> I am a Jewish woman... and Jewish women do whatever the fuck they want.
>
> —Maura Pfefferman, *Transparent*

> What a strange power there is in clothing.
>
> —Avigdor, *Yentl, the Yeshiva Boy*

WHILE FILMING THE SEGMENT of *Rabbi Jacob* set in New York—scenes that feature Dalio as Rabbi Jacob surrounded by a swarm of Hasidic-garbed actors young and old—a Hasidic man approached director Gérard Oury and asked, "What are you doing? A pornographic picture?"[1] The man may have been admonishing Oury for making a spectacle or even a mockery of Hasidic life on the Lower East Side. But while the apparent piety of Hasidic dress would appear automatically alien to the notion of porn, Hasidic performances from Israel Grodner to Woody Allen have lent the imagery a kind of subversive sexuality that affords some logic to Oury's interrogator's question.

Theories of pornography can shed light on how Hasidic garb operates as a fetish about Jewishness. Such theories can also help explicate how the garb aims to resolve while ultimately complicating a crisis of representation. Film scholar Linda Williams proposed a theory about representations of the female orgasm in hard-core pornography, offering a handy analogy for this crisis. While other filmic forms fetishize the female body, she explains, by playing "so many games of peekaboo around this body... hard core tries *not* to play peekaboo with either its male or female bodies."[2] While the stakes for women in hard-core porn are incomparable to those at play when considering popular comedies, the representational possibilities are analogous. The hard-core goal to show "everything" has a parallel in representations of the "hard-core" religious Jewish man, a man whose Jewishness, rather than flesh, is entirely on display. This is in contrast to those representations of hidden, less visible Jews whose ability to pass as gentile offers its own "game of peekaboo." Williams goes on to explain that hard-core porn ultimately fails to accomplish its show-everything goal:

> The irony . . . is that, while it is possible, in a certain limited and reductive way, to "represent" the physical pleasure of the male by showing erection and ejaculation, this maximum visibility proves elusive in the parallel confession of female sexual pleasure. Anatomically, female orgasm takes place . . . in an "invisible place" that cannot be easily seen. . . .
> The history of hard-core film could thus be summarized in part as the history of the various strategies devised to overcome this problem of invisibility.[3]

The "maximum visibility" of Hasidic Jewish attire is likewise limited to men. A woman's Jewishness is often restricted to its demonstration by other means: through her alignment with a visibly religious man; through a wig that nevertheless is designed to resemble hair (see chapter 5); through modest attire that nevertheless seeks to be fashionable and attractive (see chapter 4). Or it can be demonstrated through the means Woody Allen uses in 1997's *Deconstructing Harry*: he first desexualizes the Jewish woman and then has her verbalize her commitment to Judaism. Not only does male Jewishness not demand such measures, but, like male physical pleasure, mere seconds are all that is required to demonstrate what is elusive in the representational world of Jewish women. This chapter explores the ways in which the immediacy of male Jewish garb may be understood (again, like the male orgasm) as "limited and reductive." It also suggests that the inverse may be true for representations of religious Jewish women. Because they demand complex measures to signify their Jewishness, women may automatically evade the reductive nature of the male Hasidic garb.

The Frisco Kid and *Rabbi Jacob* both demonstrate the signifying power of the Hasidic fantasy that took hold in the 1970s: the seemingly progressive messages that fantasy conveys when actors put on and take off the garb and the precarious consequences of such costume play. Those two films employ similar strategies in divergent contexts to arrive at these same conclusions. Now we come to Woody Allen, a figure who straddles both contexts. He is one of Hollywood's most prolific filmmakers, but he simultaneously maintains "a privileged relationship with France," where he is embraced precisely for his "independence from the Hollywood machine."[4] In a fascinating overlap, not only do his characters reference the French Holocaust documentary *Le chagrin et la pitié* (*The Sorrow and the Pity*) (1969) multiple times in the celebrated comedy *Annie Hall*, but Allen himself credits the sobering documentary with influencing *Annie Hall*'s "mockumentary" style and themes.[5] Beyond such overt references and Allen's status in both France and America, his public persona and its attendant controversy also straddle the questions I ask here about sex and Jewishness. Allen has been derided in some circles for being a "self-hating Jew" and a misogynist. But the meditation on the creative process he presents in *Deconstructing Harry* provides viewers with complex women characters who offer a surprising way to explore questions about what it means to be a religious Jew.

ALLEN, ALVY, ANNIE, AND DOV: A MUDDLED LEGACY

In 2007 two billboards advertising the clothing company American Apparel —one in Manhattan and one in Los Angeles—featured the iconic image of Woody Allen dressed as a Hasidic Jew. They were taken down after less than a week when Allen complained that American Apparel had failed to obtain his permission to use the image. He later sued American Apparel for $10 million.[6] Showcasing a screen shot from one of Allen's most celebrated films, 1977's *Annie Hall*, the billboard depicted the face of Allen playing the character Alvy Singer, who, at Easter dinner with the family of his girlfriend, Annie, briefly transforms into a Hasid. The billboard contained several assumptions about the countless passersby who would view it: among them, first, that Allen would be recognizable despite his Hasidic disguise; second, that the disguise would be identifiable as that of a Hasid; and third, that the image came from his film *Annie Hall*. Above the company's logo, a Yiddish text read "der heyliker rebbe" (the holy rebbe), a moniker usually reserved for the late Lubavitcher Rebbe Menachem Mendel Schneerson. This text demanded a kind of insider knowledge, even though many viewers might be able to decipher the Hebrew letters without knowing what they spelled. Finally, the

Figure 3.1 The American Apparel billboard, Allen Street, New York (Susan Sermoneta).

viewer was expected to know, as the company's Jewish CEO, Dov Charney, later explained on his website, that the image and text were meant as an allusion to some of the legal challenges, including charges of sexual harassment, that American Apparel was facing at the time.[7] The multiple demands for familiarity with Woody Allen's persona, with the signifiers of Hasidism, with a brief scene from *Annie Hall*, with Yiddish, and with the internal politics of American Apparel necessarily limited the target audience of this billboard and thereby its apparent function: to deflect the controversy surrounding the company's brand and to promote its sales. But, as was the case for Alvy in the Easter scene in *Annie Hall*, even without these explanations, the Hasidic garb alone makes for a powerful image—a power that lies in its ability to signify Jewishness in general instantly while also yielding ambivalent messages about what Jewishness means.

The garb's signifying immediacy synthesized with its erotic potential at the moment of the billboard controversy. When Allen sued American Apparel for $10 million, Charney made an official statement on the company's website defending his use of the *Annie Hall* image:

> This was intended as a satirical spoof and not to be taken literally. Posed as a riddle, the purpose of the text was to create a parallel between the sentiment of that moment in the film and what my company and I were experiencing at the time ... the media fallout resulting from a few sexual harassment lawsuits. There were false allegations ... that were sensationalized and exaggerated to the point where my entire persona was vilified. ... Some writers characterized me as a rapist and abuser of women, others asserted that I was a bad Jew, and some even stated that I was not fit to run my company. There are no words to express the frustration caused by these gross misperceptions, but this billboard was an attempt to at least make a joke about it.[8]

Charney claimed he used Allen's image on the billboards because he identified with Alvy's predicament. He had been accused of being a "bad Jew" and a perpetrator of sex crimes—two accusations famously shared by Allen, though not by his fictional counterpart, Alvy. Charney seems to allude to Allen's charges of sexual impropriety during his public breakup from Mia Farrow and subsequent marriage to her adopted daughter, Soon Yi Previn. He elicits Allen's real-life scandal while relating to the character Allen plays in *Annie Hall*. The Jewish image becomes at once a testimony of Charney's (and Allen's?) innocence and a signifier of his and Allen's alleged sexual misdeeds and Jewish self-hatred. The Hasidic image thus opens the way for the charge of sexual hypocrisy: it gives the illusion of piety while perversion lurks beneath the beard and hat.

The lawsuit is replete with its own hypocrisies: the clothing company implicitly assumed that Allen's image was valuable enough to sell their product, but their legal defense was based on the notion that Allen's image was worthless (certainly not worth the $10 million Allen was demanding). Charney identified with Allen's sexual predicament by alluding to the Farrow/Previn scandal on his website, but he also used that scandal against Allen as a way to devalue his image in court. Ultimately, the company's threats to denigrate Allen publicly at trial—including bringing Mia Farrow to the stand as a character witness—resulted in a reduced settlement that awarded $5 million to Allen. The billboards are provocative not only for their legal repercussions but also for the underlying sexualization of the religious image that arose with the legal discourse. The Hasidic man's sexuality was called into question when Charney used the imagery in connection with his alleged sexual misdeeds and when he raised the issue of Allen's own dubious sexual ethics. Whether the image alone is erotic is debatable, but Allen's use of it, followed by Charney's appropriation, accentuates the erotic or sexual potential of the Hasidic man.

As I argued of *The Frisco Kid* and *Rabbi Jacob*, distinctive religious markers like beards, broad-brimmed hats, and peyos are a useful visual shorthand for representing Jewishness, a highly contingent and internally diverse category. But the expediency of this shorthand eclipses its complexity: the religious garb forcefully and efficiently affirms the authenticity of this type of Jew, and at the same time, the image undermines the authenticity of the garb by depicting it at the level of signifier only, depriving it of deeper meaning. In other words, a character's ability to don and remove the garb in the manner of a mask points to its superficial, surface quality and its stereotypical utility in conveying humor. This double function—the image is both full and empty, deep and superficial—contributes to the image's complexity and thereby its enduring power. It is the inherent power of the Hasidic fantasy, its openness to a multiplicity of often-conflicting meanings, that undoubtedly served as partial motivation for Allen when he chose it as a way to signify Alvy's self-conscious Jewishness in *Annie Hall*. These multiple meanings also motivated American Apparel's Dov Charney when he designed his company's controversial billboard as a means to assert how conspicuous he felt during his and his company's legal troubles.

WOODY ALLEN'S JEWISH DRAG

Annie Hall was not the first nor the only time Allen has used the Hasidic figure in his work. In his early slapstick comedy *Take the Money and Run* (1969), the crook protagonist (Allen) samples an experimental drug only to experience the bizarre side-effect of being "turned into a rabbi" for several hours—that is to say, appearing in full Hasidic garb, including a long beard. *Zelig* (1983) contains a sight gag similar to the one from *Annie Hall*. Driving home the performative quality of the Hasidic attire, a group of "rabbis" (all bearded Hasidim) stands on a cabaret stage as the chameleon-like Leonard Zelig (Allen) transforms into one of them—beard and all—before a delighted audience. Although not visibly Hasidic, the rabbi who appears in the "What's My Perversion?" sketch from *Everything You Always Wanted to Know about*

Sex (1972) has many of the signifiers of the Hasidic man discussed here, including the black hat, suit, Yiddish accent, Jewish gestures, and Jewish name. His sex fetish points to the potential—if discordant—erotic nature of the religious Jewish man. A scene from *Love and Death* (1975) includes a gag where a priest shows a young boy some sketches of Jews. The viewer does not see the sketches but can imagine them, inviting the spectator to envision the Hasidic man in his absence. Allen's 2011 one-act play, *Honeymoon Motel*, featured a rabbi who dons Hasidic garb. Finally, in 2013's *Fading Gigolo* Allen costarred with writer/director John Turturro as two Brooklyn men who start a gigolo business targeting Hasidic women clients, further demonstrating both the ongoing saliency of the Hasidic image and its continued relationship to Allen's comedic and sexual persona.

Allen's Hasidic image in *Annie Hall*, as the American Apparel billboard presumed, remains his most iconic. At Easter dinner with Annie's family, Alvy imagines himself as a Hasidic Jew at a moment when he feels his Jewishness to be exposed. As Alvy awkwardly praises Grammy Hall's "dynamite ham," the camera jumps from face to face: from Alvy to Annie to Grammy to the other Halls. When the camera points back to Alvy, he appears in full Hasidic garb. Although the image is on-screen for no more than two seconds, Alvy's beard, peyos, black hat, and caftan are projections of his fears of what the Hall family sees when they look at him.

When Alvy imagines himself in Hasidic attire, he sees himself as he believes the gentile Halls see him. From this perspective, his attempt to "fit in" with the WASPy Halls is betrayed by the Jew beneath the sports coat—the Hasidic garb reveals the "real Jew" behind the mask of assimilation.[9] On the other hand, the Hasidic garb is an intense exaggeration of Alvy's Jewishness and therefore equally artificial. Surely the beard and hat form the mask, and the "real" Alvy is the man in the sports coat. Hasidic costume play thereby presents a tension in which Alvy belongs in the garb as much as he does not belong in it.

Anthropologist Esther Newton describes what she calls the "double inversion" of drag performances by composing a formula that exposes the incoherence of the gender binary: "Drag says, 'my "outside" appearance [the costume] is feminine, but my essence "inside" [the body beneath] is masculine.' At the same time it symbolizes the opposite inversion; 'my appearance "outside" [the body, the sex] is masculine, but my essence "inside" [the self] is feminine.'"[10] The message sent by Alvy when he experiments with Hasidic drag is the same: My "outside" appearance (the Hasidic garb) is Jewish, but my essence "inside" (my authentic self) is secular/unmarked/American. My appearance "outside" (my civilized manner, my voice) is American, but my essence "inside" (my authentic self) is Jewish. Allen and Alvy, in performing Jewishness, expose it as a discursive cultural category; the simplicity with which Jewishness can be signified through the garb is destabilized by the complex and dynamic possibilities it introduces. The larger implication here is that in order to act Jewish, one must act like a certain type of Jew, a visible, Hasidic Jew, just as imitating "womanness" (for a man *or* a woman) requires the elaborate production of dress, speech, and gesture. If drag reveals that all women are performing their "womanness," then *Annie Hall* brings to light the notion that Jewishness, onstage or off, is performative.

But where do these performances of Jewishness leave the Jewish woman, both as image and as audience member? Jewish women viewers, like Jewish men, are invited to identify with this ethnoreligious imagery, forcing them into a double estrangement from what they see on-screen. According to the myth of Jewish authenticity communicated by the garb, not only do non-Hasidic Jewish women fail to affiliate with or practice "authentic" Judaism, but as women, the possibility for them to be authentic Jews does not exist in the easily identifiable realm of what a "real Jew" looks like. Just as the veracity or authenticity of the female orgasm may be called into question even in the most revealing hard-core performances of pleasure, so, too, is a woman's Jewish authenticity always called into question, as she lacks the signifying immediacy of the Hasidic man's garb.

At its origins in the 1970s and 1980s, feminist film criticism challenged the ways women characters are traditionally objects on-screen while men characters are "actors."[11] Women are "looked at" while men do the looking, or, to use John Berger's formulation, "men act and women appear."[12] During the Easter scene in *Annie Hall*, however, the Hasidic Jewish man, and not the woman beside him, is the object of the gaze. By objectifying his character (one closely identified with himself) and subverting the paradigm of the male-directed gaze, Allen also opened the door for the image's subsequent objectification on the billboards thirty years later. The billboards and the legal grievances surrounding them further confirm the objectification of the

Jewish man, in part by sexualizing or eroticizing the image. Even if Allen does not appear on the billboard as an object of sexual desire, his image is sexualized by the billboard's context, a context that reminds the viewer of Allen's alleged sexual perversion. This process of reobjectifying the Jewish man in turn unleashes a new kind of potential for how Jewish women may be represented on-screen, a potential Allen explores at length in *Deconstructing Harry*.

RECONSTRUCTING WOODY

Theories of deconstruction, to which the title of the film alludes, are always aimed at challenging discourses of authenticity. Allen's film is about the blurred boundaries between the "real-life" and fictional fantasies of its title character. But in deconstructing Harry and his relationships, the film also deconstructs Jewishness. To explore a complex variety of Jewishness that lent itself to both internal conflict and religious content, Allen created religious Jewish characters who do not immediately signify Jewishly. Because the religious Jewish man (namely, the Hasid) signifies Jewishness instantaneously, these characters had to be women—deeroticized and thereby nonobjectified women. While objectification and eroticization need not always go hand in hand, eliminating sexual desirability from depictions of Jewish women eliminates one possibility for objectification. By reconfiguring Jewishness in this manner, *Deconstructing Harry* paved the way for new readings of women, but this does not make Allen a feminist filmmaker or the film in question a feminist film. Instead, the new paradigm points to the similarities between how women and Jews are signified on-screen and how employing religious Jewish women characters helped Allen to escape Grammy Hall's gaze.

Deconstructing Harry tells the story of a writer, Harry Block (Allen), whose fictional portrayals of his already troubled relationships lead to disastrous consequences in his real life. Harry struggles to contend with three ex-wives, a self-professed sex obsession, and a near constant feeling of failure and disjointedness. Despite the success of his most recent book, Block has fallen deeper into depression and a bad case of writer's block, as his name suggests. Throughout the film, Harry's literary fiction is illustrated in vignettes, dispersed among related, often parallel scenes from his real life. Harry narrates these fictional scenes, which include crisp lighting and conventional edits.

The actors who portray Harry's creations look polished and sexy, including Harry's neurotic alter egos. The "real-life" scenes, on the other hand, are choppy and halting. Harry's fragmented existence is conveyed through jump cuts that often cut him off midsentence, replay an action several times, or leap incongruously between nonconsecutive moments. While many of the actors in these scenes are attractive movie stars, they appear more disheveled and awkward than their fictional counterparts.

Two scenes in the film, one from Harry's "real life" and one from a fictional vignette, feature religious Jewish women. The film spotlights many other Jewish characters whose names and activities mark them as unmistakably Jewish. Indeed, we might consider *Harry* to be Allen's most Jewish film for its array of Jewish personalities and references. Most of the Jewish types in the film demand insider knowledge: Jewish names, for example, are a far subtler indication of Jewishness than the Hasidic garb and Yiddish accents. The film's vulgarity—near constant sex jokes and gratuitous use of four-letter words—invited criticism from some, but Allen (not for the first time) got into the most trouble for skewering Jewishness.[13]

Allen reportedly wanted to cast actor Elliott Gould (among others) in the role of Harry, but Gould had to step down due to scheduling conflicts, so Allen ended up casting himself in the starring role.[14] During production, Allen described the film to the *New Yorker*: "It's about a nasty, shallow, superficial, sexually obsessed guy. I'm sure everyone will think—I know this going in—they'll think it's me."[15] This is not quite a denial that the film is autobiographical, and the film, which constantly calls into question how fiction and "real life" may or may not collide, does little to negate a biographical reading. In Allen's own words, "I'm always fighting against reality."[16] Whether or not we understand his relationship with Previn and the scandal surrounding it as informing the ultimate meaning of the film, audiences and critics detected an equivalence between Allen and the characters he plays, making his private (or, rather, public) affairs an important star in the constellation that makes up any reading of the film.

The film prefigures this perceived equivalence between Allen and Harry, since the main conflict hinges on the equivalence the characters detect between Harry and his fictional creations. As he negotiates the troubled waters of family and lovers, Harry's fiction is so successful that the college that once kicked him out (as Allen was from NYU) now wishes to celebrate him with an honorary degree. Accompanied by a friend and hiring a prostitute named Cookie (Hazelle Goodman) to be his date, Harry kidnaps Hilly (Eric Lloyd), his son from a previous marriage, to make the trip to the college upstate. Along the way, Harry stops at his estranged sister's house for a visit, evidence of the way he is reassessing his relationships after the publication of his latest novel. He sits down to talk with his wary sister, Doris (Caroline Aaron), who, like the other women in his life, is enraged by her image as portrayed in his writing.

We learn—through dialogue between Harry and Doris—that Doris became a religious Jew upon marrying her husband, Burt (Eric Bogosian), whom Harry refers to as a "fanatic" and "zealot." Burt sports a knit yarmulke and trimmed beard; he is far from Allen's Hasid in *Annie Hall*. Nevertheless, the beard and yarmulke are toned-down signifiers that help establish his religiosity: at the very least, he is proudly, visibly Jewish and a different Jewish type from Harry. The viewer "in the know" about Jewish politics and denominational variations will understand that Burt's particular look generally signals modern Orthodox Judaism with Zionist sensibilities (the modern clothes and trimmed beard for modern Orthodoxy, the knit yarmulke for Right-leaning Zionism). Also notable about Burt is that this minor supporting player, who has very few lines in the scene, is able to convey various messages about his Jewishness via his garb alone.

Doris's Jewishness, on the other hand, is not as immediately, visually obvious. With a simple short haircut, minimal makeup, a long, flowing skirt, and a long-sleeved blouse, Doris appears at first glance as an average-looking, markedly unsexy (especially when compared with the other women in Harry's life), middle-aged woman. Through the brother and sister's conversation, the viewer learns of Doris's turn toward Jewish observance as an adult. In the scene transcribed below, Harry sits down with his sister for a chat while his son, Hilly, his friend Richard (Bob Balaban), and his "companion," Cookie, chat outside with Burt. With eyebrows raised in a smug, defensive sneer, Doris aggressively folds napkins.

DORIS: I know what you think of me.
HARRY: Oh, please, Doris, don't start in.

Figure 3.2 Doris confronts Harry about his book (screen grab).

> DORIS: Am I wrong? It's all over your book. "Jewish." "Too Jewish." "Professionally Jewish." Of course, you attributed it all to your ex-wife, Joan, but you used the details of my life because you wanted to depict her with contempt.
>
> HARRY: Oh, I don't know what you're talking about.
>
> DORIS: You don't know what I'm talking about? You made a picture of your ex as a horror. And in order to make that picture unsympathetic and unappetizing, yes, you used some of her, but mostly, mostly you caricatured my religious dedication. Because it has always enraged you that I returned to my roots.

While Doris appears to be defending herself against the negative portrayal of one of Harry's fictional Jews, she suggests here that her variety of observant Judaism (and its fictional caricature) would be perceived by his readers as "unsympathetic and unappetizing." She believes that Harry uses religious Jewishness as a negative trait to portray an unlikeable character, indicating that Jewishness alone might be cause for disdain from readers. For Doris, the "unappetizing" quality that goes along with being Jewish—religious or not—demands no explanation. She assumes Harry already knows why she believes non-Jews see her that way. At the same time, Doris's deliberate gestures and strong, poised tone convey her confidence and pride in her choice to "return" to observant Judaism. Doris resigns herself to the "unappetizing" quality of observant Judaism as caricatured by Harry as a means to assert her pride in her religious roots.

Annie Hall and *Deconstructing Harry* are different films with different comic rhythms and different uses of sight gags, and they were created during vastly different times in the director's career. But what is significant here is that it is difficult to imagine how Allen could have employed immediately signifying visual cues to indicate Doris's Jewishness the way he was able to do with Alvy. Doris's domestic activity (folding napkins), her wig-like hairdo, and the crystal candlesticks behind her in the frame all *suggest* Jewishness but do not *insist* on it the way the Hasidic man's garb does. Likewise, it is difficult to imagine Harry carrying on such an elaborate debate with an estranged, newly religious brother (in beard and black hat) instead of a sister. Harry's blend of fascination and disgust with Doris's religious life reflects a complex internal debate between secular and religious Jewishness, a debate absent from the scene in *Annie Hall*. The man's Hasidic garb creates a signifying wall that blocks the kind of reflective dialogue featured in this scene. In both films, the characters "become" Jewish—Alvy in a fleeting imaginary flash and Doris in the manner of a *ba'alat tshuvah,* the tradition of the Jewish "returnee" who comes to religious Judaism as an adult. These two ways of becoming further reinforce the immediacy of Alvy's transformation versus the more internal and discursive process of Doris's.

Doris continues, "I'm a Jew. I was born a Jew. What, do you hate me because of that?" Harry responds with a series of reductive hypotheticals, asking how she would feel "if our parents converted to Catholicism" or "if a gentile gets hurt." "You know what?" Doris responds, looking Harry directly in the eyes. "Burt is right about you. You're a self-hating Jew." Harry replies with one of Allen's great one-liners: "Hey, I may hate myself, but not because I'm Jewish." Harry is echoing a joke Allen made years earlier in the leftist Jewish quarterly *Tikkun*. "I have frequently been accused of being a self-hating Jew," he writes, "and while it's true I am Jewish and I don't like myself very much, it's not because of my persuasion. The reasons lie in totally other areas—like the way I look when I get up in the morning, or that I can never read a road map."[17]

The echo resonated a third time when the comedian Larry David employed the same joke on his HBO series *Curb Your Enthusiasm*. In a season 2 episode of the show, a man overhears Larry whistling a Wagner melody and accuses him of being a "self-loathing Jew." "I do hate myself," Larry responds, "but it has nothing to do with being Jewish."[18] We cannot know whether David's joke was influenced by Allen, but both created characters who faced the same accusation and came up with the same defense. In fact, the jokes work because Woody's, Harry's, and Larry's denials are undermined by their telling. When repeated, the statement becomes a "Jewish joke," one about Jews who hate themselves, even while claiming that their Jewishness is irrelevant to their insecurity. Part of the joke is that Jews who hate themselves are by definition self-hating Jews. Thus, the denial reinforces the truth of the accusation, although the accusation and the admission have different implications.

Despite Harry's denial about being a self-hating Jew, the viewer knows that Harry's Jewishness is by no means incidental to his or his characters' insecurities or abhorrent qualities. Nearly every one of Harry's short story vignettes includes identifiably Jewish names: Harvey Stern, Mendel Birnbaum, Reuven, Epstein, Max Pincus, and so on. One vignette—one that particularly enrages Burt and Doris—is even set at a *Star Wars*–themed bar mitzvah celebration. Playing on Harry's hypersexual, amoral, and neurotic persona, his fictional characters tend to do despicable things: a married man "borrows" a comatose friend's apartment in order to hire a prostitute; a man having an affair with his wife's sister performs a sex act in the presence of her blind grandmother; and, most despicably, a Jewish man eats his wife and children. Such actions are clearly meant to be comically deplorable—Harry wrote them that way—and they are deplorable whether or not the characters are Jewish. But, as in *Annie Hall*, the religious Jew is brought into the cinematic conversation in order to explore how the non-Jewish gaze affects secular Jewish characters. Doris's religiosity provides a moral compass for the film, even as the viewer is asked to sympathize and identify with Harry, and even as Doris herself ultimately does.

Most of Doris's anger is directed at a specific story, which stars Stanley Tucci as Epstein. In this vignette, Epstein is a sexually depraved neurotic who is strongly attracted to his psychiatrist, Helen. Played by the leggy Demi Moore, Helen attributes Epstein's feelings to transference, until one day she terminates his treatment in order to see him socially. They fall in love and eventually marry. Everything is wonderful until their son, Hilly (also the

Figure 3.3 Helen's transformation (screen grabs).

name of Harry's "real-life" son), is born. Then, Helen becomes "what Epstein referred to angrily as 'Jewish with a vengeance.'"

Helen's appearance becomes progressively dowdier throughout the vignette. In the psychiatrist's office, her bare legs feature prominently in the shot, and her long black hair drapes provocatively over her shoulders. At home, during the early phase of their relationship, Helen wears a sexy tank top as she curls up on the couch by Epstein. After the birth of their son, her legs and shoulders all but disappear from view. Helen marches aggressively, angrily, around the kitchen in a long loose black skirt, a conservative gray blouse, and a shapeless black cardigan, although Moore's famous curves remain visible, and her top blouse button is suggestively open. She wears her hair partly tied back. As she plays out the main gag of the vignette—reciting the Hebrew blessings over wine, challah, candles, and, finally, oral sex—Helen maintains her covered-up appearance and conservative hairstyle. In bed for the punch line, she wears a loose long-sleeved nightshirt. Even the sex act itself loses its eroticism when Helen, whose fully covered body is awkwardly perched over Epstein in their dark bedroom, recites "*borey p'ri ha*—blow job."

The scene then cuts to Helen back in her office working with a new patient. The shot's composition is identical to the initial shot of Epstein as Helen's patient, except that now, Helen shows no skin at all. In stark contrast to the first scene of the vignette, her hair is completely tied back into a low bun. She wears a thick black turtleneck and large heavy shawl across her shoulders, masking her shape completely. In place of bare legs, she wears a long shapeless black skirt. In the vignette's final joke, Helen uses exactly the same language with her new patient—"an Israeli"—as she used with Epstein. She suggests they terminate treatment in order to pursue a social relationship. Like Doris, Helen's Jewish visibility requires verbalization, more screen time, and subtler costume cues than Alvy Singer's Hasidic moment in *Annie Hall*. With the hypersexualized Moore in the role of Helen, the exaggerated comedy in the vignette amplifies how religious Jewish women's garb works to undercut (albeit unsuccessfully) the eroticism of a woman's body.

When Alvy dons the beard and hat, there is no explicit comment on his sex appeal (although the Hasid's appearance, like most religious figurations, carries with it the implicit sexual piety of its wearer). Later, in light of the Farrow/Previn scandal and Charney's use of the screen shot on the billboards, the image takes on an erotic, perverse status, carrying with it dueling notions of sexual aggressor and victim of "false allegations" of a sexual nature, thereby playing on both the perceived piety and the perceived hypocrisy of the Hasid. Similarly, in Allen's 1983 mockumentary *Zelig*, when Allen's character transforms into a Hasidic rabbi, he does so onstage, surrounded by scantily clad cabaret dancers, pointing to the potential (if incongruous) erotic quality of the Hasidic man. Although Alvy and Zelig gain beards and peyos in these scenes, their transformations are not about skin and hair as much as they are about costume and disguise. Doris's outfit and especially Helen's costume changes are clearly about the act of covering up skin and shape and minimizing the sexiness of a hairstyle. In order to have a full voice and complex character, these women are forced to shed their potential erotic natures. Even the famously seductive Moore, who starred a year earlier in *Striptease*, is stripped of her eroticism even in the most ostensibly sexual moments: oral sex with her husband and subsequent cheating on him with a new patient.

As in the scene with Doris, Helen's transformation from secular to religious must be verbalized and defended. She is presented, like Doris, as angry, even irrationally proud of her tradition, but her arguments about why she maintains this pride take on a rational tone, as if Harry/Allen is arguing with himself about the value of tradition.

> EPSTEIN: God, you're like a born-again Christian, except you're a Jew.
>
> HELEN: I see my father's face in Hillel.
>
> EPSTEIN: Hilliard. His name is Hilliard. We didn't name him Hillel. We didn't name him after some rabbi. It's Hilliard Epstein.

HELEN: I'm sick of your smug cynicism. There's value in tradition. . . . I see not only meaning in Judaism but true beauty.

EPSTEIN: Helen, you're a scientist.

HELEN: Einstein was a scientist *and* he was a Jew *and* he was religious!

Helen and Epstein, Harry and Doris, present two extremes of an essentially futile debate about traditional Judaism versus secularism. Like Doris, Helen "becomes" Jewish in the manner of a ba'alat tshuvah. Harry/Allen recognizes the attraction to this kind of "return" even if he fights it. By providing Doris and Helen with rational voices in the debate, Allen allows religious Judaism to be about more than the fear of the antisemitic gaze and a visual one-liner, to which his Hasidic men had been consigned in his earlier comic films. Instead, religious Judaism is the axis around which characters' familial, collegial, and sexual relationships revolve in *Deconstructing Harry*; religious Judaism is at the (hard) core of these characters' moral, ethical, and psychological struggles.

Contrary to feminist criticism on the silenced woman's voice in literature or film, *Deconstructing Harry*'s Jewish women have voices—complicated, full voices that enable them to seem reasonable, irrational, or both at once. Alvy Singer does not have that option when dressed as a Hasid. Just as the erotic female body might silence her literary or cinematic voice, the Hasidic man's garb restricts his voice. Through the women in *Deconstructing Harry*, Allen attempts to get beneath how he's seen: to *be* instead of just *being seen*. These religious Jewish women whose lifestyles as depicted by Harry/Allen seem restrictive nevertheless invite the viewer to consider the complex multiple options that Jewishness presents. These women who are deeroticized by virtue of their clothing, hair, and mannerisms expose the attractiveness of Judaism by articulating its virtues as ba'alei tshuvah. Allen has not quite recovered women from the male gaze in this film. Instead, he uses these religious Jewish women in order to explore nuanced approaches to religion, an exploration that would not be possible for his characters who are men.

ENGENDERING MASQUERADE

According to feminist film theory, in order for women viewers of mainstream narrative films to receive pleasure from their objectified images on-screen, they have basically two options: to identify masochistically with the objectified woman or to make a "transsexual" or "transvestite" identification with the male performer who "controls the look."[19] Mary Ann Doane builds on these ideas for the spectator, introducing her take on Joan Riviere's idea of the masquerade. "Masquerade" refers to the notion that "womanliness is a mask which can be worn or removed."[20] The religious transformation that Moore's character undergoes exemplifies the womanly masquerade via its removal (reversing the more common trajectory in film where through a "makeover," a frumpy woman becomes more feminine). Helen's transformation also suggests that Jewishness, like womanliness, is a mask that may be assumed or rejected at will.

Likewise, Allen's Hasidic men who don and remove the Jewish "mask" leave the spectator wondering which face constitutes the mask and which the "real Jew." One answer to that conundrum—as with the fiction of the womanly masquerade—is that both the womanly and the less womanly, the assimilated Jew's clothing and the Hasidic attire, are masks. Or, alternatively, neither is a mask. The audience's ability to laugh at (or, in dramatic instances, be moved by) such garb switching owes in part to the confusion of the masquerade's powerful dynamics, or, as I described earlier, the way in which Alvy belongs, as much as he does not belong, in the garb.

Doane characterizes the masquerade in terms of proximity. Hasidic garb, to adopt her language, "doubles representation" and "effects a defamiliarisation" of Jewish iconography by inventing a distance between the Jew and himself, as it does between the woman and herself. She begins by referring to one of Freud's lectures in which he compared women to hieroglyphic language, explaining that "the relationship between signifier and signified is understood as less arbitrary in imagistic systems of representation than in language 'proper.'" For Freud, women, like hieroglyphics, lack the gap between signifier and signified present in phonetic language: "Too close to herself, entangled in her own enigma . . . she could not achieve the necessary distance of a second look."[21] The masculine, according to this formulation, contains this distance; it can examine itself, return for a second look, and represent itself. The feminine, on the other hand, "cannot describe itself . . . in formal terms, except by . . . losing itself."[22]

Based on their claims, it appears Freud and possibly even Doane are making the case for a transcendental condition of womanhood or femininity—a case that the arguments made here about Jewishness, race, and ethnicity must logically reject. There do exist, however, standards and expectations for the representation of women, ones that Freud's and Doane's metaphors help to explicate. We can draw an analogy between Doane's description of Freud's "feminine" and the Hasidic or religious Jewish fantasy. The facility with which a Jewish man can be signified—a facility demonstrated in the screen shot from *Annie Hall* and its reappropriation on American Apparel billboards—indicates that the fantasy of the Hasidic man maintains the necessary distance for a second look. The religious Jewish woman, however, is so close to herself, so enigmatic, that she cannot be described or represented in "formal terms." This is why in *Deconstructing Harry*, there is no quick way to visualize Doris's and Helen's Jewishness; in both cases, it must be verbalized.

But the analogy only takes us so far: as in the Hasidic man's case, the inverse also appears to be true. If we reimagine Doane's theory applied to Jews, the gender roles are reversed. Here, it is the Hasidic man, like hieroglyphic language, whose signifying garb lacks the arbitrariness of phonetic language. Hasidic men's signifiers (the hat, beard, peyos, and caftan) are so closely intertwined with their signified—Jewishness—that the image becomes enigmatic and objectified. As Doane claims of the feminine, "The iconic system of representation is inherently deficient—it cannot disengage itself from the 'real,' from the concrete."²³ Such is the case for the Hasidic man, an iconic image so entangled with ideas about Jewishness that an equivalency is created for spectators between "real" Jews and Hasidic men. Here, I use the term "real" in both its senses to mean "real-life" Jews (as opposed to players on-screen) and "authentic" Jews (whose perceived piety lends them an air of religious authority).

Doane explains: "While the hieroglyphic is an indecipherable or at least enigmatic language, it is also and at the same time potentially the most universally understandable, comprehensible, appropriable of signs."²⁴ Like hieroglyphics and Doane's claims about representations of the erotic feminine, the powerful dynamism of Hasidic men's iconography lies in its contradictory status. The Hasidic man is indecipherable, enigmatic, *and* universally understood by spectators. This is why his image is open to use on billboards, while the multifaceted meaning of the billboards remains obscure.

Understood in these theoretical terms, the religious Jewish woman on-screen, as we see in *Deconstructing Harry*, does not suffer from the problem of proximity. Despite the fact that they must be deeroticized, Allen's Helen and Doris are represented in such a way that they invite the "second look" that Doane claimed only men on-screen summon. Lacking iconic (or hieroglyphic) signifiers like the black hat or beard, these religious Jewish women are presented as complex, complete characters. They are at once rational and irrational, angry and affectionate, prudent and irresponsible.

A dialectic surfaces: imagery of the Hasidic Jewish man projects Jewish authenticity, restricting Jewishness to a single type. Doubly estranged from the image on-screen, the Jewish woman spectator is alienated by this image because the potential for Jewish authenticity is limited to men. However, these limitations ultimately liberate the Jewish woman, at least at the level of representation. Not confined to the immediately recognizable Hasidic garb, the religious Jewish woman on-screen is unfettered by iconography and can be represented in any number of complex—and, I would argue, interesting—ways.

Feminist and Jewish critics have attacked Allen from every angle, particularly after the Farrow/Previn scandal. I have suggested, however, that the religious Jewish women in *Deconstructing Harry* enable Allen to play out debates about Judaism that are foreclosed by his emblematic image as a Hasid in *Annie Hall* and other films. In the years following the scandal, not just women but Judaism has acquired complex new characteristics in Allen's comic oeuvre. Moving away from questions about misogyny or Jewish self-hatred, I have located an opening for a liberating reading of Jewish women on-screen, an opening made possible, ironically, by the iconic status of the Hasidic Jewish man. When Linda Williams boldly contends that the history of hard-core pornography may be summarized as a "history of the various strategies devised to overcome [the] problem of invisibility," she may just as well have been writing about the history of Jews in film. The "problem of invisibility" that the Jewish man's Hasidic attire resolves unravels when the lens is directed toward religious Jewish women.

BACK TO BLACK (HATS)

Six years after Charney's legal troubles with Woody Allen, he returned the Hasidic man to the center(fold) of his company's advertising campaign. Between pages of scantily clad, seemingly underage models, the American Apparel catalog featured male model Yoel Weisshaus. Hailing from Brooklyn,

Weisshaus is a Satmar Hasid, one of the largest and most religiously rigid of the Hasidic sects. He poses in the magazine wearing the company's menswear. His black pants, shiny black shoes, and white collared shirt are customary Hasidic attire. His beard reaches down to his chest, and so do the curled peyos he wears in front of his ears. His head, partially covered by a large black velvet yarmulke, is shaved according to Satmar convention. In the photo editorial, Weisshaus crouches grinning on a stool; he stands with his hands behind his head wearing a tall fur shtreimel (his own, not a company product); and in three especially compelling photos, he lies in various poses on a white bed.

Charney clearly understands the signifying immediacy of Hasidic attire and the powerful dissonance this symbol of piety elicits when juxtaposed with the other hypersexual, spandex-clad models in the company catalog. This clever approach to advertising drew a spate of attention from both the Jewish and general presses, with the *Jewish Daily Forward* calling Weisshaus "the most unorthodox American Apparel model ever."[25] Charney seems to relish the mass appeal of the type of irony the *Forward*'s wordplay exposes. Like the Woody Allen billboard before it, his use of Hasidic imagery acknowledges the not-so-hidden erotic potential of the Hasidic man. But unlike the billboard, the Weisshaus ad campaign is not about uncovering the covert Hasid beneath the secular Jew. It is not about taking an "unmarked" secular Jew and exposing the immutable Jewishness behind the mask of assimilation. Instead, Weisshaus's photos begin with the marked thing—the real-life Hasid!—and make him into something more generalized, a vessel for menswear that is featured on a marked body but available to anybody. A similar claim could be made of the black American Apparel nail polish called "Hassid."

Earlier that same year, *Harper's Bazaar Indonesia* carried a fashion photo editorial featuring a Hasidic-attired man alongside a blond model with a crown of braids. Photographed in deliberately sensual poses—holding hands, undressing, sharing a bed—these images behave differently from the American Apparel ads because the Indonesian readers would have far fewer encounters with Hasidim (or Jews in general) than an American readership. Perhaps a commentary on the allure of guilty pleasures, images of an illicit affair become more haunting and more illicit when the man is stylized to be

Hasidic.[26] The erotic potential of the Hasidic man is not limited to the United States and western Europe. Even in a southeastern Asian nation with only a handful of Jews, the figure of the Hasidic man presents a sensual enigma. Like so many images of women, the Hasidic man appears in front of the lens for "looking at."

The *Annie Hall* billboard was not the first American Apparel advertisement to cause legal troubles for Charney and the company. Accusations about underage models, misogynistic depictions of women, and crude behavior by Charney behind the scenes led to lawsuits and journalistic exposés years before Allen's settlement and concluded with Charney's ultimate removal as CEO from the company he founded.[27] While Charney meant Allen's Hasidic image to offer a commentary—a profession of innocence—concerning Charney's ongoing legal battles, the image from *Annie Hall* bears a resemblance not just to the Hasidic model Weisshaus but also, theoretically, to the problematic photographs of topless or underage girls whose controversy it seeks to minimize. The figure of the Hasidic man and the woman's photographed flesh share a signifying immediacy that results in objectification. This operation invites a host of conflicting readings as it forecloses certain ways of looking at the images.

NOTES

An earlier version of this chapter was published as "Reconstructing Woody: Representations of Religious Jewish Women in *Deconstructing Harry*," in *Woody on Rye: Jewishness in the Films and Plays of Woody Allen*, ed. Vincent Brook and Marat Grinberg (Lebanon, NH: Brandeis University Press, 2014), 171–189.

1. Gérard Oury, *Ma grande vadrouille* (Paris: Plon, 1988), 94.
2. Linda Williams, *Hard Core: Power, Pleasure and the "Frenzy of the Visible"* (Berkeley: University of California Press, 1989), 49.
3. Ibid.
4. Gilles Menegaldo, "Woody Allen and France," in *A Companion to Woody Allen*, ed. Peter J. Bailey and Sam B. Girgus (Malden, MA: Wiley-Blackwell, 2013), 53–71.
5. Bill Desowitz, "The Long Shadow of 'The Sorrow and the Pity,'" *New York Times*, May 7, 2000.
6. On the billboards and subsequent lawsuit, see Bloomberg News, "Woody Allen Sues Clothing Maker," *New York Times*, April 1, 2008; "Woody Allen Sues Company over Rabbi Billboard," *HuffingtonPost*, April 9, 2008; Ed Pilkington, "Woody Allen v American Apparel Trial Opens Tomorrow," *Guardian*, May 17, 2009; Larry Neumeister, "Woody Allen's Sex Life SLAMMED by American Apparel," *HuffingtonPost*, April 16, 2009; C. J. Hughes, "For $5 Million, Woody Allen Agrees to Drop Lawsuit," *New York Times*, May 18, 2009; US District Court, Southern District of New York, Complaint, "Woody Allen against American Apparel, Inc.," 08 CV 3179.

7. Dov Charney, "Statement from Dov Charney, Founder and CEO of American Apparel," Americanapparel.net, May 18, 2009. http://employment.americanapparel.net/presscenter/dailyupdate/index.asp?m=5&y=2009, accessed January 8, 2013.

8. See Williams, *Hard Core*.

9. One of Annie's most famous lines from the movie is "You're what Grammy Hall would call a 'real Jew.'"

10. Esther Newton, *Mother Camp: Female Impersonators in America* (Chicago: University of Chicago Press, 1972), 103; cf. Judith Butler, *Gender Trouble* (New York: Routledge, 1999), 174.

11. Groundbreaking contributions to feminist film theory include Laura Mulvey, "Visual Pleasure and Narrative Cinema," *Screen* 16, no. 3 (1975): 6–18; Mary Ann Doane, "Film and the Masquerade: Theorising the Female Spectator," *Screen* 23, nos. 3–4 (September–October 1982): 74–87; Luce Irigaray, "Women's Exile," *Ideology and Consciousness* 1 (May 1977): 62–76.

12. John Berger, *Ways of Seeing* (London: Penguin, 1972), 47.

13. For an example of a Jewish critique of *Harry*, see Elliot B. Gertel, *Over the Top Judaism: Precedents and Trends in the Depiction of Jewish Beliefs and Observances in Film and Television* (Lanham, MD: University Press of America, 2003), 92–94. For an interesting example of a feminist critique of Allen, see Elayne Rapping, "A Feminist's Love/Hate Relationship with Woody Allen," *Cineaste* 33, no. 3 (1998): 37–38. *Harry* was received with particular outrage from journalist Maureen Dowd, who, in a clear reference to the Farrow/Previn scandal, saw the film as an assertion that "ordinary ethical standards do not apply to people who produce extraordinary art." In her piercing critique, Dowd could not resist reading Allen's film in light of his personal life. Maureen Dowd, "Liberties; Grow Up, Harry," *New York Times*, January 11, 1998.

14. Peter Bailey, *The Reluctant Film Art of Woody Allen* (Lexington: University Press of Kentucky, 2001), 244. According to Eric Lax, Robert De Niro and Albert Brooks were also considered for the Harry role. See Lax, *Conversations with Woody Allen* (New York: Alfred A. Knopf, 2007), 147.

15. John Lahr, "The Imperfectionist," *New Yorker*, December 9, 1996, 82.

16. Ibid., 70.

17. Woody Allen, "Random Reflections of a Second-Rate Mind," *Tikkun*, January–February 1990, 15. A notable public accusation against Allen includes a half-dozen published letters to the editor responding to his op-ed piece in the *New York Times* about Israeli brutality against Palestinians called "Am I Reading the Papers Correctly?," January 28, 1988.

18. *Curb Your Enthusiasm*, "Trick or Treat," dir. Larry Charles, HBO, October 7, 2001.

19. Doane cites Mulvey's "Afterthoughts . . . Inspired by *Duel in the Sun*," *Framework* 15–17 (Summer 1981): 13. In her work *The Desire to Desire*, Doane addresses the "excessive" (if imagined) desire and pleasure inherent to women's spectatorship with reference to Allen's film *The Purple Rose of Cairo* (1985), about a woman spectator and male actor who cross the boundaries of reality/fantasy and looking/being looked at. See Doane, *The Desire to Desire: The Woman's Film of the 1940's* (Bloomington: Indiana University Press, 1987), 1–2.

20. Doane, "Film and the Masquerade," 82.

21. Ibid., 75–76.

22. "The masculine can partly look at itself, speculate about itself, represent itself and describe itself for what it is, whilst the feminine can try to speak to itself through a new language, but cannot describe itself from outside or in formal terms, except by identifying itself with the masculine, thus by losing itself" (Irigaray, "Women's Exile," 65). Cf. Doane, "Film and the Masquerade," 80.

23. Doane, "Film and the Masquerade," 76.

24. Ibid.

25. Debra Nussbaum Cohen, "American (Hasidic) Apparel," *Jewish Daily Forward*, September 8, 2013.

26. Nicoline Patricia Malina, photographer, "Black Code," *Harper's Bazaar Indonesia*, May 2013.

27. Editorial staff, "American Apparel: A Timeline of Controversy," *Week*, June 25, 2010. On Charney's dismissal, see Jim Edwards, "Inside the 'Conspiracy' That Forced Dov Charney out of American Apparel," *Business Insider*, August 21, 2015.

4

CINÉMA JUDÉITÉ

Projecting Jewish-Muslim Romance

> France without Jews would no longer be France.
> —Prime Minister Manuel Valls, January 13, 2015

> The leitmotif of their messages revolves around the idea that when Muslim women are free to sleep with as many men as they want to, then they will be integrated. Liberty is measured by the number of sexual acts they engage in.
> —Dounia Bouzar, arguing against the headscarf ban in 2003, quoted in Joan Wallach Scott, *The Politics of the Veil*

THE COLLECTIVE CRY OF THE MAY 1968 protesters in France, "We are all German Jews!" echoed in the words of French journalists and the general public when they expressed solidarity with the American victims of the September 11, 2001, terrorist attacks. "Nous sommes tous Américains" (We are all Americans) was the tearful pronouncement on France 2's eight o'clock news show on the evening of 9/11 in France. The phrase was repeated as a headline on the front page of *Le Monde* on September 13.[1] Taking a cue from the '68ers' slogan, the French allied themselves with a radically shaken America by sharing in the nation's victimhood.

In January 2015, following the deadly attacks on the satirical weekly paper *Charlie Hebdo* and the Hypercacher market in Paris, another newspaper, *Libération*, plastered its cover with the words, "Nous sommes tous Charlie" (We are all Charlie). The proclamation connects explicitly to the "German Jews" slogan from 1968, since *Libération* was founded by Jean-Paul Sartre and Serge July as a journalistic response to the events of May 1968. But that slogan was quickly subsumed by a related one that emerged less than an hour

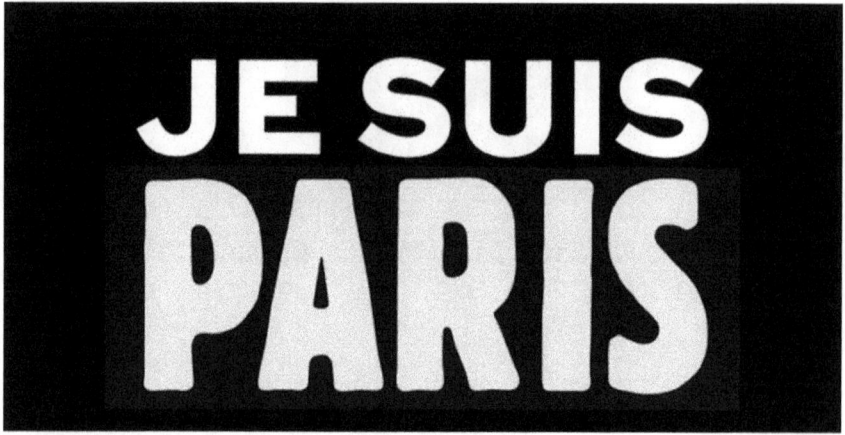

Figure 4.1 The #jesuisParis logo and slogan, modeled after the #jesuisCharlie tweet (public domain).

following news of the attacks. The French artist Joachim Roncin designed a simple black rectangle with bold white and gray letters that read "JE SUIS CHARLIE" (I am Charlie). He posted the image to his Twitter page, where the slogan rapidly evolved into a globally retweeted hashtag with several related offshoots: #jesuisflic ("I'm a cop," for the two police officers killed in the attacks), #jesuisAhmed ("I am Ahmed," one of the police officers and, significantly, a Muslim), and #jesuisjuif ("I'm a Jew," for the Jewish victims targeted at the kosher market). Paris was terrorized again less than a year later when in November 2015 at least 130 civilians were brutally massacred and several hundred more injured in an orchestrated series of attacks in and around Paris. With the *Charlie Hebdo* carnage still fresh in the memories of the French people and their allies around the world, a worldwide response came in the form of the all-inclusive new hashtag, #jesuisParis (I am Paris). The *nous* of 1968 had been definitively overtaken by the "je" of 2015.[2]

This outpouring of international support was a touching display of solidarity appropriate to the age of the "selfie." But some critics were reluctant to participate in this Twitter protest movement. The sociologist Shmuel Trigano wrote, "If 'I' am all these people, then, in effect, I am no one in particular. . . . I am choosing not to assume who I am . . . to face the aggressor in order to prevail in this struggle."[3] For Trigano, the "I" slogans were a claim of helplessness and a refusal to be held accountable in the fight against terrorism. An American reporter critiqued the implicit selfishness of the "#Iam" movement: "While #IAm often begins as a way to grant a voice to the voiceless ... it's also designed to grant a platform to another silenced demographic: ourselves."[4]

But the "je" in "je suis Charlie/juif/Paris" does more than extirpate individuals from any responsibility to "face the aggressor" or give a (sometimes self-serving) voice to empathizers. It also takes the "nous sommes tous / we are all" of 1968, which cut across age, class, and gender to form a cohesive sociopolitical front, and transposes it into a "je/I," a fragmented valley of individuals. If *Rabbi Jacob* preaches that everyone is the same because everyone is different, it does so by acknowledging certain varieties of difference: Jew, Arab, Catholic, and so on. The move from the '68ers' "nous" to the "je" of 2015 follows the path to an idealized version of abstract individualism, a value at the heart of French republicanism. It pushes the idea that everyone is the same to its logical extreme. *Rabbi Jacob* fails to acknowledge that not all differences are equal. #JesuisParis refuses to acknowledge difference at all. So long as every French person is seen by the law and society as an "I," an individual, every French person will be treated equally.

The threat to this system comes when the person pronouncing the "je" professes something else that aligns her with a community, a community smaller than "France" but larger than "je." Community affiliation, sometimes called communalism (*communautarisme*), threatens a system that struggles to protect individuals under the law only as individuals. On the other hand, the nation's convoluted free speech laws (handing down hefty fines and jail time, for example, to those accused of Holocaust denial or racist speech) sometimes appear to protect certain groups but not others.

Film has become a forum for testing the limits of communautarisme in France, and the box-office success of "ethnic comedies" (*comédies communautaires*) demonstrates a public urge to zoom in on ethnic differences in France. In the thirty years since the famous Jewish-Muslim handshake in *Les aventures de Rabbi Jacob* discussed in chapter 2, Jews and Muslims have been placed in r elation to each other in French film comically, tragically, and, in the first decade of the twenty-first century, romantically. The heterosexual romances in these movies—on the surface, conventional romance narratives—and the prospect for reproduction that they present construct a fantasy future for France, one in which religious, ethnic, and national differences disappear when races and religions mix, specifically, the presumed ethnic enemies of Jews and Muslims.

Beginning with *Rabbi Jacob* and extending through the recent blockbuster *Qu'est-ce qu'on a fait au bon Dieu?* (2014), ethnic films disproportionately feature Jews and Muslims reluctantly forming friendships (as these two films do) or romantic relationships. In an analysis of French ethnic films, sociologist Fabrice Montebello argues that "these comedies stand in opposition to institutionalized republican discourse, wherein one mustn't exhibit one's differences publicly."[5] Another film scholar, echoing the messages of *The Great Family of Man* exhibition, critiqued by Roland Barthes, sees such films for their restorative powers: "Difference is merely superficial. If we move beyond it, we find we have fundamental things in common: friendship, love, starting a family, etc."[6] Ethnic films in France, then, are a form of resistance against the reigning values of republicanism and a means to build social cohesion among different kinds of peoples.

But, as with *Rabbi Jacob*, most of these ethnic comedies cannot escape certain conservative standards of what it means to be French. I begin this chapter with an analysis of two such comedies, *Mauvaise foi* (*Bad Faith*, 2006) and *Le nom des gens* (*The Names of Love*, 2010), and the implicit and explicit messages they convey about how to be Jewish or Muslim in France. Then I turn the lens back toward the depiction of religious Jews in film, evaluating the tragic outcomes for the Jewish and Muslim characters in 2005's *La petite Jérusalem* (*Little Jerusalem*). While all three films feature Jewish-Muslim romances, only the film with religious Jews shows that relationship to be unsustainable. In what ways do the happy conclusions of the comedies and the dramatic ending of *La petite Jérusalem* depend on the presence or absence of religious garb? What are the limits of ethnic "difference" in determining who may lay claim to the "je" in #jesuisParis and who remains excluded? How do filmic representations of Jews and Muslims—from *Rabbi Jacob* to *La petite Jérusalem*—help explain the shift from "nous" to "je" in French conceptions of national identity?

Film theorist Carrie Tarr writes of Western cinema that it "normally works to (re-)produce ethnic hierarchies founded on the assumed supremacy of white metropolitan culture and identity, largely through the absence or marginalizing of the voices and perspectives of its troubling ethnic Others."[7] Exploring Jews and Muslims in French film draws out the specific varieties of "troubling" otherness facing France. While filmmaking is always a collaborative process, the three films explored here were written and directed by members of the very marginalized voices Tarr implies are mostly silenced. Their voices from the margins challenge the ethnic hierarchies in place, but they also echo some of those same notions of supremacy she describes. These films attempt to make an intervention into the national discourse about immigration and ethnic difference. They open up taboos via romantic confrontations between Jews and Muslims and enable loaded political debates to play out on-screen. But despite the different outcomes of the comedies and drama, all three films ultimately reinforce the superiority of French republicanism.

SEX AND THE COMÉDIE COMMUNAUTAIRE

In *Mauvaise foi*, Roschdy Zem (who also directed) stars as the sensitive and sensual Ismael. When his longtime girlfriend, the nominally Jewish Clara (Cécile de France), becomes pregnant, they struggle to find ways to reconcile the religious differences they had not realized mattered until her pregnancy. When Clara first tells her parents she is seeing someone seriously, her mother says, "Il est de chez nous?" (Is he one of us?). Clara does not (or pretends not) to understand and answers, "Oh, yes, he's French." Already, her answer rings false. Technically, the character is French-born, but according to the dominant discourses in France, as the son of Moroccan immigrants he, too, would be labeled an immigrant. Of course, Clara's mother was not asking if he was French but whether he was Jewish. Clara's mother presses, "OK, but is he . . ." Like Louis de Funès in his interview about *Rabbi Jacob* and his character's wife, Germaine, in the film, the mother hesitates to insert the controversial predicate, as if "Jewish" were a dirty word (as "antisemite" was for de Funès and, in Germaine's case, "Arab"). Clara answers no and asks if this will pose a problem for her parents. Her mother responds, "No no no, not at all! We like Sephardim too!" And her father chimes in, "Sephardim are a Jew's best friends!" The joke works because the question Clara's mother dared not utter was not the expected "Is he Jewish?" but rather "Is he Jewish the way we are Jewish, or is he the other kind of Jew?" Already the parents' condescending, classist answer about Sephardic Jews hints at the ethnic hierarchies they've established, hierarchies that will place a Muslim like Ismael at the bottom.

Clara's quiet, bourgeois parents do not practice Judaism and even avoid using the term "Jew." When her father accidentally calls Ismael "Israel" (these names rhyme in French), the audience laughs at the awkward way the family's discomfort with their own Jewishness and with Ismael's Arabness seethes beneath the surface. Apparently surprised by her parents' uneasiness, Clara becomes progressively more torn about what her Jewishness means to her. She puts a mezuzah on the apartment door she shares with Ismael, playing down this sudden expression of Jewishness by explaining to him that it is just tradition, and it is only there for good luck.

Ismael hesitates to tell his own mother about their relationship, seemingly less naive about how she might react to her son having a child with a Jewish woman. Each time he attempts to broach the subject with her in their compact apartment in the projects, he is interrupted by neighbors, the imposing portrait of his dead father, a TV news story about Palestine, or a Ramadan feast. He, too, becomes torn between his professed "Frenchness" and his family's traditions. Responding to Clara's mezuzah, Ismael begins (unsuccessfully) fasting for Ramadan for the first time since he was a boy and informs Clara that they will name the child after his father.

It hardly seems plausible that a Jewish-Muslim couple would never have addressed the political, emotional, and historical heft of their relationship, even if they did choose to suppress their differences in favor of the identity they call "French." During one dramatic confrontation, Clara's mother asks, "Will your child be Jewish or Muslim?" to which Clara responds, "He'll be French." Her answer contains within it the denial of the possibility to be both "French" and Jewish or "French" and Muslim, drawing a line between these communal identifications and the incompatible French national identity. Laura's response to her mother reflects the famous words of the count of Clermont-Tonnerre in 1789: "The Jews should be denied everything as a nation, but granted everything as individuals."[8] Jews attained French citizenship at the expense of their collective particularities as a "people." In this way, the very ideology that leads Clara to claim that her child will be French (and not Jewish or Muslim) is the same one that makes it possible for there to be French Muslims and Jews, citizens of France.

Clara's response to her mother implies that Frenchness demands the erasure of overt ethnic and religious identification. But her relationship with Ismael belies this promise of what Frenchness can mean. While Clara's name, appearance, and class might enable her to pass as gentile, Ismael's difference is marked by those very things: his name, his skin color, and his class mean that he will always be first seen as an "immigrant" and will have to fight to make the case for his Frenchness.

After breaking up several times and one dramatic almost-abortion scene, the film ends at Clara and Ismael's apartment. Ismael carries a baby boy in his arms as an older girl runs around. Both children have French names. The doorbell rings, and the two grandmothers, women who signify Ismael and Clara's obligations to their family histories and traditions, burst through the door smiling, chatting, offering kisses and hugs. The ending seems to assert that in France, it *is* possible to move beyond the chains of history, what the French commonly call "origins," and that the most improbable of peoples may come together successfully as long as they do so as French men and women. Despite the anxieties that emerged during Clara's pregnancy about what the child would "be," the couple found their way back to the place they were before she was pregnant—where their differences were irrelevant to their compatibility. Their journey to parenthood was filled with ethnic and religious conflict, but the film's end, where love conquers all, fails to resolve the conflict, making their journey essentially moot.

In *Le nom des gens* from 2010, the gender and ethnic identities we saw in *Mauvaise foi* are swapped. Here, the man is Jewish and the woman is Arab (and Muslim when it suits her). The protagonists are facsimiles of their creators, the screenwriter couple Michel Leclerc (who also directed) and Baya Kasmi. First, the film introduces Arthur Martin (Jacques Gamblin). This name, he explains in the opening scene, is one he shares with more than fifteen thousand Frenchmen. Baya Benmahmoud (Sara Forestier), the woman who will change his life, says she is the only person in France to have her name. Arthur represents quiet moderation and accommodation—his political position, career, and relationships all reflect his aversion to risk or excess. Arthur's father is French Catholic. His Jewish mother was orphaned when her parents were deported to Auschwitz, a family story about which she has taken great pains to remain utterly silent. Silence is the modus operandi at the Martin family home, not unlike Clara's Jewish family in *Mauvaise foi*.

Baya is Arthur's polar opposite: she is politically and sexually radical, her wardrobe is provocative. She has made it her life's work to convert right-wing French men to her leftist politics by seducing them, manifesting the sixties motto to "make love not war" as literally as possible. Her father is an Algerian immigrant refugee, and her mother is a French former Catholic, but Baya loudly embraces her Arabness. While the Martins (and Clara's family in *Mauvaise foi*) are quiet, polite, and distant, the Benmahmouds (like Ismael's family) are loud, intimate, physically close, and excessively emotional. Their working-class home is always crowded, and the people inside it talk openly about politics and sex. At the Martin home, on the other hand, Arthur works hard to structure conversations so as to avoid anything controversial, even something as banal as mentioning the oven or summer camp for fear of eliciting Auschwitz.

When Arthur finally confesses his secret family history to Baya, she is delighted. "Auschwitz?" Baya relishes. "Well, that's brilliant! Look, you're Jewish, I'm Arab. And what's more, we both have a bunch of dead people in our families at the hands of French cops!" Arthur vehemently denies that he is Jewish, and Baya denies that she is Muslim. Like Clara and Ismael, these characters negate their identifications as a "Jew" or a "Muslim" even as they can't quite work out the content of the thing they're denying. Also like Clara and Ismael, their "origins" end up being the *most* important thing about who they are, the thing around which their relationship evolves, breaks, and comes back together again. As in *Mauvaise foi*, this film ends with a baby—Baya and Arthur have a son, whom they decide to name Chang. When the nurse starts to ask if the boy has Chinese origins, the couple responds, "Screw his origins!" Chang Martin-Benmahmoud represents an attempt to retain the family's legacies (in his hyphenated last name) while depriving these legacies of any meaningful content (in his seemingly random Chinese first name).

In what we might imagine to be a typically French maneuver, heterosexual sex—and the babies that come from it—is meant to resolve the historic divide between Jews and Muslims and between these groups and the hegemonic ideal of French Catholic whiteness. Because these babies are neither Jewish nor Muslim, neither white nor Arab, they will presumably evade the anxieties their parents faced, opening the way to world peace, as Baya suggests. These improbable relationships signify French collaboration and colonization, inviting the French audience to nod to the two black marks on France's past but move beyond them through the promising product of the couples' racially, religiously, and ethnically mixed babies. These films, which are about the value or at least the burden of ethnic and religious difference, these films, which assert the importance of "origins" in shaping an individual's identity, conclude with the denial of those origins to the children the couples produce.

WHEN THE JEW IS MARKED: *LA PETITE JÉRUSALEM*

In both comedies, the Arab/Muslim characters are marked—their names alone reveal their origins. In contrast, the origins of the Jewish characters are concealed beneath bourgeois behaviors and French names. Jewish "passing" in the French worlds constructed in these comedies is an expected feature of Jewish life. So what happens to the narrative when the Jew in the relationship is marked not subtly but explicitly as Jewish? What if the various and powerful messages conveyed by religious Jewish garb are manifested on the Jew's body in a Jewish-Muslim romance? *La petite Jérusalem* from 2005 experiments with both Jewish garb and Jewish-Muslim romance, a combination that results not in comedy but in tragedy. Rather than the (re)productive outcomes and happy endings of ethnic comedies like *Mauvaise foi* and *Le nom des gens*, the dramatic *La petite Jérusalem* concludes with a broken relationship. As much as it presents a careful, respectful version of religious life for immigrants in France, the film also presents this life as a tragic bind, pitting the characters' community affiliations against Frenchness. The movie's thematic focus on desire and pleasure—common tropes for French cinema—creates filters for exploring a much larger question about French society, that of integration.

For the romance to take place between a religious Jew and a Muslim, the relationship had to be between a Jewish woman and a Muslim man. As I argued of *Deconstructing Harry*, religious garb in film produces heavily gendered outcomes for the characters who wear it and the spectators who view it. Functioning as objects and not subjects, Hasidic men on-screen read as either extreme piety or extreme perversion (or they vacillate between the two), and they do so with symbolic immediacy. Religious Jewish women, on the other hand, generally use language to express their religiosity, since their options for garb are subtler—a wig that looks like hair, a long skirt, and so on. Similar to the Hasidic man, a Muslim woman's hijab operates as a severe, immediate marker of her Muslimness and invites the various associations that go along with it. In France, this means she is perceived as communitarian, as an obstruction to secularism, and, regardless of where she or her parents were born, as an immigrant. Like the Hasidic man's attire, the hijab raises ideas about sex, specifically, the suppression of desire (usually at the behest of Muslim men). The Muslim woman's hijab and Hasidic man's black hat would create roadblocks to a romantic narrative that was anything other than farce, as their garb removes French liberal ideas of what qualifies as sexy from the characters. As *La petite Jérusalem* features a Jewish woman and Muslim man, their ethnic markers are subtler. Thus, the potential for sex surfaces, and the audience's ability to see the characters as sexy becomes possible.

The filmmaker Karin Albou, who wrote and directed *La petite Jérusalem*, is Jewish, the daughter of an Algerian immigrant. Her voice from the margins—like Zem's for *Mauvaise foi* and Leclerc and Kasmi for *Nom*—would seem to open the way for a tender, empathetic look at one religious Jewish community in France. But the film's depiction of insular, rigid minority groups also "works to justify dominant negative perceptions of communitarianism."[9] In her attempt to intervene into the national discourse about immigration and ethnic difference by opening up these taboos in romantic confrontations between a Jew and a Muslim, Albou's film ultimately reinforces the superiority of the French ideal of *laïcité* (which imprecisely translates to "secularism"). While Albou depicts her characters lovingly and realistically, the film upholds a French value system that works against many of those who live there, a fact that may help account for the film's popularity.

The film tells the story of a family of Tunisian Jewish immigrants living in Sarcelles, one of the largest of the Parisian *banlieues* (suburbs). Known for its sizeable Jewish population, one neighborhood within Sarcelles has earned the nickname Little Jerusalem. Two sisters, Laura and Mathilde, inhabit a cramped apartment with their widowed mother in one of Sarcelles's imposing towers, along with Mathilde's husband, the Ashkenazic Ariel, and their four young children. Young Laura (Fanny Valette) studies philosophy at a university in Paris where the film quickly establishes an opposition between *la philo* (philosophy) and the Judaism of her family. When not studying or in school, Laura works as a janitor at the nearby Jewish preschool. There, despite the school's status as a religious Jewish institution, the crowded locker room captures the mythic French ideal of harmonic racial diversity, "Black-Blanc-Beur" (black, white, Arab), a catchphrase meant to celebrate the diverse origins of the world champion French soccer team members in 1998.

Figure 4.2 Laura undresses as Ariel chants the morning prayers (screen grab).

Laura finds herself unexpectedly attracted to Djamel (Hédi Tillette de Clermont Tonnerre), who also works at the school. They eye each other as she takes her regular evening walk through the neighborhood; she nervously smiles as the pair stands back-to-back changing into their janitorial uniforms in the locker room. They begin a passionate, quiet love affair against the wishes of her family (her mother is on the hunt for a Jewish husband for her), against Jewish custom (prohibiting premarital touching), and against the philosophical ideals she embraces (rejecting desire and refusing to be enslaved to passions).

As Laura and Djamel's relationship develops, Mathilde (Elsa Zylberstein) learns that her husband has been having an affair when she discovers a blond hair on his suit. The devotedly modest Mathilde visits with the wise woman (Aurore Clément) at the *mikvah*, the Jewish ritual bath, and Laura joins her. There, the women learn that sexual pleasure is indeed permissible within the bounds of Jewish law and that in order to save her marriage, Mathilde must find a way to "let go" and give her husband the kind of sex he wants (in this case, touching his genitals). Eventually, Mathilde is convinced that her own religious modesty need not prevent her husband's (and her own?) sexual pleasure. The marriage is saved! If this feels like a somewhat heartbreaking and sexist outcome for Mathilde, the film does not portray it as such. Her reluctant path toward fulfilling her husband's sexual desires is framed by the film as liberating for *her*, even though the film does not quite show Mathilde discovering her own sexual fulfillment.

Taking an Orthodox, legalistic position as espoused by the mikvah woman, the film shows how Mathilde must acquiesce to her husband's sexual needs, despite her discomfort, and that she must take responsibility—sexual responsibility—for his affair. Sex saves the marriage, but at Mathilde's expense. At the same time, the film also makes an argument for the redemptive potential of what we might call "French" sex, that is, sex that fulfills desire and creates pleasure. Sex—done the French way—saves their marriage! For Mathilde, the two opposing worldviews, Orthodox and French, lead to the same conclusion: staying married to a sexually gratified husband. Whether Mathilde benefits or is wounded by the process depends on which of the two perspectives the spectator adopts.

Laura's affair with Djamel also presents double readings. Orthodox patriarchy stands in the way of Laura's desires for Djamel. At the same time, in spite of the relationship's brevity and the strictures of religion, Laura emerges from her sexual exploration more mature and independent. As one reviewer writes, "In contrast to how the film's characters regard Laura's actions, the filmmaker treats Laura's affair in a more classic French style; it marks her transition to being a fully mature adult."[10] If desire and pleasure are ultimate ideals, the two relationships at the center of *La petite Jérusalem* impart to viewers that religion suppresses and (French) sex liberates these very ideals.

LEGISLATING FRENCHNESS

Heterosexual sex appears in *La petite Jérusalem* as it did in *Mauvaise foi* and *Le nom des gens* as a means to resolve interethnoreligious tensions and minority-majority tensions; but the outcome of the Jewish-Muslim romance for Laura and Djamel is far more ambivalent than in the ethnic comedies. The film frames desire and pleasure as universal human values posited against the particularities of Jewish and Muslim values, where law and family are shown to come first. Where *Rabbi Jacob* regulated Frenchness by regulating religious dress and neighborhoods, *La petite Jérusalem* regulates Frenchness by regulating sex. Where *Rabbi Jacob* solved the problem of where Jews belong in France via a process of "separate but equal (so long as visibly identifiable)," *La petite Jérusalem* does the opposite maneuver: Jews and Muslims are not separated out and identified, they are thrown together into the most intimate spaces. The characters' naked bodies and the ways they are used to experience (or not) sexual pleasure determines whether (or not) they can find a place in French society.

In some ways, *La petite Jérusalem* addresses the socioeconomic questions that *Rabbi Jacob* sought to ignore. The working-class North Africans, both Jewish and Muslim, who came in waves to France beginning in the late 1960s were effaced by *Rabbi Jacob*, especially as the film fantasized about the slick, sexy, secular Slimane, who became the head of state in a newly liberated, unnamed North African nation. The fantasy provided a safe and inviting place for Arabs well outside French borders. But in 2005, the year *La petite Jérusalem* came to screens to critical acclaim, such a fantasy was moot. By that time, the Muslim minority and their "culture" (by no means homogeneous) were being subjected to intense scrutiny from the press, popular culture, and even lawmakers.

The year before *La petite Jérusalem* came to theaters, the French government enacted a law banning "conspicuous" religious symbols in public schools. The law was directed overwhelmingly at Muslim schoolgirls who wear the hijab, although the text also mentions skullcaps, turbans, and "large crosses." The controversy over the ban on wearing the hijab in French public schools and the 2005 riots that were the culmination of anti-Muslim sentiment and widespread poverty in immigrant communities form the backdrop to the tragic fantasy that is *La petite Jérusalem*. Joan Wallach Scott explains in *The Politics of the Veil* that the Muslim headscarf was the site where questions about divergent cultural standards—particularly those standards pertaining to sex—could play out. According to Scott, "French norms of sexual conduct [are] taken to be both natural and universal." In contrast, she argues, "Muslim sexuality [is represented as] unnatural and oppressive when compared to an imagined French way of doing sex."[11] Through the normative practices of French heterosexual sex, Laura and Djamel, like Clara and Ismael, Arthur and Baya, are rescued from their subordinate status as "immigrants," and their conflicting histories are overcome. As long as Jews and Muslims can have sex the French way, they can lay claim to being real French men and women.

The double fantasy of Jewish-Muslim harmony and French unity is realized in *La petite Jérusalem* as Djamel and Laura challenge their communities by pursuing each other sexually. Scott unearths the connection between religious garb, notions of French sex, and national identity when she interrogates the language of the headscarf ban. She looks specifically at the law's distinguishing between "ostentatious" religious symbols and "discreet" ones: "When 'ostentatious' . . . refers to an excessive display on or by a body, especially if it's a woman's body, it conveys a sense of erotic provocation. 'Discreet' is the opposite of ostentatious. . . . [A] discreet object doesn't call attention to itself. . . . [I]t is somehow neutral—asexual." From a Muslim perspective, the headscarf qualifies as "discreet"; from the dominant French perspective—and the legal system that bolsters it—the headscarf qualifies as "ostentatious." Mining deeper into the meaning of the ban, Scott points to its central paradox: "There was something sexually amiss about girls in headscarves; it was as if both too little and too much were being revealed."[12] Similarly, the frequent conversations about modesty in *La petite Jérusalem* do more to expose modesty's potential for eroticism than to assert its other possible outcomes, which include protecting unmarried men and women from eroticism.

The French Jewish essayist Alain Finkielkraut weighed in on the headscarf ban at the outset of the controversy in the 1980s. In an interview, Finkielkraut said, "Back in 1989, on the 200th anniversary of the revolution, I signed a petition against the Islamic headscarf. For me it had to do with the notion of secularism, which is running into criticism around the world these days. France believed at the time that this was a model for the world, and is today reminded of its distinctiveness. It is no longer a question of exporting our model. We have to remain modest, yet steadfast." Finkielkraut refers to modesty here, but this is *French* modesty, that is, modesty in the face of decreasing French influence around the globe. For him, laïcité may not be a successful export, but it remains a crucial value of the Republic. He insists that "this has nothing to do with aggression against Muslims" and is "merely asking for a bit of restraint on everyone's part."[13] The "restraint" in this case does not refer to Muslim restrictions on overt sexuality but rather to demands that Muslim girls restrain their urge to dress like Muslim girls.

Just as the discourse surrounding the headscarf ban introduces multiple possible meanings for modesty, the film's characters are likewise conflicted about the meaning and function of modesty. Laura and Mathilde's mother recounts to her family how she smuggled her precious ring with her to France from Tunisia, explaining how she hid it in her bra. The family laughs at the idea of a much younger woman hiding this secret in a very private place from the French police and (Muslim) Tunisians, who "wouldn't dare touch it." "Tunisian men are very modest," the mother says. When a child asks, "What does modest mean?" Mathilde struggles to find an answer. "What does modest mean? It means . . . what does modest mean? It means shy, embarrassed." "Not daring [*n'oser pas*]," adds her mother. "Why wouldn't they dare?" challenges Laura. Mathilde inserts herself again: "It's clear, Arab men are modest, they don't. . ." she trails off. "Oh, Arab men are modest now?" Laura laughs, clearly thinking of her own immodest encounter with the Arab Djamel. For Mathilde and her mother, modesty is a virtue the Jews and Arabs of Sarcelles share against, we might imagine, the conspicuous sexuality of the "real" French, those who do not have visible origins as immigrants.

This conversation about modesty positions the Jews of *La petite Jérusalem* as victims (at least) twice over: first at the hands of the oppressive and antisemitic French colonizers and again at the hands of Muslim antisemitism, as the Jews are targeted by their own neighbors in the film. Following an antisemitic attack, when thugs beat up Ariel as he plays a game of soccer with some neighborhood children, Ariel instructs Laura to abandon her regular evening walks. But their conversation quickly devolves into a confrontation between Laura and Ariel about his extramarital affair. The characters' threatened sex lives weigh more heavily than the threat of violence around them. "I did it because I respect her. I won't ask her to do things only I like, you see?" explains Ariel. A conversation meant to be about the dangers of being Jewish in the banlieue is eclipsed by a conversation about the twin dangers of Jewish women's sexuality: too ostentatious, and modesty is compromised; too modest, and marriage is compromised.

VESTIGES OF THE GARB ON NAKED BODIES

In 2003 a scandal affected French public schools when some girls adopted a fashion of exposing their thong underwear by wearing low-cut jeans. While a handful of girls were sent home to change, and some discussion arose about the pressures on girls to follow the latest fashions, no government action was taken. The *affaire du string* (thong incident) was an unfortunate footnote that provoked a minor media stir and a discussion about school uniforms, but "there was a vast difference between the overt acknowledgment of desire and its suppression."[14] Hypersexual teenage fashion, while taken to be a lamentable distraction in certain cases, was not nearly as dangerous as teenage suppression of sexuality, as the Muslim headscarf was imagined to convey. "Thongs at School, So What?" read an op-ed headline in *Libération*.[15] The thong incident incited talk-show debate, whereas the headscarf demanded federal legal action. Concealing sexuality in France was seen as far more threatening than its overexposure. In this system, a woman's covered body draws more attention to that body's potential sexuality than a woman's naked or suggestively uncovered body. This compelling paradigm operates in direct opposition to the Jewish and Muslim designated function for modest women's attire: to obstruct the woman's eroticism. It also elicits questions about what a naked woman's body means, if in this case it carries less erotic potential than her covered body. This reflects the central contradiction of Roland Barthes's essay about the striptease: "Woman is desexualized at the very moment when she is stripped naked."[16]

La petite Jérusalem experiments with this paradigm of the erotic potentials of nudity versus modesty. As with *The Frisco Kid*, *Rabbi Jacob*, *Annie Hall*, *Deconstructing Harry*, and others, dressing and undressing from religious garb on-screen constructs and tests the limits of Jewishness, religious piety, and modesty. The film presents Laura getting dressed in the beginning and undressing to put on her pajamas later. Mathilde undresses completely at the mikvah, and Ariel slowly removes his religious garb as he asks his wife for forgiveness. Several times, the camera zooms in on Laura and Djamel as they put on and take off their janitorial uniforms at the preschool. How far down past the garb does Jewishness reach? To the flesh? Can the viewer still see modesty or piety even on the religious Jew's naked body?

If we take the naked body to be universal—in the same vein as the other universals purported by *The Great Family of Man* museum exhibit, critiqued by Barthes (see chapter 2)—then the erotic appeal of Laura's and Mathilde's nudity in *La petite Jérusalem* should be equivalent, the same as the bodies of Clara and Baya in the ethnic comedies discussed here, the same as any other naked woman's body. But bodies have histories and contexts; standards of beauty change over time and place. Still, republican universalism rejects history and context when it holds that eliminating the headscarf puts Muslim girls on par with all other girls in the classroom, that a girl's visible Muslimness can be removed with her hijab. Detaching what Barthes would call the "exotic barrier" and revealing her hair should return the woman to her presumed "natural state."

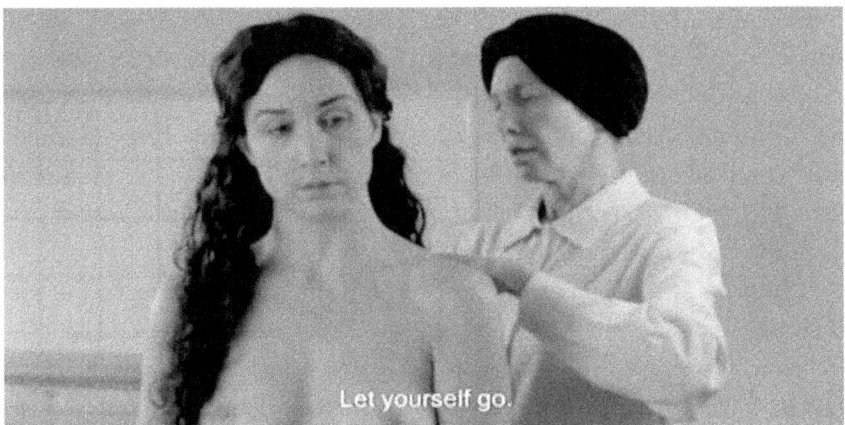

Figure 4.3 The mikvah woman advises Mathilde (screen grab).

While *La petite Jérusalem* asserts certain French notions about the universality of sex, it also defies this notion of universalism when *the very thing that makes the sexual encounters sexy is the fact that they take place between a Muslim and a Jew*. In other words, the appeal of Laura's nakedness in the film lies in the knowledge that she is a religious Jew. Stripping away the external markers of her religiosity from her body does not eliminate their presence in the mind of the viewer. Albou drives this point home during one scene where the camera switches between a praying Ariel, donning *tefilin* (phylacteries) with a large *tallis* draped over his head, and Laura, slowly undressing from her modest attire and putting on her nightshirt (fig. 4.3). As Ariel gyrates in the unmistakably sexual style of traditional Ashkenazic prayer custom, the camera cuts to Laura rolling down her thick stockings, unbuttoning her blouse, and pulling off her skirt. Ariel's religious garb and prayerful sway contextualize Laura's slow undressing, reminding the viewer of her pious lifestyle, connecting her naked body to the particular sounds of Jewish prayer. Additionally, the decidedly erotic back-and-forth motions customary to Ashkenazic prayer become profoundly sensual when positioned alongside what amounts to a striptease.

In late 2015 a real-life, politicized version of this striptease scene from *La petite Jérusalem* took place. Two radical feminist activists from the protest group FEMEN charged a conference stage—topless—during a presentation by two imams about women in Islam. In this gendered, sexualized protest, the FEMEN activists knowingly objectified their bodies. Their protest was intended to liberate Muslim women from what they see as the patriarchal structure, which forces these women to hide their bodies. But one consequence of this protest technique is the way it promotes one kind of objectification (the one that values the aesthetic beauty and arousing power of a woman's bare breasts) over another kind of objectification (the one that asserts that women's bodies are dangerous for men's piety).

La petite Jérusalem participates in a filmic protest similar to the one carried out by the members of FEMEN. The film's focus on the sensuality of religious Jewish women and the erotics of everyday Jewish life in the banlieue highlights the apparent incongruity between religious piety and women's sexuality (or, more broadly, women's bodies). Like the FEMEN protest, the film injects women's naked bodies into scenes of religious life. In one such scene, Laura is at the apartment alone. She opens up a book of hymns and begins chanting. She clutches the pearl necklace Djamel gave her as a gift as she turns his name into its own prayerful meditation. "Djamel, Djamel," she intones. The shaky camera zooms in on her face as she begins to unbutton her blouse. In a moment of ecstasy—the film remains ambivalent as to whether this climax was spiritual, sexual, or both—Laura rips the necklace off, and the pearls fly across the room. Just like the FEMEN protesters' scene at the conference about Islam, this scene stresses the discordance between the piety of religious practice and the eroticism of women's bodies.

FEELING FRENCH, FILMING FRENCHNESS

In Laura and Djamel's romance, ostentatious religiosity (the central language of the headscarf ban) and ostentatious sexuality meet. Protecting the body from its own sexuality seems to draw attention to that body, especially in the context of liberal French society. The film's very first shot is a close-up of Laura's hair as she bends down to pull her thick, wool tights over her legs. The scene's sensuality is unmistakable as the camera jumps around Laura's body from her hair to her lips, buttons, legs, back, and underwear. This opening shot seeks to confirm what religious Judaism and Islam maintain: that a woman's hair has the potential to arouse sexual desire. Albou corroborated this notion in an interview: "I wanted us to be immediately on the flesh that she conceals. She puts on her tights, her blouse . . . then we see nothing of her face except her mouth and her hair: those things which are the most sensual, and which she will not cover up."[17]

The film straddles the line between intimacy and claustrophobia; nearly every scene is shot in close-up. There are no expansive landscapes as in *The Frisco Kid*, no imposing monuments as in *Rabbi Jacob*. There are no crisp fantasy scenes as I described for *Deconstructing Harry*. Refusing to back away from its characters and offer them (and the viewers) some room to breathe, *La petite Jérusalem* invites the kind of confusion at play in the prayer/masturbation scene. Close-ups of faces and hair also enable the filmmaker to avoid providing the critical information, the kind hard-core porn attempts to convey (see chapter 3). For example, did Laura and Djamel actually have sex, or were they just embracing? And is there a significant difference for these characters? Was Laura masturbating or meditating? Albou explains her choice to film in close-up not as a mechanism to obscure but as a means to show up close people who are rarely, if ever, shown on film. She positions her film in opposition to Amos Gitai's 1999 Israeli ultra-Orthodox drama, *Kadosh*, where "the camera is intentionally always kept at a distance" from its subjects.[18] Albou does not just want to show viewers a rarely seen world; through her filmmaking, she wants to invite them inside it and ask them to identify with it. Tellingly, the only scene where the camera appears to pull back from the actors' faces and bodies is when Djamel brings Laura to meet his religious Muslim aunt and uncle. Albou's screenplay and her camera can insert themselves into the heart of a Tunisian Jewish family, but she maintains a certain distance from the family of Algerian Muslim immigrants. "It eventually becomes clear that she doesn't quite know who Djamel is," writes critic Nathan Lee of Albou.[19]

Recalling the words of Clara from *Mauvaise foi*, Albou insists in an interview, "I'm the product of a mixed marriage. I feel French above all else."[20] Only someone with non-French origins would need to insist they "feel French," a kind of declaration that would be alien to the racist, nationalist caricature we saw in *Rabbi Jacob*'s Victor Pivert. When Albou asserts that she "feels French," she is also asserting that she feels that way in spite of her Algerian Jewish father. Because of him, she can zoom in on Laura and her family and get at the heart of a religious Jewish experience she was not raised with. Because of him, she films Djamel and his family from a distance as an outsider. The viewer has the opportunity to identify with Laura, but not with Djamel.

Unlike the joyful wedding scenes that conclude *The Frisco Kid* and *Rabbi Jacob* and the gurgling new babies at the end of *Mauvaise foi* and *Le nom des gens*, in the world of *La petite Jérusalem*, a happy ending is simply an impossibility. Djamel is not a legal resident of France and depends on the generosity of his uncle to make a life there. When he naively brings Laura to meet his family, they interrogate her in Arabic, which she does not speak: "What is your name? Which family are you from?" Djamel answers for Laura, and his aunt replies, "That's not an Arab name." Her suspicions aroused, she continues, "Where in Tunisia were you born?" Djamel answers, "Djerba," and Laura adds in French, "Near the synagogue." This subtle act of coming out Jewish is met with silent condemnation from Djamel's family. His uncle then pulls him aside and insists that if Laura wants to live in the house with them, she will need to convert to Islam. Djamel refuses to ask this of Laura, but, acknowledging that they can neither live in Laura's home nor afford to live alone, he breaks off his relationship with her. Laura responds by taking an overdose of sleeping pills.

If sex is a means to establish a Muslim or a Jew's Frenchness, then Djamel's uncle shuts out the possibility for Djamel both to stay in France and to continue to have (French) sex. In this way, the Muslim Djamel can never be truly French, an option that remains open to the Jewish Laura by the end of the film. Once Laura comes home from the hospital, Ariel makes the unilateral decision that the family will make *aliyah*, move to Israel. Laura stays behind, and her mother offers her the ring Laura's mother carried with her from Tunisia as a means to put a down payment on a studio apartment in Paris. The film's final shot shows Laura standing motionless on the moving sidewalk inside one of Paris's large commuter rail stations. As she moves toward the metropolitan center and away from the too-close quarters of Sarcelles, her potential for future sexual encounters, for "doing sex the French way," expands.

French and Jewish sexual norms have the capacity to coexist in France in ways inaccessible to Muslims. Partly, this is due to French Jews' open embrace of republicanism. In his semiautobiographical novel *Lehaïm: A toutes les vies*, Michaël Sebban describes the compromises his religious Jewish character, Éli, had to make in order to complete the training to become a philosophy professor. When classes were held on the Sabbath, he writes:

I had two hours of math on Saturday mornings. . . . I told the teacher that I couldn't come that day. I promised her I'd make up the work, I'd do extra homework. She didn't want to hear any of it. "Just try to miss even a single class," she told me, "and I'll send you back to high school." I still remember all those Saturdays when I would come to class in my white shirt and hat. When I would sit in the front row without writing anything. I sat there, arms crossed, listening to algebra lectures that I had no use for.[21]

Published in 2004, Sebban's book at once mourns and challenges this version of French republicanism that demands religious compromise as a prerequisite to integration. Éli's compromise was a form of silent protest; yes, he would come to class on Shabbat, but he would not pick up his pencil and write. And he would enact this quiet refusal from the front row. Describing the anti-French and antisemitic slurs he encounters at the high school in the banlieue where he teaches, the protagonist resents his Muslim students for their unwillingness to make the same kinds of concessions he made in order to be successful. His Muslim student Karim rejects the very possibility of ever being considered French. "You seen where we live?" Karim probes his teacher over coffee. "You seen what happens at school? You've got to let it go, sir. You think with this face I could become French? . . . For the French, I'll always be an Arab." But Éli refuses to surrender. He tells the boy: "Karim, integration is a machine wherein you can put a little Jew whose father speaks Arabic and doesn't know how to read French. And twenty-five years later, he becomes a professor of philosophy for the national education system and a functionary of the Republic. I know this machine is broken, Karim. . . . But I tell myself that if it can work for me, it can work for you."[22] Karim replies that not only can he never be considered French, but he does not even *want* to be considered French. Like *La petite Jérusalem*, in *Lehaïm* the question of what it means to be French is one that a Jew and a Muslim explore together in an intimate setting and in relation to each other. The outcome for Sebban's novel and the film is the same: integration is possible for Jews but not for Muslims. Éli and Karim both come from the same place in Oran; they share racial, ethnic, linguistic, and national origins. The only factor that appears to separate them is their religion, a difference that in the eyes of their militantly secular contexts in France should render them utterly equivalent. So why is it that Éli was able to emerge successfully from the integration machine while Karim rejects even the prospect of trying? Why was Laura able to leave Sarcelles with enough money and support to begin an independent life in Paris, while her ethnosocioeconomic equal, her lover, Djamel, would be condemned to a life as a janitor in his uncle's cramped apartment in the projects?

The answer does not lie only in racial difference. Karim's insistence that it is his face, his race, that prevents him from ever being French is undermined by *La petite Jérusalem*, in which a white man is cast in the role of the Muslim-Arab Djamel and the non-Jewish actor Bruno Todeschini plays the Orthodox Ariel. Neither does the answer lie only in some Muslim Arabs' refusal to participate in republicanism—this system rejects them before they can reject it. The answer cannot be found only in a history that harks back to the colonial era, when Jews in North Africa succeeded in shaking off the stigma of the *indigène* (indigenous) label, claiming a place on a higher rung of the colonial hierarchy than Muslims. Certainly, the headscarf ban codified the widespread conception that "Islam [is] an obstacle to full integration."[23] But neither the ban's supporters nor its critics offered a clear explanation as to why this is so. Along with these complicated ethnic and political histories, one explanation for Djamel's and Laura's divergent potentials in France lies in the ways Jews and Muslims are represented in film, television, and literature.

OF HATS AND HEADSCARVES

French struggles with postcolonial integration took many forms, not just the reactionary sentiments that led to the headscarf controversy. In the 1980s the socialist government worked toward a policy of embracing the immigrants' cultural particularities under the slogan "le droit à la différence," the right to difference, or what Americans would call diversity. Part of this policy included injecting funding into teaching France's regional languages, like Breton. In this case, accepted forms of *différence* are restricted to what may be called "native" forms of difference. Anthropologist Kimberly Arkin explains: "While on one level absolute homogeneity of cultural practice had ceased to be the centerpiece of the national project by the 1980s—no one, excepting some Bretons themselves, thought that the inhabitants of Brittany were not 'French'—on another, it continued to index fitness for national belonging for nonwhite, non-Christian populations."[24]

The Muslim population was not entirely neglected by these new policies, however. Part of the 1980s agenda to address the growing populations from

North Africa was manifested in a state-funded variety show aired on Sunday mornings called *Mosaïque*. The program had two adverse outcomes for the audience it ostensibly aimed to integrate. One was developing cultural homogeny for a diverse population of Arabic-speaking immigrants. Recognizing difference in this case required consolidating it. Another was the program's not-so-hidden agenda of eventually returning these populations to their countries of origin by keeping them immersed in these countries' cultural output. The government actors funding *Mosaïque* even worked with leaders from North African nations in developing programming.[25]

Where did Jews from North Africa, like those featured in *La petite Jérusalem*, fit into these ongoing conversations about integration? Rather than emphasizing their commonalities with the Muslim immigrant populations, the way Sebban's Éli attempted to do with his student, many North African Jews consistently insisted on their relative "nativeness" to France over and against the Muslim Arabs. Arkin even catalogs a trend among Sephardi Jewish teenagers laying claim to being racist, openly hating "Arabs" in part as a way to distinguish Sephardic populations from Muslim Arab ones. When the Holocaust became an official component of the national curriculum in 2000, the lessons it offered in accepting difference also solidified the Jewish place within the national community.[26] No such curriculum exists to address the brutality of French colonialism and its aftermath, once more leaving Arab Muslims outside of the national narrative. For these reasons, Prime Minister Manuel Valls was able to pronounce to the National Assembly after the attacks at the Hypercacher, "France without Jews would no longer be France."[27] No one has dared to make such a statement about French Muslims.

Along with these complex threads that combine to explain the more favorable outcomes for the Jewish characters in *Lehaïm* and *La petite Jérusalem*, the relative success of Jewish integration over Arab/Muslim integration may be explained, at least in part, by the very representations of religious Jews and Muslims we see in films like *La petite Jérusalem*. Just as the Jews of France, including that relatively new category of "North African Jews," may be swept up beneath the charming, nonthreatening, Ashkenazic shtreimel worn by Rabbi Jacob, so have the Muslims of France and their eponymous "culture" been swept up beneath the much more sinister symbol of the Muslim woman's "veil"—language that captures its furtive power to both conceal (the woman's body) and reveal (the woman's difference). Djamel is depicted as being a mystic, rejecting the constraints of organized religion. We never, for example, see him praying or engaged in any other kind of religious ritual. In spite of this, his name, his family, his country of origin, and his neighborhood all condemn Djamel to being an accomplice in a threatening French caricature of "Muslim culture." The "hidden danger of women's repressed sexuality" is a danger embodied by extreme terrorist acts but is also located on the flesh of secular Muslim men like Djamel.[28] This is a danger that the film captures when Djamel's aunt, her hair covered with an embroidered golden turban, frowns suspiciously as she quizzes Laura. It is a danger that is manifested when Djamel's decision to leave Laura nearly kills her.

As for Laura, her experiences in Sarcelles could not be further removed from *Rabbi Jacob* and the quaint rue des Rosiers of that film. But the same xenophobic logic that connects Djamel to girls in headscarves and headscarves to violence and murder connects Laura to Rabbi Jacob and his family. The republican ideal that aims to erase difference and unify all French people as individuals instead unifies all Jews and all Muslims against all "real" Frenchmen and women.

Both the Muslim headscarf and the Hasidic hat and beard reveal as they conceal, but beards make Jewish bodies visible, while headscarves "veil" Muslim bodies.[29] The Hasidic garb in *Rabbi Jacob* resolved the anxiety caused by Marcel Dalio's invisibility in Nazi propaganda posters from the 1940s. The film reflected a French demand in the 1970s that as long as Jews "show" themselves as Jews, they may be tolerated. The demands made on Muslims in the first decade of the twenty-first century are quite the opposite. In this case, French republicanism demands that Muslim women "show" themselves, but not by showing their Muslimness and wearing the headscarf. Instead, they must show themselves *as women* by removing the headscarf and displaying their bodies. For Jewish men, Jewish invisibility is a deception. For Muslim women, Muslim visibility is a threat. The hypocrisy at work here is about more than a complicated history of colonialism and Jewish-Muslim relations. Becoming French is about becoming men and women in the appropriate ways. It is about men displaying origins and women displaying bodies. *La petite Jérusalem* purports to ask a deeply philosophical question about what constitutes liberty. While it vacillates between a liberty rooted in obedience and one that hinges on "letting go," the unspoken message it conveys about liberty is decidedly sexual. Films like *La petite Jérusalem* that place a Jew and a Muslim in sexual relation to each other expose the limits of French belonging for France's Jewish and Muslim populations.

The effect of coupling Laura's nudity with Ariel's prayer reinforces the ways in which removing religious garb from a body does not remove the traces of that garb. This echoes what some opponents of the headscarf ban have asserted: removing the hijab from a Muslim schoolgirl's head does not remove the French gaze that sees even her bare head as Muslim. Discussing the headscarf ban, Finkielkraut argues that miscegenation is a prerequisite for integration: "A woman who wears the veil effectively announces that a relationship with a non-Muslim is out of the question for her."[30] Not only does the responsibility for integration lie in the hands of Muslim women, but Finkielkraut treats the headscarf as a personal rejection. Taking off the headscarf becomes a sign of her availability for French sex, not a sign that she is suddenly passing as non-Muslim. In this formulation, the headscarf signals both a passive submission to Islamic patriarchy and an aggressive, preemptive rejection of non-Muslim French desire. Vehemently ignoring the voices of the girls who wear the headscarf and what it means to them, men like Finkielkraut make clear that the scarf is about sex: whom the girls will (or will not) have sex with, how they will have it, and the risks their sexuality poses to the Republic.

#QUISUISJE?

If being French after the Parisian attacks of 2015 means, in part, joining in a movement of individuals in saying #jesuisParis, then we might imagine the fictional Laura, now a few years into her twenties, participating in this "je" cry; but she is only able to do so after having first abandoned the particularities of her Jewish experience and leaving the banlieue for Paris, the Torah for philosophy. Mathilde, on the other hand, who remains committed to religious life, is banned from the "je" slogan and therefore from France itself. Beyond that, while we may imagine the Laura of 2015 tweeting #jesuisParis, Djamel—undocumented, consigned to living on Paris's periphery, Muslim, it seems, in spite of himself—may not lay claim to Paris in the same way.

Les aventures de Rabbi Jacob heeded the call of the "We are all Jews" protest of 1968. Pivert, a symbol of the racist old guard in France, the type against whom the '68ers rallied, was converted to the 1970s multiculturalist model through his interactions with Jews and Arabs. But that film shows that

"We are all Jews" so long as what we mean by "Jews" are the quaint, easily detectable Hasidim of Paris's Jewish quarter. *Rabbi Jacob* offers Jews a place in France's cultural landscape as Jews—a limiting variety of Hasidic Jewish. In contrast, as 2015's cries of #jesuis echo throughout the world, twenty-first-century France welcomes Jews to lay claim to Frenchness while demanding their complete integration and invisibility. Religious Jews, those residing in the banlieue or those dwelling in the urban centers, are always peripheral to Frenchness, or, in recent years, like *La petite Jérusalem*'s Mathilde, these Jews are imagined as always already on their way out of France and toward Israel. Ironically, Jews like Laura are welcome to pronounce "#jesuisjuif," but only if they do so as individuals and not as actual Jews.

As with the ethnic comedies that have made a splash at the French box office in the past twenty years, *La petite Jérusalem* defies the #jesuis movement, the anticommunautariste system, by literally zooming in on communal differences and showing Jewish religious practices in France up close. The film asks the viewer to acknowledge Jewish communal difference *and* see the community's members as individuals. However, the film's conclusion about its main characters belies the impossibility of Jews becoming "je" *as Jews*. *La petite Jérusalem* celebrates Jewish difference by highlighting its sensuality, its humanity, in close-up. But it cannot resolve the tension between community affiliation and French individualism, leaving the characters no choice but to abandon their Jewishness or abandon their France.

NOTES

1. Jean-Marie Colombani, "Nous sommes tous Américains," *Le Monde*, 13 September 2001.
2. Digital librarian Nick Ruest collected and analyzed Twitter hashtags in the month following the attacks on *Charlie Hebdo* and the Hypercacher market. #NoussommeCharlie was tweeted around 130,000 times, while #jesuisCharlie garnered a staggering 8 million tweets. #JesuisAhmed was tweeted roughly 377,000 times, more than twice as many as #jesuisjuif (141,993 tweets). #JesuisMusulman did not make it into the top ten tweets and therefore was not analyzed by Ruest. See Ruest's blog, http://ruebot.net/post/exploratory-look-13968293-jesuischarlie-jesuisahmed-jesuisjuif-and-charliehebdo-tweets, February 3, 2015.
3. Shmuel Trigano, "Pourquoi la manifestation du 11 janvier est un événement inquiétant," *Actualité Juive*, January 15, 2015.
4. Amanda Hess, "#IAm: The Default Mode of Showing Solidarity in the Hashtag Era," *Slate*, January 9, 2015.
5. Quoted in Camille Jourdain, "Les comédies 'communautaire,' la recette gagnant du cinéma français," *Slate.fr*, May 28, 2014.
6. Laurent Jullier, quoted in ibid. See chapter 2 on Barthes and *The Great Family of Man*.

7. Carrie Tarr, "French Cinema and Post-colonial Minorities," in *Post-colonial Cultures in France*, ed. Alec Hargreaves and Marc McKinney (New York: Routledge, 1997), 59.
8. "Debate on the Eligibility of Jews for National Citizenship (December 23, 1789)," in *The Jew in the Modern World: A Documentary History*, comp. and ed. Paul Mendes-Flohr and Jehuda Reinharz (New York: Oxford University Press, 2011), 115.
9. Tarr, "French Cinema," 79.
10. Alyssa Sepinwall, "Sexuality, Orthodoxy and Modernity in France: North African Jewish Immigrants in Karin Albou's *La petite Jérusalem*," in *The Modern Jewish Experiences in World Cinema*, ed. Lawrence Baron (Lebanon, NH: Brandeis University Press, 2011), 343.
11. Joan Wallach Scott, *The Politics of the Veil* (Princeton, NJ: Princeton University Press, 2007), 10.
12. Ibid., 152.
13. Alain Finkielkraut, interview with Mathieu von Rohr and Romain Leick, *Der Spiegel Online International*, December 6, 2013.
14. Scott, *The Politics of the Veil*, 112.
15. Philippe Moreau, "Le string à l'école, et alors?," *Libération*, October 10, 2003.
16. Roland Barthes, *Mythologies*, trans. Annette Lavers (New York: Hill and Wang, 1972), 72.
17. Karin Albou, extract from the film's press release, reprinted at *cinémotions.com*, n.d.
18. Karin Albou, interview with Audrey Khalifa, *Audrekhalifa's Blog*, March 24, 2009, https://audreykhalifa.wordpress.com/2009/03/24/interview-de-karin-albou-realisatrice-de-la-petite-jerusalem/.
19. Nathan Lee, "Film in Review: *La petite Jérusalem*," *New York Times*, January 27, 2006.
20. Albou, interview with Khalifa.
21. Michaël Sebban, *Lehaïm: A toutes les vies* (Paris: Hachette, 2004), 216.
22. Ibid., 211.
23. Scott, *The Politics of the Veil*, 149.
24. Kimberly Arkin, *Rhinestones, Religion, and the Republic: Fashioning Jewishness in France* (Stanford, CA: Stanford University Press, 2014), 60.
25. Angéline Escafré-Dublet, "L'état et la culture des immigrés, 1974–1984," *Histoire@Politique: Politique, culture, société* 4 (January–April 2008): 15.
26. Arkin, *Rhinestones*, 1–14, 64.
27. "Sans les juifs de France, la France ne serait plus la France" (Manuel Valls, "Discours de Manuel Valls à l'Assemblée nationale en homage aux victimes des attentats," national address, French National Assembly, January 13, 2015).
28. Scott, *The Politics of the Veil*, 158.
29. "Of course, beards have a lot to do with sexuality; the difference was that beards were visible, while women's bodies were disguised by veils" (ibid., 157).
30. Finkielkraut, interview with von Rohr and Leick.

5

WHAT LIES BENEATH THE WIG

Hester Street and Adaptation

> The story that is told in this storybook [*mayse-bikhl*]
> has the name of what is called in Russian Poland *shterntikhl*.
> That same woman's pearl adornment was called in other places
> *shtern-bindl, kop binde, bindalik*, and so on with other phrases.
> Today, we've rid our heads of this madness,
> and Jewish women go around like other
> ladies with a false braid [or wig]
> . . . .
>
> Maybe soon the *shtreyml* and *spodek* [Hasidic fur hats]
> will also be preserved in formaldehyde, so
> we can remember what they were.
>
> —Israel Aksenfeld, *Dos Shterntikhl* (*The Headband*), 1861

> How can I let you see me, past and future,
> blemishes and dust? Must I
> shear away my hair and wear
> the wig the wisemen say? Will you
> receive me, rejoice me, take me for your wall?
> To any man not blind, a wig is false.
>
> —Ruth Whitman, "The Marriage Wig," 1968, in *Laughing Gas*

"IN AMERICA THEY DON'T WEAR WIGS." These are among the first words that Jake speaks to his wife, Gitl, when she arrives in New York from Russia in Joan Micklin Silver's immigrant drama *Hester Street* (1975). The disparaging words convey both Jake's lack of compassion for his wife and his short memory; only a few years earlier he was in her place as a conspicuous new immigrant. These words also reveal the reigning tension among immigrants to America at the turn of the twentieth century—the need to "become" American rapidly, to shed the immigrant mentality, beginning with the immigrant's dress. More telling than this utterance, however, is Gitl's response. Her face washed with astonishment, confusion, and shame, she replies in Yiddish, "No? I have a kerchief." Gitl (Carol Kane) understands Jake (Stephen Keats) to mean that the custom in America is for Jewish women to wear a kerchief rather than a wig, incapable as she is of imagining the alternative: a married woman who "go[es] around in [her] own hair." By the film's end, Gitl wears neither a wig nor a kerchief but a stylish updo, and she is a far cry from the dowdy greenhorn the viewer first meets in the immigration hall. In *Yekl* (1896) by Abraham Cahan, the novel upon which the film is based, the author describes the rapidity with which Gitl and immigrants in general adapted to America (as they perceived it). At the end of the tale, Cahan wrote, Gitl had "that peculiar air of self-confidence with which a few months' life in America is sure to stamp the looks and bearing of every immigrant."[1]

What Cahan wrote about and what he experienced in his own life, coming to America as a young man in 1882, has been variably labeled by historians of this era as acculturation, assimilation, Americanization, integration, or secularization. Scholars cannot agree on the appropriate terminology to describe what it means that "they don't wear wigs," both the phenomenon to which the utterance points (the fact that most Jewish women stopped wearing wigs) and the circumstances of the utterance itself (a husband urging his wife to stop wearing her wig). Each of the terms explains elements of the story of how Jews became Americans and can be applied to the particular story told in *Yekl* and *Hester Street*. But another term captures Jewish immigrants' transformations as recounted in this particular narrative: adaptation. In this chapter, I argue for exploring *Hester Street* as an adaptation in two senses: as the translation of Abraham Cahan's 1896 immigration novel into film and as the Americanization of its Jewish immigrant characters. Like the other French and American films discussed here, the processes of asserting national belonging and testing Jewish authenticity are expressed through taking off and putting on religious garb.

Reviewers of the film praise Silver's loyalty to the Cahan story. For example, historian Hasia Diner describes how the film "hewed quite closely to Cahan's short story"; Sonya Michel calls the film "generally faithful" to the book; and Joyce Antler goes so far as to describe *Hester Street* as "scrupulously adapted from [the] 1896 story."² Given how other famous Jewish films have veered from their source texts (Barbra Streisand's *Yentl* comes to mind as a particularly controversial adaptation), these reviewers were not wrong.³ Loyalty and fidelity are powerful, emotionally charged concepts, intensified by *Hester Street*'s focus on Jewish traditions that the characters either preserve or abandon, as well as the infidelity that destroys Jake and Gitl's marriage. Removing the moral imperative toward loyalty in the context of *Hester Street*—that Silver's script diverges in some ways from Cahan's novel is not the same kind of tragedy as Jake's extramarital liaisons—introduces the possibility of questioning how and why differences arise between these "texts." A critical obsession with the minor ways films veer from novels generally plagues readings of adaptations, but here, these small differences are precisely what make Silver's retelling of Cahan's story revealing of its particular historical moment for both American Jews and American women.⁴ Silver's adaptation sheds light on the complicated politics of 1970s multiculturalism and the similarly complex and seemingly incompatible politics of second-wave feminism.⁵

Analyzing *Hester Street* as an adaptation is especially productive when studying the story of Jewish Americanization, itself a process of adapting to a new culture. Adapting requires translating one's lifestyle and language while attempting to remain faithful to an "original." Adaptation is thus more poignant a term in this case than its sister concepts, assimilation and acculturation, which do not carry the historical Jewish imperative toward continuity. But adaptation theory—whether applied to film or to cultural processes—carries its own set of problems. As film scholar Robert Stam explains, adaptation theory tends to establish a hierarchy wherein the novel maintains a privileged status over the film (which takes priority over television, which is higher than the Internet, etc.).⁶ Or, as Linda Hutcheon writes, "Whether it be in the form of a videogame or musical, an adaptation is likely to be greeted as minor and subsidiary and never as good as the 'original.'"⁷

Focusing on *Hester Street* as an adaptation, I rely on Stam's ideas about the implicit (or explicit) hierarchies of adaptation in film criticism to understand how related hierarchies in the Jewish Americanization process may have influenced Silver's choices to preserve or reject elements of Cahan's original story. Here, I consider how the stories Jews tell about the adaptation process differs for Jewish men and women as storytellers and as characters within the story. If the image of the Hasidic man serves as a site for locating and displacing ambivalences about what it means to be both Jewish and American, in *Hester Street* the spotlight is redirected toward the religious Jewish woman. As with the religious imagery from *Annie Hall*, *The Frisco Kid*, and *Les aventures de Rabbi Jacob*, the conflict hinges on religious visibility and Jewish garb. As with *La petite Jérusalem* and *Deconstructing Harry*, questions about Jewish identity and authenticity are curtailed by the Jewish woman's body, whose hair and flesh act as their own kind of garb.

ADAPTATION AND THE SYMBOLIC ORDER

Stam identifies three sources for the prejudice that falsely prioritizes literature over film, each of which has a parallel in the realm of traditional Jewish thought. One is the "older is better" argument, which may be applied to the arts in general and which is a core, if often unspoken, precept of traditional Judaism. Next is "dichotomous thinking," which places literature in a "bitter rivalry" with film. Again, such a prejudice also applies to the other adaptation in question, from "Jewish" to "American." The notion that these categories are incompatible lies at the heart of every representation of religious Jews explored in these chapters—the central conflicts in the films discussed here would be absent without the presumption that a character must choose between being Jewish and being American or French. Finally, Stam points to "iconophobia" as a phenomenon he ties to Judaism's prohibition against "graven images."[8] The letter takes priority over the image in film adaptation theory just as Judaism values the sanctity of the word and disparages imagery as idolatry.

Stam concludes, "Film and other visual media seem to threaten the collapse of the symbolic order, the erosion of the literary fathers, patriarchal narrators, and consecrated arts."[9] Stam critiques those who find the visuality of film threatening to the invisible, sacred order commanded by the written word. Similarly, Jewish immigrant adaptation rests on the question of the visual, how Jewish an individual looks. When Jews shed their Jewish signifiers, they also threaten a symbolic order—the ethnic/racial one that organizes Americans into categories. These categories, in author Cahan's lifetime a source of shame for Jews who wished to "blend in," became a source of pride in filmmaker Silver's lifetime for Jews who wished to "stand out."

It is therefore no stretch to connect Stam's assessment of the prejudices at play in adaptation criticism to similar prejudices at play in religious Jewish evaluations of the Americanization process. Stam and Hutcheon work to break down these false hierarchies for film and move away from discussions of fidelity, loyalty, loss, and shame often associated with adaptations. Stam acknowledges the potential of a film, for example, to offer new, sometimes richer insights into a story than the written word. My own experience with *Hester Street* corroborates his argument: I saw the film before I read the novel, so the book was an adaptation of the film for me, confirming that adaptation does not always follow a unidirectional course. If we accept that adaptation is not a hierarchical process, then questioning how and why adaptations divert from their sources may help us better understand *why* the old is privileged over the new, tradition over modernity, authentic over reproduction, original over adaptation.

ADAPTATION AND SHAME

In the Charlie Kaufman film *Adaptation*, Susan Orlean (Meryl Streep) and John Laroche (Chris Cooper) discuss what it means to adapt, to "figure out how to thrive in the world." Orlean says that while adaptation may help plants thrive, in people, "adapting is almost shameful, it's like running away." Jake's experience with adapting to American life in both *Yekl* and *Hester Street* captures this element of "running away" and the shame that accompanies it. The speed and focus with which he adapts to become "a *regely* Yankee"—however unsuccessful the project—fill him with shame when he is confronted with the past he left behind. But Gitl's shame is different; it stems instead from her *inability* to adapt. Thus, shame is at the center of the adaptation process in both cases, but it is inverted within the couple. Shame appears to be an inevitable by-product of adaptation, since adapting demands both sufficient loyalty to an "original" and sufficient distance from that original. Or, put another way, the adaptation should fastidiously approximate the original while still being "original," a critique lodged against *Hester Street* in the *New York Times* review, which declared, "There is nothing very original about *Hester Street*."[10] Throughout the couple's adaptation to America, Gitl cleaves too intensely to her Old World ways, while Jake creates too much distance. The result is a failed marriage.

Hester Street's success as a film owes to the filmmakers' choices of precisely where to maintain loyalty to Cahan and where to veer from it. In fact, despite its tiny budget and independent production, *Hester Street* reached a wide audience and was even recognized at the Academy Awards (Kane was nominated for best actress). The story told in *Yekl* and adapted into *Hester Street* continues to resonate, and the US Library of Congress declared the film "culturally, historically, or aesthetically significant" in 2011.[11]

Both the book and the film turn the lens toward the destructive potential of immigration at the most intimate level of family. Yekl comes to America with the goal of bringing over his wife, Gitl, and their baby boy, Yossele. He quickly adjusts his appearance by donning stylish American attire and shaving his beard, adopts English as his primary means of communication (even with other native Yiddish speakers), and changes his name to Jake. He works in a sweatshop and saves his money to send to Gitl, but he does not send her all of it. He spends some of it on leisure activities, attending dancing school and entertaining single ladies, particularly the sophisticated Mamie Fein, in the guise of a bachelor. When he receives news of his father's death, Jake readjusts his priorities. He borrows money from Mamie and refurbishes his living space to welcome his family. But when he sees Gitl for the first time in the immigration hall, he is overwhelmed with embarrassment by her "greenhorn" appearance and practices. He urges her to follow his example by removing her dowdy wig and quickly learning the English language. However, even when she takes measures to look "more American," Jake is disgusted by her and maintains his feelings for Mamie. When they ultimately agree to divorce, Jake must rely on Mamie's money to pay for the settlement with Gitl.

At the end of both the film and the book, Gitl, newly wealthy from Mamie's savings, plans to marry Mr. Bernstein, their scholarly, observant boarder who works at the sweatshop with Jake. She mourns her failed marriage but looks forward expectantly to a future with her new husband and the grocery they plan to open with Mamie's savings. Jake and Mamie, on the other hand, are broke and defeated, and Jake's newfound "freedom" from Gitl is met with the immediate obligation to his new wife, Mamie. While Gitl does not adapt to American culture with Jake's enthusiasm (or desperation), her transformation by the film's and book's end is clear. She attends the religious divorce proceedings "in her own hair," wearing a stylish dress and hat. She has even taken to calling their son by his American name, Joey.

When Gitl initially arrives in New York, both book and film vividly convey Jake's shame and embarrassment at seeing his wife for the first time in years. In *Yekl* he spots her in the crowd but wills himself to believe it is not really her. In *Hester Street* Gitl sees Jake first and runs up to him, shouting his name and smiling, reaching for him through the wire fence that separates the new immigrants from the Americans on the other side. Jake lets out a slight smile upon seeing his son but remains silent in the face of Gitl's excitement. Gitl's delight at finally seeing her husband is mixed with shock at his new look. "You shaved your beard," she says in Yiddish. "I didn't know you, I thought you were a nobleman!" Jake almost immediately insists that Gitl change her dress and remove her wig. She gives in by replacing her dowdy brown wig with a kerchief, a resignation that Jake greets with even greater shame. "In America no one wears wigs, a kerchief," becomes a trope throughout the film recited at least twice by Jake and several times by their nosy and brash neighbor Mrs. Kavarsky (Doris Roberts). Jake soon snips off his son's peyos, and a horrified Gitl screams while she looks on (a scene without a parallel in the novel). Hair—exposing it by shedding a wig or concealing it through shaving or cutting—is at the center of the Jewish Americanization process in *Hester Street*. Adaptation is gendered in these key filmic moments, as the wig signifies differently from the peyos and beard. Hair on men signifies piety, while hair on women signifies sexuality. Not unlike the demands placed on French Muslims ensnared in the headscarf debates, becoming American means the woman must expose her hair, while the man must conceal his.

GITL'S WIG, GITL'S HAIR

The way *Hester Street* challenges Stam's hierarchies that place tradition over modernity or original over adaptation is no better conveyed than in the scene where Gitl removes her dowdy wig and dons a stylish hairdo. When Jake comes home to find his wife with a modern American hairdo, he violently attacks her, attempting to rip off what he perceives as a wig. "It's my real hair!" a terrified Gitl squeals. That Gitl's *real* hair is the adaptation, seen by her own disbelieving husband as a wig, introduces the question of which comes first, the tradition or its adaptation, the wig or the hair.

According to Jewish law, the wig is meant to conceal hair. But the scene in the film only works because the wig looks like hair. The wig is thus a slippery signifier because its role is to mimic. The wig should be mostly indiscernible from a woman's hair while also being detectable enough to convey her piety (rather unlike the man's head-covering, which may only be concealed beneath an even larger head-covering, as in the contemporary practice of wearing a baseball cap over a yarmulke). Jake's adaptation, on the other hand, is shocking at first but incontestable. When Gitl first sees Jake at the immigration hall, she is surprised by his new look, but she does not grab Jake's skin or hair, believing these to be a false veneer where once there was a beard and yarmulke. Gitl's Americanization is more volatile because her initial Jewish signifiers are less secure or obvious, making her visible adaptation subtler. In this way, Gitl's wig and Gitl's hair are two versions of the same thing; and for Jake, they both fail. Because a wig looks like hair, the imperative toward modesty is lost when the modest attire so closely resembles the immodest. Furthermore, both Gitl's wig and her real hair repel Jake, suggesting that the thing meant to conceal her sexuality is gratuitous, because he is incapable of seeing her as a sexual being.

By the end of the film, Gitl attends the ritual divorce at the rabbi's house not only in her own hair but with a stylish hat and form-enhancing dress. Conforming to the American audience's desire to see a beautiful swan at the end of such a film, Gitl's adaptation is partly a visible trajectory toward physical beauty, even though her adaptation is also a feminist one. As Joyce Antler asserts, "The film implies that . . . women will have a powerful hand in determining their families' American futures."[12] Gitl's escape from the abusive Jake and her self-determination reinforce Antler's claim. Even so, despite changes in her physical appearance, Gitl remains an observant, traditional Jew, a position that requires a man in order to be complete. After Gitl removes the final vestige of her Old World attire, her embrace of tradition in America can only be visually asserted through her alignment with another man—the bearded, yarmulke-wearing Bernstein, to whom she is engaged by the film's end.

DO I LOOK LIKE A JEW?

Silver's film and Cahan's book illustrate how the processes of Jewish adaptation to America are contingent upon gender both at the level of the Jewish family and at the cosmetic level of Jewish garb. Riv-Ellen Prell argues that Jewish women have historically served "as a medium for representing difference, excess, and desire."[13] Prell's book explores how the Jewish minority's perceptions of its relationship to the Protestant majority in America are reflected in the way Jewish women are represented and imagined by Jewish men: "However [Jews] march toward, or are barred from, a place at America's table, their stories about and images of one another bear the imprint of that journey. That imprint takes shape within relations between men and women, who are at once separated by their genders and joined by their group's differences from others."[14] This "conflict between intimates" is exemplified by *Yekl* and *Hester Street*, both stories about Jews as told by Jews.[15] Jews historically pushed back against antisemitic stereotypes either by appropriating these stereotypes pridefully or by producing counterrepresentations on the page, stage, and screen.[16] Likewise, because *Hester Street* is a woman's adaptation of a story told by a man, Silver "talks back," to use Prell's language, against certain elements of Cahan's version of the narrative, particularly in the alterations she makes that both embolden and soften Gitl's character.

Hester Street exemplifies Prell's claim that representations of Jewish women are fruitful tools for expressing Jewish difference, since the film is devoid of any gentile representations (save the brief appearance of an immigration officer when Gitl first arrives). Nevertheless, a phantom gentile haunts the entire film. The gentile is the imagined figure that Jake aspires to resemble, the one he believes Gitl keeps him from becoming. In an essay about Cahan's *Yekl*, Cheryl Malcolm draws on the words of a character from Bernard Malamud's story "Black Is My Favorite Color."[17] "If you ever forget you are a Jew," the character cautions, "a goy will remind you." Malcolm explains that in *Yekl*, "in place of a Gentile," it is the Jewish woman, Gitl, who serves to remind Jake of his Jewishness.

Returning to the hierarchical structures at play in the adaptation process, Jake cannot escape his Jewishness, as he is reminded of it from both "above" (the invisible gentile world into which he attempts to blend) and "below" (the Jewish woman to whom he is legally and emotionally bound). Jake's imagined bind traps him in a middle position, and he cannot make the upward progress that adaptation seems to demand. But Jake survives by moving sideways, finding a different species of Jewish woman, just as Gitl survives by finding a different species of Jewish man.

Indeed, neither Jake not Gitl "becomes" American by becoming "gentile," although twice in the film Jake insists on his success at doing so. As he encourages Bernstein to shave and become more American, Jake asks, "Do I look like a Jew? Just from looking at me, could you tell I am a Jew?" Later in the film, he repeats the trope: "Take a look on me. Am I a Jew or a gentile? Just by what you see." These questions, absent from Cahan's book, are a product of the story's adaptation to a visual medium. Jake's words force the viewer to look at his body and ask what it means to be visibly Jewish and what the alternatives to "looking Jewish" might be. The question "Could you tell I am a Jew?" contains its answer in the asking. It is not unlike when *La petite Jérusalem*'s director Albou insists that she "feels French"; only a Jew can ask such a question, and in asking it, he exposes the very Jewishness he wishes to conceal.

For Prell, Jews became Americans in part through the ways conflicts played out between Jewish men and women, "because acts of differentiation were acts of Americanization."[18] The scientific process of adaptation depends on striking a balance between differentiating/mutating and conserving. Too much differentiation, and the new species develops into something unrecognizable from its ancestors, rendering the old species extinct. Too little mutation, and the animal or plant cannot survive. The biological fact that both too much and too little transformation can lead to extinction disrupts the conversation about hierarchies when applied to nonbiological processes of adaptation, but it does not eliminate these hierarchies from the discourse.

INCOMPLETE ADAPTATIONS

Consenting to hierarchies that privilege the past, those who represent American Jews on page, stage, or screen employ strategies to mask processes of change by couching the new within the old. In this manner, those "shameful" elements of adaptation are concealed by an insistence on continuity. Such insistence suppresses major instances of change while maintaining the religious imperative toward tradition (or the illusion of it). *Hester Street* beautifully illustrates and complicates this couching procedure. Filmed in black and white, often with a handheld camera, and with the characters speaking (subtitled) Yiddish most of the time, the film sets itself up as an authentic representation of 1890s immigrant New York, looking almost like a documentary. The meticulous set design and ragtime soundtrack re-create in detail a noisy, crowded, gritty Lower East Side ghetto, a moving picture version, as Silver herself declared, of Roman Vishniac's famed photographs.[19] The film thereby asserts its loyalty both to the past it represents and to the book upon which it is based, privileging these earlier iterations of the narrative.

However, this documentary style belies the film's modern feminist tropes and the ways in which it veers from Cahan's story. For example, while the characters in the film speak to one another in Yiddish, *Yekl* was written entirely in English, employing stylistic turns in dialogue and font markers meant to convey when characters switch languages. During the novel's opening dialogue among Yekl, Mr. Bernstein, and some other men at the sweatshop where they work, Yekl expounds upon his knowledge and love of America. The narrator informs the reader—in English—that Yekl is speaking in Yiddish: "He spoke in Boston Yiddish, that is to say, in Yiddish more copiously spiced with mutilated English than is the language of the metropolitan Ghetto in which our story lies."[20]

Jake's first words look like this: "When I was in Boston . . . I knew a *feller.**" The asterisk directs the reader to the bottom of the page, where it is written, "English words incorporated in the Yiddish of the characters of this narrative are given in italics."[21] If Cahan's English novel was intended, at least partially, to invite an English-speaking readership into an unfamiliar Yiddish-speaking world, his editorial maneuver ultimately has a defamiliarizing effect: the reader's gaze is forced downward to the bottom of the page, and she is invited to read twice.[22] The italicized English takes some getting used to; for example, Jake proclaims: "Once I live in America . . . I want to know that I live in America. *Dot'sh a' kin' a man I am!* One must not be a greenhorn. Here a Jew is as good as a Gentile."[23] The irony of Jake's statement lies in his insistence *in fluent Yiddish* that he is fully American, given away to the reader through the mutilated and accented English. Jake's incomplete adaptation is mirrored by Cahan's incomplete translation of a Yiddish moment into English.

Another moment of incomplete or inadequate adaptation materializes upon a close reading of *Hester Street* as an adaptation. In the film, Mrs. Kavarsky argues to Gitl that even observant Jewish women do not cover their hair in America. "Look at me," Mrs. Kavarsky implores. "Am I a *goye*? I'm as pious as you anyhow. And I go with my own hair, don't I? Plenty of time for the *patch* [wig] when I get old. When I'm young, I'm young, and that's all!" Notably, in *Hester Street*, Mrs. Kavarsky makes her case to Gitl in English. She uses Yiddish only to express those terms that are particular to Yiddish culture—*goye* and *patch*—and that lack a reliable English translation. In *Yekl* the author employs the complete opposite narrative device. Rather than a speech given in English and peppered with Yiddish terms, this specific monologue is meant to be understood as spoken in Yiddish, with a few American terms

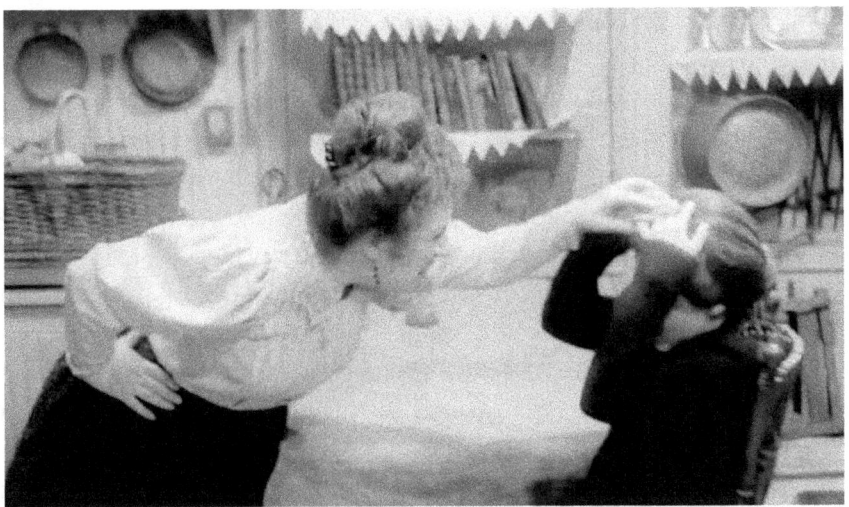

Figure 5.1 Mrs. Kavarsky advises Gitl to remove her wig (screen grab).

interspersed. Cahan's italics indicate which words are spoken in English: "Look at me! I should think I was no Gentile woman, either. I am as pious as you *anyhull*. . . . *Vell*, and yet I am not afraid to go with my own hair. . . . Plenty of time for putting on the patch [meaning the wig] when I get old; *but as* long as I am young, I am young *an' dots ull!*"[24] This conversation is about what it means to be visibly marked as Jewish in relation to some imagined, neutral, unmarked position. The indeterminacy of what counts as marked or unmarked is reflected in the language itself, inverted in book and film. Cahan marks Yiddish with English and English with italicized phonetic dialect. Those rare times when he employs actual Yiddish words, he includes a footnote defining the term or, as in the monologue above, a bracketed translation. Silver mainly uses subtitled Yiddish in her film, defamiliarizing the non-Yiddish-speaking audience who must read in order to follow a conversation. But even when the characters speak English, as in this scene with Mrs. Kavarsky, the audience remains defamiliarized via the deeply accented English and the smattering of Yiddish terms, which, because it is film, cannot be accompanied by bracketed or footnoted explanations.

In the book and the film, the markings (italics, phonetic dialect, accented language, subtitles) indicate what is "native" and what is "other," or, to use the language of adaptation, what is original and what is mutation. The marked thing is that which is alien to the language of the telling. In the case of Cahan, the language of the telling is literary English (as a code for Yiddish), and the alien voice is the ghetto English of the immigrant speakers. In Silver's film, the language of the telling is Yiddish, and the English is marked in various ways, including the different accents and grammatical errors of the characters. In both cases, the reader and viewer are consistently estranged from the language. A particularly revealing example is the way in which the awkward phrasing "Gentile woman" is no less marked than the Yiddish "*goye*," a word that demands it not be translated. The book, written in English for a non-Yiddish-speaking readership, and the film, subtitled for the same reason, seem unable to avoid the awkwardness or alienating quality of telling a story in a language that is not its own.

The different but related issues concerning language in the book and its adaptation on-screen reveal that what counts as "marked" is highly variable. This holds true not just for Cahan and Silver as storytellers but also for their characters. For Gitl, in the language of self-representation, the wig qualifies as unmarked. When she dons her real hair, the result for Jake is like trying to translate *goye*. The wig is so deeply enmeshed with her identity that when viewing her real hair, Jake cannot capture what he might see when he sees another woman without a wig. Gitl's wig is alien to the version of America Jake embraces, but Gitl's hair, for Jake, is alien to her body. This is why he attempts to rip off her hair as if it were a wig. The hierarchies that place old over new, original over adaptation, or authentic over synthetic are muddled by what counts as marked for the audience and what qualifies as marked for the characters in the film.

INADEQUATE TRANSLATIONS, ABSENT ORIGINALS

The film's actual bilingualism as opposed to the novel's implied bilingualism serves to make the film a "more authentic" representation of history than the book. Translation theorists use the term "retroversion" to describe the process of translating a text back into its original language. Texts like the New Testament, however, have a *presumed* original language, in this case, Hebrew or Aramaic, making retroversion efforts partly a performance in recovering an alleged lost original text. Naomi Seidman explains this special process: "Retroversion or pseudo-retroversion, the most coveted effect of New Testament translation into Jewish languages, is both a strategy, since retroversive effects work to establish the Jewish credentials of the New Testament as they obscure its long Christian associations, as well as a performance, since the results, a conflation of Jewishness and Christianness, embody their own argument."²⁵ The effects Seidman describes—redirection, obscuration, conflation—work to hide the fact that a Hebrew translation of the New Testament is just another translation, a new edition of an old text; there is nothing to "recover." Silver employs the same strategy to establish the "credentials" of her film—the historical credentials and the "Jewish" credentials. Like Seidman's example of efforts to render the New Testament into Hebrew, Silver's black-and-white filming, her set design, and particularly her Yiddish translation of an English novel are part of an authenticating strategy, rendering the film adaptation a seemingly "truer" version of the immigrant tale than its original telling by Cahan. These tactics obscure the film's "newness"—notably, that it is not documentary footage from the 1890s but a fictional feature film produced in the 1970s.

Gitl's hair reveals the lie of the pseudoretroversive text. When Gitl exposes her hair with the fashionable hairdo, her new look is simply another (always inadequate) translation of the "original" hair she wore beneath the wig. If the wig is a slippery translation of Gitl's actual hair, then the American hairstyle is a similarly slippery performance of Gitl's hair. The wig asserts her Jewish piety, but only partially, since it looks so much like the thing it is there to conceal. The hairstyle asserts her Americanness, but only partially, since it fails to make her more attractive to Jake. Both the hairstyle and the wig are inadequate translations of Gitl's actual hair or her actual body, as inadequate as translating the richly textured *goye* with the descriptive but one-note English "Gentile woman." In fact, Gitl's "actual body" is a concept the reader or viewer may imagine but never see. Just as there is no Hebrew New Testament to recover, there is no "original" Gitl.

This film's apparent authenticity masks the other ways Silver's adaptation deviates from Cahan's novel. Hasia Diner points out that *Hester Street* reflects the second-wave feminism of its era, a concept impossible to apply to Cahan's story, even if the main character, Gitl, comes out on top at the end of Cahan's tale. Arranging for her divorce in the film, Gitl negotiates a large settlement from Jake's lawyer, subtly forcing the sum upward. In the book, she has no say in the amount of money she receives (although she still receives a healthy sum). But the film conceals this feminist triumph. Gitl's agency in the scene with the lawyer is hidden behind the couple's traditional Jewish divorce ceremony—a ceremony that requires a woman's consent but does not permit her agency—as well as Gitl's near immediate betrothal, this time to an observant Jew. The film's feminist achievements—the substantial financial settlement she skillfully obtains and her choice to (re)marry for love—perform a balancing act with the film's "traditional" feel, not only its documentary style and language but also the ways in which Gitl remains loyal to traditional Judaism throughout her Americanization process. These techniques help the viewer gloss over the feminist messages of the story and the potential the film opens for American Jewish women to "have it all" (money, family, romance, and tradition). Gitl's small victories help the Jewish viewer of 1975 celebrate the "authentic" immigrant past that many were so eager to claim as their own.

RECOVERING ROOTS

The film's "pseudoretroversive" outcome of feeling more like a recovery than an adaptation coincides with the widespread desire among young Americans in the 1970s to "recover" their ethnic origins. This "roots phenomenon," as it came to be called after the popular miniseries and novel *Roots*, stirred a national passion for genealogy and ethnic pride. The ethnic revival stemmed from the civil rights movement, when white Americans followed the example of black nationalism in part due to "whites' consciousness of their skin privilege, rendering it not only visible but uncomfortable." These whites "quit the melting pot. Italianness, Jewishness, Greekness, and Irishness had become badges of pride, not shame."[26]

Hester Street, like many works of literature and film at the time, participated in the ethnic renaissance both in telling a story set in the world of Jewish immigrants and in retelling a story written by a Jewish immigrant. A similar example, Henry Roth's now canonized Jewish immigrant tale, *Call It Sleep* (1934), was "discovered" first by critic Irving Howe in a review in 1960 and then republished in paperback in 1964, going on to sell over a million copies.[27] Howe, as it turns out, later participated in the canonization of the immigrant experience in a second significant way when he published *World of Our Fathers* in 1976. Howe framed the history of the Jewish Lower East Side with the collective, possessive "our," and its success as a *New York Times* best seller indicates how eager a generation of Jews was to connect to their immigrant past.[28]

Similarly, Anzia Yezierska, who had great success as a writer (and screenwriter) during the first two decades of the twentieth century, was largely forgotten and subsequently "rediscovered" in the 1970s during this same charged movement toward claiming Jewish roots.[29] Yezierska is an important benchmark for this period because she was a woman. Like *Yekl*, her novel *Bread Givers* was reread by second-wave feminists as a piece of feminist literature.[30] Feminists, like Jews, were seeking roots in the immigrant era and found them in literary expression. Yezierska was seen by some as a feminist counterpart to Howe. Matthew Frye Jacobson calls *Bread Givers*'s 1975 republication an example of "world-of-our-mothers feminism."[31] In this way, the quest for cultural roots not only coincided with but confronted and even challenged the pursuit of equality for women in the late 1960s and early 1970s.

As Jacobson explores in his book, some understood feminism and the multiculturalist movement to be fundamentally at odds. He cites noted feminist Katha Pollitt, who writes, "You could say that multiculturalism demands respect for all cultural traditions, while feminism interrogates and challenges all cultural traditions."[32] *Hester Street* not only "stands out as [a] perfect exemplar of the social and cultural trends that prevailed" at this time, as Diner writes, it also stands at the crossroads of these movements."[33] The feminist elements of Gitl's story present a challenge to Jewish tradition. But the way Gitl ultimately preserves a traditional Jewish lifestyle, particularly her eventual marriage to the religious Mr. Bernstein, challenges antipatriarchal feminist leanings. Jacobson points out, however, that it has never been possible or desirable for feminists to reject their cultural origins. In fact, feminism of the 1970s depended largely upon women seeking out "*counter*traditions—feminist 'roots.'"[34] In other words, women looked to their cultural traditions to draw out those women who, within the confines of patriarchy, rebelled, revolted, or pursued an alternate lifestyle. These women became the "mothers" for feminists who desired a history (or *her*story) as much as their male counterparts. This more nuanced perspective eliminates *Hester Street*'s ostensible self-contradictions and replaces them with messages fully aligned with feminist-multiculturalist leanings.

"Gitl's agency," writes Diner, "her ability to chart her own future, allows her to organically blend her commitment to tradition and her adoption of aspects of American culture." This blending is precisely what feminist multiculturalism demands. Diner describes how Gitl "strives for a synthesis that keeps her connected to the authentic."³⁵ *Hester Street*, by couching feminist tropes in a Jewish immigrant story, injects this ideology into the Jewish past, offering Jewish feminists the elusive "roots" that so many sought at the time. The inverse reading also holds true: the film makes Jewish tradition more palatable to a 1970s American audience by couching Jewish traditionalism within a feminist plotline. It is possible to foreground the feminist turns the story takes, enabling the film's old-fashioned style and conservative conclusion (marriage, Jewish observance) to empower traditional Judaism by making it the appealing "winner" in the film and entirely compatible with the 1970s women's liberation movement. Adaptation in *Hester Street* is thus backward looking but forward moving. It looks backward toward Jewish immigrant roots and forward toward Jewish women's liberation, placing value in both trajectories. Silver makes the same maneuver in her adaptation of the novel: she moves backward by injecting Yiddish into an English tale and forward by injecting feminism into a realm where patriarchy was the norm.

A TALE OF TWO GITLS

Silver's choice to cast then-newcomer Carol Kane in the role of Gitl is a place where the film's adaptation reflects the demands of its particular context and medium. In Cahan's book, Gitl is described as "stout" and "short," "naturally dark of complexion," with "inky little eyes."³⁶ Carol Kane, on the other hand, is slight and blond; her complexion is pale and is often the lightest shade of gray in the black-and-white film. In an interview decades after the film's release, Silver contended that casting Kane was "one way [Silver] really did change the story." While she attributes the casting to Kane's "phenomenal" and "very affecting" performance and her "wonderful reading" at the audition, Gitl's softer, lighter, blonder beauty in the adaptation carries over into other elements of Silver's adaptation. In the book, Gitl is brassy and melodramatic.³⁷ She frequently inserts exaggerated interjections into conversations ("Woe is me!" "A pain upon me!" "A weeping to me!") or swoons histrionically ("with another pitiful outcry, she fell on his breast").³⁸ Cahan's Gitl is an example of the "ghetto girls" described in Prell's history of representations of Jewish women in America. These "girls" are often marked by excess, both physical and emotional.³⁹ Cahan's Gitl fits this stereotype perfectly. Her inability to contain her emotions in the expected American manner, her religious and superstitious excesses, and her physical excess—she is dark skinned and plump—prevent her from complying with the sophisticated American mold.

Kane's Gitl, on the other hand, is "big-eyed, scared, and inaudible."[40] She raises her voice only when Jake physically attacks her, maintaining uncanny poise throughout her dramatic transformation. The film's Gitl internalizes her most intense emotions, and it is a credit to Kane's acting that the viewer is able to observe this internalization. Even when she invites a peddler into their home in order to purchase a love potion, a clear indication of her Old World superstition, Kane's shyness and quiet shame in this scene demonstrate her capacity to follow "the rule of bourgeois respectability."[41]

In the book, no such scene with a peddler exists. There, Gitl briefly toys with the idea of seeking out a peddler to purchase a love potion but abandons the idea, concluding, "Who knows whether there are in this terrible America any good Jews or beggar women with love potions at all!"[42] The Gitl of the novel is more observant of the world around her than her adaptive counterpart. Although she is as bewildered as any new immigrant, she employs "timid irony" or "hidden sarcasm" when addressing her husband. Cahan's Gitl lacks the wide-eyed doe-like quality of the film Gitl, whose naïveté may well be her defining characteristic.

When Mamie Fein surprises Gitl and Jake by showing up at their home unannounced and demanding the twenty-five dollars Jake owes her, neither book nor film Gitl is able to follow the conversation between the paramours, as it takes place in English. But the Gitl of the novel was "racked with jealousy and all sorts of suspicions."[43] Cahan's Gitl looks to Mr. Bernstein and Mrs. Kavarsky for reassurance that her husband still loves her and is not cheating on her, but she maintains her suspicions throughout. When Jake ultimately rejects her and yells at Mrs. Kavarsky that he hates Gitl and "can not bear the sight of her," Gitl rushes out of their bedroom (in Cahan's words, she "bursts out of the darkness of her retreat"). "May you and your Polish harlot be jumping out of your skins and chafing with wounds as long as you will have to wait for a divorce!" Gitl "explode[s]."[44] The same scene in the film is slightly altered. There, Gitl pronounces the same curse in Yiddish, "May you and your Polish whore be jumping out of your skins!" but she leaves it at that. Kane's Gitl can hardly be said to "burst" from the bedroom, and even in this intense, charged moment, she retains her quiet poise. While Jake brings up the idea of divorce in the book, Gitl is the first to do so in the film. Without using the word, she quietly whispers to Mrs. Kavarsky that she does not want Jake back and that she's had "enough."

These differences between book and adaptation expose the limits of their individual contexts. By the mid-1970s, the darker, brassier Jewish woman figure was ubiquitously, if cruelly, represented as either the overbearing Jewish American Mother or the entitled Jewish American Princess.[45] In casting the light, airy Kane in the role of Gitl, Silver took measures to avoid the Jewish American Princess stereotype (a kind of updated version of the ghetto girl), which caught on in the 1970s. The Gitl of *Hester Street* had the feminist foresight and agency to demand a divorce herself, but she also had the quiet reserve of a woman who is not "too" aggressive, obnoxious, or unlikeable. Cahan's telling of the same story, on the other hand, does not seem invested in creating characters the reader will "root for." Instead, his detailed descriptions maintain a grittier texture, and the story feels less triumphant than tragic, as all parties struggle and contend with great losses in adapting to the New World.

The filmgoing audience expected a beautiful leading lady, someone well-mannered and likeable by American standards. Kane's inoffensive, poised interpretation of the hysterical, melodramatic Gitl of the novel helps fulfill filmgoers' expectations. Kane's Gitl is a woman they can root for because she is a woman to whom they can relate (or to whom they desire to relate). The roots-seeking Jewish audience may have wished to imagine a time when the "the rule of bourgeois respectability" was resisted, but they would have resisted identifying with the cruder version of Gitl from the novel. By playing Gitl as a woman racked with shame at her failure to adapt, Kane's performance helps the audience avoid feeling ashamed of her—and their—vulgar Jewish heritage. In this manner, Silver's casting, Kane's acting, and the audience's expectations of its cinematic heroines place the same kinds of demands on Cahan's Gitl as Jake did: when the book was adapted to the film, Gitl was forced to adopt a bourgeois brand of femininity, the American ideal, from the first moment she appeared on-screen.

Gitl allows Mrs. Kavarsky to style her hair and dress her in a corseted dress in Cahan's tale, but Jake does not come home and attempt to rip off her hair. Rather, upon seeing her new look—a transformation he demanded—he announces, "It becomes her like a wet cat."⁴⁶ While such verbal abuse is both powerful and cruel, the physical abuse that the film's Jake effects on Gitl turns her into an unquestionable victim. Again, this adaptive measure provides the viewing audience with another film convention: not only does Gitl transform from ugly duckling to beautiful swan by the film's end, but she also transforms from victim to hero.

JEWISH MUTATIONS

Gitl's garb, specifically her wig, is at the center of both of these transformations. Men characters who dress and undress from their Jewish garb often leave the hat (a fedora, shtreimel, or yarmulke) as the last item either to put on or to remove, using it as an instrument in a game of revealment and concealment. Religious garb serves to expose the character's Jewishness even as it covers up his body, as in the famous scene from *Annie Hall*. Likewise, shedding the garb exposes the body but conceals the figure's Jewishness, as in Rabbi Belinski's dramatic turn in *The Frisco Kid*. The library of Jewish symbolism is vast and is certainly not limited to religious garb. However, even with additional semiotic cues (e.g., Jewish accents, big noses, bookishness), film and fiction that employ Jewish religious imagery establish the primacy of male Jewish headgear as a signifier of Jewishness in general. When a Jew dresses up like a Jew, the comic or absurdist element surfaces when putting on a costume coincides directly with the message that he is revealing his hidden self. As he adds a black hat, caftan, even a beard and peyos, the character is covering up his body as he exposes it. Philip Roth captures this absurdist quality beautifully in his story "Eli, the Fanatic" when the assimilated character Eli stands naked in front of a mirror with only a large black hat on his head.⁴⁷

Silver's *Hester Street* offers an alternative to these varied literary and filmic representations of Jewish men. Her film presents women's headdress, specifically the wig and headscarf, as an alternate site for exploring ambivalence about Jewish religiosity and authenticity. Like Roth's character Eli, Gitl has a moment in the film where she stands in front of her mirror wearing little but a hat. After Mrs. Kavarsky has given her an initial makeover, tightly tying a corset beneath her drab Old World frock and crowning her with a feathered hat, Gitl waits at home expectantly for her husband to return and see her new look. When their boarder, Mr. Bernstein, returns to the house first, attempting to soothe a visibly disappointed Gitl with lies about how "it's the busy season" and Jake is working late, Gitl seems to suspect what the audience knows: that Jake is out with another woman. She storms into her bedroom, removes her dress, rips off the restrictive corset, and sinks into her bed in front of the mirror. When she looks up, she sees the same ridiculous image the audience sees: Gitl, wearing nothing but a modest slip and her *patch*, is crowned with the flamboyant feathered hat. To adopt language from the science of adaptation, Gitl looks like the Darwinian "missing link," that funny species between shtetl Jew and American lady (or *lada* in Cahan's accented English). This particular permutation—or Darwinian mutation—of Gitl's American self links old with new.

"If mutation is the means by which the evolutionary process advances," Stam writes, "then we can also see filmic adaptations as 'mutations' that help their source novel 'survive.'"[48] The film, of course, helps the novel survive by introducing Cahan's nineteenth-century narrative to a late twentieth-century audience. And the story's very survival is dependent upon the ways in which it was adapted for the new medium. Gitl's financial coup, her budding romance with Bernstein, her swan-like transformation, and her quiet, genteel manner—all absent from the book—ensure the story's success for a moviegoing audience who expects genre conventions to be met and desires a beautiful, quiet hero but also a woman who makes feminist advances. The film's pseudoretroversive use of Yiddish to adapt an English-language novel helps an audience in search of Jewish and feminist Jewish roots see themselves in this seemingly authentic representation of their past.

Stam's claim about mutations applies at the level of character as well. Gitl's transformation helps preserve the past in part by demonstrating to the audience the impossibility of completely erasing it. Looking at her image in the mirror, (nearly) naked with the fancy hat, she lets out a sigh and a chuckle at her image, just as Eli does in Roth's story. "What a silly disappointment to see yourself naked in a hat," Roth writes of Eli. "Especially in that hat."[49] But once again, Gitl's experience in front of the mirror is a gendered one. Instead of the hat drawing out the Jewishness of an "invisible" American Jew like Eli, Gitl's hat does the inverse and makes the conspicuously Jewish woman more like other American women. On the other hand, throughout the makeover and mirror scene, Gitl retains her unfashionable wig, as if it (and therefore her Jewishness) were an extension of her very body, the wig becoming like

Figure 5.2 Gitl laughs at her own image in undergarments, wig, and fashionable hat (screen grab).

a vestigial limb. Stam continues, "Are adaptations not a hybrid form . . . the meeting place of different 'species'?"[50] Here, the different species are the two media, novel and film, and the two identity categories, American and Jew. Gitl's sigh in front of the mirror is the visual embodiment of the fashionable hyphen that many place between Jewish and American.[51]

As with adaptation, the processes at work for promoting messages about feminism and multiculturalism are subject to hierarchical structures. While the multiculturalist message is dependent upon the classical Jewish hierarchy that places old above new, the feminist one is dependent upon a hierarchy that places renegade above faithful, subversive above loyal. The question is not whether such incongruities can coexist—the film and its success attest to the fact that they can do so effectively—but which elements of Jewish tradition and which elements of feminist rebellion "win" at the film's end. In *Hester Street*, bourgeois ideals of femininity and beauty defeat the traditional Jewish wig and kerchief. At the same time, the religious, scholarly, visibly Jewish man, Mr. Bernstein, triumphs over the invisible, assimilationist Jake.

As demonstrated in chapter 3, the religious Jewish man in film may be desirable and attractive, while filmmakers make attempts to desexualize the religious Jewish woman—an approach inverted by *La petite Jérusalem*'s

Albou when she draws attention to the sensuality of religious Jewish women's naked bodies. The Hasidic garb on a man is often a signal of his suppressed and therefore excessive sexuality or perversion, one of the underlying implications of the American Apparel billboards that lingered long after they were taken down. Religious Jewish garb on a woman is often a signal of her inaccessibility, as Finkielkraut claimed of Muslim women in headscarves. In *Hester Street*, Gitl sheds her markers of what the French might call ostentatious religiosity in favor of American standards of feminine beauty. But she maintains those markers by proxy in her affiliation with the religious-looking Bernstein. Bernstein makes no visible transformation in the film. We learn in an intimate conversation between Gitl and Bernstein that the reason he came to America was because he "could not take [his] mind off of vanities," explaining that as he studied Talmud in the Old Country, he thought constantly of women. The religious Jewish man in this film, as in *Annie Hall* and *Deconstructing Harry*, as well as in films not explored in these chapters—*A Stranger among Us* (1992), *A Price above Rubies* (1998), *Holy Rollers* (2010), to name a few—signifies both piety and perversion. No alterations in the religious man's visibility are necessary for him to be an object of sexual desire or an agent of sexuality. Gitl dramatically changes her appearance before becoming Bernstein's wife, while Bernstein retains all the markers of Jewish visibility—the yarmulke, beard, and dark conservative clothing.

Adaptation is both a process and a product. Reading *Hester Street* as an adaptation forces us to look beyond it, toward the adapted *Yekl*, even if the film has taken on the status of a "new original" to adopt language from translation theory. The same holds true of reading Gitl and Jake's experiences as adaptations; the question of which characteristics remain in their "original" state and which are mutations plagues these figures throughout the tale. Does Jake look like a Jew or a gentile? Does Gitl's modern hairstyle at the end of the film make her indiscernible from the illusory *goye* who haunts the film? Where does the film veer from the novel, and in what ways do the Jews veer from their "traditional" positions? What happens when a narrative written by a man is adapted and retold by a woman? How are these gender differences reiterated in the different approaches that Jake and Gitl take to adapting to America?

REAL HAIR, REEL JEWS

> I was very interested in Woody Allen when I was growing up, but I don't think of myself as a Jewish writer. . . . I'm more from the '70s than I am from Judaism.
>
> —Charlie Kaufman, screenwriter, *Adaptation*

Signifying religious Jewish women is slippery, whereas signifying religious Jewish men is opaque. As discussed in chapter 3, while Woody Allen has been lambasted for being a misogynist, his religious Jews give way to an unexpected feminist reading. *Hester Street*, on the other hand, is an ostensibly feminist film, written and directed by a woman and self-proclaimed feminist and featuring a woman who triumphs over her abusive spouse and the patriarchal confines of her time. However, by reading the film as an adaptation and examining the alterations made to Cahan's novel, some of Silver's feminist impulses are undermined by filmmaking choices that more often than not reflect the historical moment of the film—the multiculturalist, roots-seeking 1970s—and the demands of the medium. As we saw with *Les aventures de Rabbi Jacob*, the value that multiculturalist ideology places on difference comes at the expense of historical specificity as differences between groups are equated and thereby flattened out. *Hester Street*, a work of historical fiction, takes measures in its use of black-and-white film and Yiddish to create an "authentic" version of Jewish-American history. The multiculturalist moment is part of the reason why *Hester Street* succeeded as a pseudoretroversion of *Yekl*. By infusing the Jewish immigrant past with feminism and romanticism, Silver helped Jewish feminists "recover" their roots.

The Frisco Kid explored the seemingly incompatible categories "Jewish" and "American" by linking a Hasidic rabbi with a Wild West bandit; *Hester Street* explores these same incompatibilities through the lens of husband and wife. Confirming Prell's hypothesis, Jake and Gitl's "conflict between intimates" is a mirror image of the (supposed) broader national conflict between Jews and gentiles, an image investigated in the comic pairing of Rabbi Belinski and Tommy Lillard (not to mention Alvy Singer and Annie Hall and, in the French national context, Victor Pivert and Slimane, Baya and Arthur, Clara and Ismael, Laura and Djamel). Although these are wildly different films, they employ strikingly similar techniques to arrive at similar conclusions. For example, both Gitl and Rabbi Belinski must make certain religious compromises in order to become successful Jewish-Americans. The compromises are exercised through costume play as Gitl and Belinski remove and replace religious garb throughout the films.

The Frisco Kid concludes with a wedding, while *Hester Street* ends with a divorce. One is a celebration of the hyphen between Jewish and American, the other a eulogy to what is lost when adopting a hybrid identity. Both films and both outcomes—like the eventual breakup between Alvy and Annie in *Annie Hall* and the marriage at the end of *Rabbi Jacob*—are made possible by their historical moment in the 1970s and early 1980s. The convergence of Jewishness and national identities like American or French, whether the convergence is comic or tragic, always comes at the expense of the purity of the originary species, a purity embodied by the Jew in religious clothing. Jewish filmmakers preserve these "pure products," in the words of poet William Carlos Williams, by featuring him (or her!) on-screen.[52] Like a Barthesian museum piece, film "preserve[s] in formaldehyde," as Yiddish poet Aksenfeld writes in this chapter's epigraph, the relics of bygone Jewishness. In this way, the filmic text risks prematurely embalming a still-thriving species. Preservation implicitly acknowledges the figure's obsolescence, cementing her and celebrating her only as a figure of the past. In doing so, the past becomes "our" past, as in Howe's *World of Our Fathers*.

The will to preserve also has the (undesired) outcome of revealing that there is no "pure" Jewishness onto which roots-seeking Jews may cling. How far back must they look? Too far, and the figure is no longer relatable; too close, and the figure lacks the "necessary distance of a second look."[53] The very process of adaptation—its incremental pace, its subtle mutations—creates an infinite space between original and adapted, countless points on the grid between zero and one. Gitl's hair gives the lie to the myths and hierarchies that govern how adaptation is understood. Her various iterations of hairdo and wig call attention to the fact that there is no "original" Gitl to recover, most pointedly when Jake attempts to rip off her "real hair." The impossibility of retrieving an "original" Gitl plays out on a larger scale as an analogy for American Jews in search of their origins. Silver's film participates in this recovery project. She uses Yiddish language, black-and-white film, and a story written in 1896 to expose, rescue, or recover what lies beneath the wig. But what emerges for Silver, as with Gitl, is but another version of the same thing, a translation of a translation.

NOTES

Many thanks to Naomi Seidman for her translation of *Dos Shterntikhl*'s rhyming prologue.

1. Abraham Cahan, *Yekl: A Tale of the New York Ghetto*, in *"Yekl" and "The Imported Bridegroom" and Other Stories of Yiddish New York* (1896; Mineola, NY: Dover Publications, 1970), 1–92.

2. Hasia Diner, "The Right Film at the Right Time: *Hester Street* as a Reflection of Its Era," in *The Modern Jewish Experience in World Cinema*, ed. Lawrence Baron (Lebanon, NH: Brandeis University Press, 2011), 98–105; Sonya Michel, "Yekl and Hester Street: Was Assimilation Really Good for the Jews?," *Literature/Film Quarterly* 5 (1977): 142; Joyce Antler, "Hester Street," in *Past Imperfect: History According to the Movies*, ed. Marc Carnes (New York: Agincourt Press, 1995), 178.

3. On *Yentl* as an adaptation, see Stephen Whitfield, "Yentl," *Jewish Social Studies* 5, nos. 1–2 (Autumn 1998–Winter 1999): 154–176; and Whitfield, "Fiddling with Sholem Aleichem: A History of *Fiddler on the Roof*," in *Key Texts in American Jewish Culture*, ed. Jack Kugelmass (New Brunswick, NJ: Rutgers University Press, 2003), 105–125.

4. Freud may have called this "the narcissism of minor differences," a term he employs in relation to Jews in *Civilization and Its Discontents*, trans. James Strachey (New York: W. W. Norton, 1961), 72.

5. Cf. Diner, "Right Film," 98.

6. Robert Stam, "Introduction: The Theory and Practice of Adaptation," in *Literature and Film: A Guide to the Theory and Practice of Film Adaptation*, ed. Robert Stam and Alessandra Raengo (Malden, MA: Blackwell, 2005), 1–52.

7. Linda Hutcheon, *A Theory of Adaptation* (New York: Routledge, 2006), xii.

8. Stam, "Introduction," 3–6.

9. Ibid., 5.

10. Richard Eder, "*Hester Street* (1975), Pathos and Wit Light Up 'Hester St.,'" *New York Times*, October 20, 1975.

11. News from the Library of Congress, "2011 National Film Registry More Than a Box of Chocolates," Library of Congress, December 28, 2011, http://www.loc.gov/today/pr/2011/11-240.html.

12. Antler, "Hester Street," 181.

13. Riv-Ellen Prell, *Fighting to Become Americans: Assimilation and the Trouble between Jewish Women and Jewish Men* (Boston: Beacon Press, 1999), 209.

14. Ibid., 20.

15. Ibid., 176.

16. See, for example, Sander Gilman, *Jewish Self-Hatred: Anti-Semitism and the Hidden Language of the Jews* (Baltimore, MD: Johns Hopkins University Press, 1990).

17. Cheryl Malcolm, "Othering the Other in Abraham Cahan's *Yekl: A Tale of the New York Ghetto*," *Amerikastudien / American Studies* 46, no. 2 (2001): 225; Bernard Malamud, "Black Is My Favorite Color," in *The Stories of Bernard Malamud* (New York: Macmillan, 1983), 73–84.

18. Prell, *Fighting to Become Americans*, 20.
19. Silver claimed in an interview that Vishniac's photographs served as her inspiration for the visuals created by the film, despite their setting in 1930s eastern Europe. Joan Micklin Silver and Kenneth Turan, "A Wig, a Fence, and One White Horse," *Pakn Treger*, Fall 2003, 32.
20. Cahan, *Yekl*, 2.
21. Ibid., 3.
22. Geoff Brown writes of *Yekl* that it was "seemingly concocted for non-immigrant readers: footnotes explain Yiddish expressions and customs, and characters' dialogue is transcribed with academic precision" ("Hester Street," *Sight & Sound* 45, no. 1 [Winter 1975–1976]: 58).
23. Cahan, *Yekl*, 5.
24. Ibid., 57.
25. Naomi Seidman, "'A Gift for the Jewish People': Einspruch's *Der Bris Khadoshe* as Missionary Translation and Yiddish Literature," paper presented at the annual meeting for the Society of Biblical Literature, November 19–22, 2011.
26. Matthew Frye Jacobson, *Roots Too: White Ethnic Revival in Post–Civil Rights America* (Cambridge, MA: Harvard University Press, 2006), 2. See also, Alex Haley, *Roots: The Saga of an American Family* (New York: Doubleday, 1976).
27. Harold Ribalow, "The History of Henry Roth and *Call It Sleep*," introduction to *Call It Sleep* (Paterson: Pageant Books, 1960), xix.
28. Irving Howe, *World of Our Fathers: The Journey of the East European Jews to America and the Life They Found and Made* (New York: New York University Press, 2005). See also Hasia Diner, *Lower East Side Memories: A Jewish Place in America* (Princeton, NJ: Princeton University Press, 2000), 92–94.
29. Anzia Yezierska, *Bread Givers* (New York: Persea Books, 2003).
30. Diner, *Lower East Side Memories*, 70.
31. Jacobson, *Roots Too*, 271.
32. Ibid., 270. Cf. Katha Pollitt, "Whose Culture?," in *Is Multiculturalism Bad for Women?*, ed. Susan Moller Okin (Princeton, NJ: Princeton University Press, 1999), 27.
33. Diner, "Right Film," 98.
34. Jacobson, *Roots Too*, 271.
35. Diner, "Right Film," 100.
36. Cahan, *Yekl*, 34.
37. Silver and Turan, "A Wig," 32.
38. Cahan, *Yekl*, 36.
39. Prell, *Fighting to Become Americans*, 21–57.
40. Eder, "Pathos."
41. Diner, *Lower East Side Memories*, 173.
42. Cahan, *Yekl*, 42.
43. Ibid., 51.
44. Ibid., 70.
45. Alan Dundes, "The J.A.P. and the J.A.M. in American Jokelore," *Journal of American Folklore* 98, no. 390 (October–December 1985): 456–475; Prell, *Fighting to Become Americans*, 177–208.
46. Cahan, *Yekl*, 68.
47. Philip Roth, "Eli, the Fanatic," in *Goodbye, Columbus* (New York: Vintage Books, 1959), 285.
48. Stam, "Introduction," 3.

49. Roth, "Eli, the Fanatic," 285.
50. Stam, "Introduction," 3.
51. See Sandra Gilbert, "Mysteries of the Hyphen," in *Beyond the Godfather: Italian American Writers on the Real Italian American Experience*, ed. A. Kenneth Ciongoli and Jay Parini (Hanover: University Press of New England, 1997), 51, 52. Cf. Jacobson, "Hyphen Nation," in *Roots Too*, 11–71.
52. William Carlos Williams, *Spring & All* (Paris: Contact Publishing Company, 1923), discussed in James Clifford, "Introduction: The Pure Products Go Crazy," in *The Predicament of Culture: Twentieth-Century Ethnography, Literature, and Art* (Cambridge, MA: Harvard University Press, 1988), 1–17.
53. Mary Ann Doane, "Film and the Masquerade: Theorising the Female Spectator," *Screen* 23, nos. 3–4 (September–October 1982): 75–76.

EPILOGUE

Hijab, Habit, and Hasid

> *"I nearly reached the point of believing"*: that is the formula which sums up the spirit of the fantastic. Either total faith or total incredulity would lead us beyond the fantastic: it is hesitation which sustains its life.
> —Tzvetan Todorov, *The Fantastic*

> It was one of our earliest lessons: smaller hats always showed deference to larger ones.
> —Shulem Deen, *All Who Go Do Not Return*

MORE THAN A CENTURY AFTER GRODNER took the stage in Romania to sing "The Jolly Hasid" wearing peyos and a caftan, Wyatt Cenac reported on the eruv on *The Daily Show*. Cenac's report indicates the continued comic utility and freedom both Jews and non-Jews have to play with Hasidic garb in the twenty-first century. I have argued in these chapters that the Hasidic fantasy signifies ambiguously. It signals Jewish racial difference *and* whiteness, Jewish particularism *and* national belonging, Jewish authenticity *and* Jewish performativity. Hasidic imagery's power lies in this opaqueness (it is not legible; we cannot see beyond the beard, hat, peyos, and caftan), a characteristic that opens up compelling representational options for Jewish women.

The Hasidic image has a rich history that coincides with the birth of Jewish theater, whose origins (while mythical) point to Jewishness as a performative category. Both the Nazi abuse of Hasidic imagery and the 1970s Jewish multicultural movement that adopted the Hasidic man as a figurehead (at least in film) support my thesis that Hasidic attire presumes transparency while being symbolically illegible. I have argued here that the Hasidic figure on-screen, although ostensibly easy to decipher, generates an overlapping set of complex and contradictory codes about Jewishness, gender, and national identity. Epitomizing these ambiguities, Alvy Singer's secular Jewishness in *Annie Hall* (and Woody Allen's in real life) lends his Hasidic moment a textured humor that invites the viewer—in the two seconds the image appears on-screen—to acknowledge the multilayered nature of this Jewish performance. But as a close reading of Allen's *Deconstructing Harry* reveals, the signifying immediacy of Alvy's garb excludes a similar expression of Jewishness from women.

The visual shorthand offered by Hasidic performances is not restricted to the Jewish case. Examining the garb in its French context instantly introduces the much more politically pertinent question of Muslim women's attire, where the legal restrictions on women's headgear continue to materialize in public debate. The signifying power of the Muslim hijab and Catholic habit, like the Hasidic fantasy, emblematize cultural and religious difference as they conceal individual specificity. However, different theoretical concerns emerge when religious visibility is signaled on the woman's body rather than on the man's. Marjorie Garber ties Jewish visibility's association with men to the historical anti-Jewish notion of Jewish men as always already womanly. She addresses the "cultural misreading" of male religious garb, easily mistaken for women's clothing when terms like "robe" and "frock" are used to describe it.[1] In this way, the (Hasidic) Jewish man is not only already something of a woman because of the "effeminate" quality assigned to him by antisemites (and then embraced by figures like Woody Allen) but also like a woman because of his long curls and dress-like frock.

But the symbolic power of religious garb for Jews, Catholics, and Muslims has implications beyond the Jewish man's "womanliness." Habits, hijabs, and the Jewish woman's wig indicate modesty. The Hasid's beard, hat, and peyos, on the other hand, signal piety. This distinction between modesty (covering a woman's flesh) and piety (exposing a man's religious devotion) recalls the substantial ways gender affects acts of dressing and undressing. When Gitl removes her wig in *Hester Street*, she reveals her body/hair. When Jake shaves his beard, he conceals his Jewishness.

Non-Jewish appropriation of the Hasidic fantasy, such as Cenac's, also points to Jewish successes with multiculturalism beginning in the 1970s. If this ethnically marked imagery was a way for Jews to assert their American-ness, as Matthew Jacobson argues, then its use by non-Jewish-Americans situates it firmly as one legitimate (white) face along the diverse landscape of national identity. When the Hasidic fantasy appears on *The Daily Show* with the presumed blessing of the show's Jewish host and executive producer, Jon Stewart, it crystallizes the gulf between secular Jews like Stewart and Jews like the ones in Cenac's Hasidic graphic (Figure Intro.1). But those who make use of the Hasidic image tend to police themselves for political correctness. Is it merely a coincidence that this story, which asks audiences to laugh at both Hasidic and secular Jews, was reported by the black Cenac?

While I was writing this book, *New York Magazine* published a photographic essay featuring black Hasidim and other black Orthodox Jews from Crown Heights called "The Black Orthodox: Double-Consciousness and the Pursuit of G-d."[2] From *Annie Hall* to their reconfiguring on the American Apparel billboards, Hasidic signifiers have become commonplace in American media. But this sense of familiarity is disrupted when the garb is featured on the bodies of black men and women. Hasidic signifiers tend to serve specific objectives: as punch lines, as a means to raise questions about gender and sexuality, as markers of national belonging or alienation, and as shorthand for authenticity. So what makes the individuals in *New York Magazine* worthy of photographing? As the essay's subtitle asserts, they reflect the double consciousness of blackness and Jewishness. If Jewishness, via the Hasidic image, has become a widely accepted fixed feature of the American social landscape, it only functions as such when restricted to the bodies of white men. On a black body, the garb seems to signal more costume than an external expression of an internal Jewishness. The signifying immediacy of the Hasidic garb conflicts with the signifying immediacy of black skin in America. As Michael Rogin says of Jews in blackface, "Jews could represent blacks, but not the other way around."[3] The photographs in *New York Magazine* are a curiosity precisely because the people in them come across as blacks in Jewface rather than what they are, black Jews.

The difference between imagining the religious garb on the expected white secular Jewish body and the same garb on the religious black body is the difference between drag and disguise. Drag promotes messages about the disharmony of the costume and the person wearing it, messages that disrupt any notion of gender coherence. Adopting Esther Newton's analysis,

I demonstrated how the Hasidic garb fosters a similar message, disrupting any notion of Jewishness as a coherent category. I considered the various consequences of the French Catholic character Pivert donning the Hasidic costume in *Rabbi Jacob*, but his survival in the film and the lesson in tolerance he learns would not have been possible or plausible if he were black. The black Jews pictured in *New York Magazine* challenge the incoherency of the category "Jewish" that surfaces when characters play with Jewish drag. For *The Frisco Kid*'s Avram Belinski, the "kosher cowboy," the joke/fascination depends on the reification of the categories "Jewish" and "cowboy." The photographs of the black Hasidim perform a related operation: reifying the categories "black" and "Jewish" by highlighting their incompatibility when envisioned on a single body.

The photographic essay in *New York Magazine* signals new possibilities for the Hasidic fantasy—possibilities that appear in more recent films as well. The Coen brothers' 2009 film *A Serious Man* features a Hasidic-looking rabbi who has new and unexpected characteristics. His somber, cavernous office at the synagogue is sprinkled with scientific curiosities and globes, signposting worldliness—a characteristic usually foreign to images of the provincial Hasidic type. His intimidating silence counters earlier images of jolly, dancing Hasidim like the ones on the rue des Rosiers in *Rabbi Jacob*. The cryptic advice he gives to a bar-mitzvah student is gleaned from a popular rock song, not the Talmud. These new possibilities—black Hasidim, rock-and-roll rabbis—do not preclude the more familiar version of the Hasidic fantasy. In fact, as Hasidic imagery becomes increasingly pervasive in the American popular culture lexicon, modifications to it, such as Cenac's eruv hat, become increasingly possible.

As I was writing this conclusion, I continued to track fictional and other media portrayals of Hasidim, with new iterations of a century-old fantasy coming to screens large and small on a regular basis. A "Hasid or Hipster" photo blog on Tumblr encourages those looking at it to guess which of the photographs feature Hasidic men and which Brooklyn hipsters.[4] This intersection of two competing cultural phenomena and its later retelling on a late-night talk show, like American Apparel's Hasidic model, call attention to the ways the non-Hasidic world continues to view Hasidic garb ambivalently: the garb signifies piety and isolationism, while at the same time, the garb is just clothing, even fashion.

Nothing in recent media reports expresses the ongoing power and signifying ambivalence of Hasidic attire more than the way that some Hasidim have themselves come to acknowledge its signifying capacity. In 2015 a Hasidic antigay organization went so far as to hire Mexican day laborers to protest the New York City Gay Pride Parade on the organization's behalf. Considering the events at the parade too lewd for yeshiva boys to witness, the group outsourced their protesting needs, providing the paid individuals with signs. More significantly, they also dressed the non-Jewish protesters in Hasidic attire, including tzitzit, black hats, and faux peyos. Just as the maskil Israel Grodner understood that his staged critique of Hasidism would be more powerful (and entertaining!) if he performed in Hasidic garb, the antigay organizer behind the protests knew that his message would be more powerful and garner more media attention if it was performed in the garb.[5] Hasidic garb's performative quality—both as powerful, immediate signifier of Jewish authenticity and as mere artifice—persists from the nineteenth-century Romanian Yiddish theater to the twenty-first-century political protest arena.

M. Gordon's satirical question from 1869, "What do you need with your old granddad's garments?" challenged religious Jews to alter the aesthetics of their Jewishness. The challenge revealed much about his moment at the height of the eastern European Jewish Enlightenment. Its parodic performance in Hasidic garb (or performances of similar poems) presents at least one kind of response to the question: secular Jews need "granddad's garments" as a mechanism to distinguish themselves spatially and temporally from Hasidic Jews. At the same time, secular Jews embalm the Hasidic image through performance, asserting ownership of their quaint past while asserting the figure's obsolescence. The question's continued reiteration through film, television, advertisement, photo essay, and political protest maintains many of its nineteenth-century predecessor's meanings: piety, authenticity, history, tradition, superstition, Jewish specificity. As national ideologies transform and historical trauma strikes, the garb is continually imbued with new and often contradictory meanings: Holocaust, "roots," sexual oppression/archaism, sexual perversion, jolly dance, hipster fashion, and so on.

Hasidic garb is exceptional for its signifying potential as a myth that is always open to new meanings. But it is not alone. More and more, the Muslim woman's hijab is a site for opening up, as it "veils" political, religious, sexual, and national discourses. Like (men's) Hasidic attire, the hijab forecloses certain nuanced readings of images in favor of meanings associated with its signifying immediacy. But unlike Hasidic garb, the hijab is open to modification. Consider, for example, recent iterations of women wearing hijabs adorned with the colors of the French flag or the American Stars and Stripes.[6] Popular film has not yet caught on to the comic, dramatic, political, religious, national, and erotic signifying potential of the hijab. But I would not be surprised to see a version of *Annie Hall*'s Easter dinner scene with a secular Muslim appearing, for a mere second or two, in the hijab. With Islamophobia on the rise in both the United States and France, using Muslim women's garb as a comedic device on-screen might lead to Islam gaining a welcome (if still problematic) space in these nations, just as Hasidic garb did for French and American Jews in the 1970s.

The Haskalah dictum to "be a Jew at home and a man on the streets" acquires new dimensions when considered alongside the eruv, a ritual device that transforms "the streets" into a legal extension of "home." The multiculturalist movement beginning in the 1970s constructed an eruv around the entire nation, fashioning an American homeland for Jews, as long as they live as "Jews." While this limited type of difference is required by the American multiculturalist agenda, the French films show that Jewish difference is reluctantly tolerated there so long as it is (1) restricted to the Hasidic type and (2) geographically delimited (to the rue des Rosiers in *Rabbi Jacob* and the banlieue in *La petite Jérusalem*). Jews who look more like WASPs or white Catholics than rabbis are marginalized by both formulations, as are Jewish women, both religious and secular. The popular films discussed here police the boundaries of multiculturalism's eruv through games of revealing and concealing. The eruv's circular architecture is a useful image with which to close a discussion of the Hasidic fantasy. I cannot pinpoint a singular overarching meaning for the imagery of beards, hats, and caftans nor call out a singular implication of the fantasy for Jews or other Americans and French people. Instead, reading the fantastic Hasid is a circular process that invites constant hesitation.

NOTES

1. Marjorie Garber, *Vested Interests: Cross-Dressing and Cultural Anxiety* (New York: Routledge, 1992), 210, 224–226.

2. Molly Langmuir and photographer Wayne Lawrence, "The Black Orthodox: Double-Consciousness and the Pursuit of G-d," *New York Magazine*, December 23, 2012, http://nymag.com/news/features/black-jews-2012-12/.

3. Michael Rogin, *Blackface, White Noise: Jewish Immigrants in the Hollywood Melting Pot* (Berkeley: University of California Press, 1996), 251.

4. http://hasidorhipster.tumblr.com/. Jimmy Kimmel featured a version of this game called Hipster or Hasidic? during Back to Brooklyn Week on *Jimmy Kimmel Live!*, ABC, October 22, 2015.

5. Some debate emerged as to whether the group behind the mercenary protesters was actually an organization or just the work of a single homophobic extremist. In either case, his choice to outfit the protesters in the garb maintains its signifying power. Andy Newman and James Estrin, "Jewish Group, with Hired Protestors, Opposes the Parade," *New York Times*, June 28, 2015. See also Emily Shire, "Meet the One-Man Homophobia Machine," *Daily Beast*, July 1, 2015.

6. See the cover of Joan Wallach Scott's *The Politics of the Veil* (Princeton, NJ: Princeton University Press, 2007) for an example of the French flag hijab. Various news outlets covered Saba Ahmed's appearance on Fox News's *The Kelly File* while wearing an American flag hijab. For example, Christina Cauterucci, "This Woman Wore an American Flag Hijab on Fox News. That's a Revolutionary Act," *Slate.com*, November 18, 2015.

FILMOGRAPHY AND BIBLIOGRAPHY

FILMOGRAPHY

Adaptation (dir. Spike Jonze, 2002)
An American Tail (dir. Don Bluth, 1986)
Annie Hall (dir. Woody Allen, 1977)
Les aventures de Rabbi Jacob (dir. Gérard Oury, 1973)
Blazing Saddles (dir. Mel Brooks, 1974)
The Chosen (dir. Jeremy Kagan, 1981)
Crossing Delancey (dir. Joan Micklin Silver, 1988)
Curb Your Enthusiasm (HBO, 1999–)
The Daily Show with Jon Stewart (Comedy Central, 1999–2015)
Deconstructing Harry (dir. Woody Allen, 1997)
Der ewige Jude (dir. Fritz Hippler, 1940)
Everything You Always Wanted to Know about Sex (dir. Woody Allen, 1972)
Fading Gigolo (dir. John Turturro, 2013)
Fiddler on the Roof (dir. Norman Jewison, 1971)
The Frisco Kid (dir. Robert Aldrich, 1979)
Gentleman's Agreement (dir. Elia Kazan, 1947)
Hester Street (dir. Joan Micklin Silver, 1975)
History of the World: Part I (dir. Mel Brooks, 1981)
Holy Rollers (dir. Kevin Asch, 2010)
Il était une fois . . . Les aventures de Rabbi Jacob (dir. Auberi Edler, 2009)
The Jazz Singer (dir. Alan Crosland, 1927)
Jimmy Kimmel Live! (ABC, 2003–)
Kadosh (dir. Amos Gitai, 1999)

La petite Jérusalem (dir. Karin Albou, 2005)
La règle du jeu (dir. Jean Renoir, 1939)
La vérité si je mens! (dir. Thomas Gilou, 1997)
Le monocle rit jaune (dir. Georges Lautner, 1964)
Le nom des gens (dir. Michel Leclerc, 2010)
L'homme est une femme comme les autres (dir. Jean-Jacques Zilbermann, 1998)
Love and Death (dir. Woody Allen, 1975)
Mauvaise foi (dir. Roschdy Zem, 2006)
Mosaïque (FR3, 1977–1987)
A Price above Rubies (dir. Boaz Yakin, 1998)
The Purple Rose of Cairo (dir. Woody Allen, 1985)
Qu'est-ce qu'on a fait au bon Dieu? (dir. Philippe de Chauveron, 2014)
A Serious Man (dir. Joel Coen and Ethan Coen, 2009)
Some Like It Hot (dir. Billy Wilder, 1959)
A Stranger among Us (dir. Sidney Lumet, 1992)
Striptease (dir. Andrew Bergman, 1996)
Take the Money and Run (dir. Woody Allen, 1969)
To Be or Not to Be (dir. Ernst Lubitsch, 1942)
Tootsie (dir. Sydney Pollack, 1982)
Ulzana's Raid (dir. Robert Aldrich, 1972)
Woody Allen: A Documentary (dir. Robert Weide, 2011)
Yentl (dir. Barbra Streisand, 1983)
Zelig (dir. Woody Allen, 1983)

BIBLIOGRAPHY

Newspapers and Periodicals

Actualité Juive (1982–)
Business Insider (2009–)
Charlie Hebdo (1970–1982; 1992–)
Chicago Sun Times (1948–)
Daily Beast (2008–)
Der Spiegel Online International (1994–)
Guardian (1821–)
Ha-Meliz (1860–1903)
Harper's Bazaar Indonesia (2012–)
Huffington Post (2005–)
Jewish Daily Forward (1897–)
Le Figaro (1826–)
Le Huffington Post France (2012–)
Le Monde (1944–)
Libération (1973–)
Los Angeles Times (1881–)
New Yorker (1925–)
New York Magazine (1968–)
New York Times (1851–)
NPR.org (2007–)
Slate (1996–)
Slate.fr (2009–)
Tikkun (1986–)
Variety (1905–)
Week (2007–)

Selected Sources

Abrams, Nathan. *The New Jew in Film: Exploring Judaism and Jewishness in Contemporary Cinema*. New Brunswick, NJ: Rutgers University Press, 2012.

Aksenfeld, Israel. *The Headband*. In *The Shtetl: A Creative Anthology of Jewish Life in Eastern Europe*. Translated and edited by Joachim Neugroschel. New York: Overlook, 1989. 49–172.

Antler, Joyce. "Hester Street." In *Past Imperfect: History According to the Movies*. Edited by Marc Carnes. New York: Agincourt Press, 1995. 178–181.

Arkin, Kimberly. *Rhinestones, Religion, and the Republic: Fashioning Jewishness in France*. Stanford, CA: Stanford University Press, 2014.

Aschheim, Steven. *Brothers and Strangers: The East European Jew in German and German Jewish Consciousness, 1800–1923*. Madison: University of Wisconsin Press, 1982.

Bailey, Peter. *The Reluctant Film Art of Woody Allen*. Lexington: University Press of Kentucky, 2001.

Barthes, Roland. *The Eiffel Tower and Other Mythologies*. Translated by Richard Howard. New York: Hill and Wang, 1979.

———. *Mythologies*. Translated by Annette Lavers. New York: Hill and Wang, 1972.

Bassnett, Susan. *Translation Studies*. 3rd ed. New York: Routledge, 2003.

Berger, John. *Ways of Seeing*. London: Penguin, 1972.

Berkovitz, Jay. *Rites and Passages: The Beginnings of Modern Jewish Culture in France, 1650–1860*. Philadelphia: University of Pennsylvania Press, 2007.

Berkowitz, Joel, and Barbara Henry, eds. *Inventing the Modern Yiddish Stage*. Detroit: Wayne State University Press, 2012.

Bhabha, Homi K. *The Location of Culture*. 1994; London: Routledge, 2005.

Bial, Henry. *Acting Jewish: Negotiating Ethnicity on the American Stage and Screen*. Ann Arbor: University of Michigan Press, 2005.

Bialik, Haim Nahman. "*Halachah* and *Aggadah*." In *Revealment and Concealment: Five Essays*. Jerusalem: Ibis Editions, 2000. 45–87.

Birnbaum, Pierre. "*La France aux Français*": *Histoire des haines nationalists*. Paris: Seuil, 1993.

Bouzar, Dounia, and Saïda Kada. *L'une voilée, l'autre pas*. Paris: Albin Michel, 2003.

Boyarin, Daniel. *Unheroic Conduct: The Rise of Heterosexuality and the Invention of the Jewish Man*. Berkeley: University of California Press, 1997.

Breines, Paul. *Tough Jews: Political Fantasies and the Moral Dilemma of American Jewry*. New York: Basic Books, 1992.

Brodkin, Karen. *How Jews Became White Folks: And What That Says about Race in America*. Piscataway, NJ: Rutgers University Press, 1998.

Brook, Vincent. *Something Ain't Kosher Here: The Rise of the "Jewish" Sitcom*. Piscataway, NJ: Rutgers University Press, 2003.

Brook, Vincent, and Marat Grinberg, eds. *Woody on Rye: Jewishness in the Films and Plays of Woody Allen*. Lebanon, NH: Brandeis University Press, 2014.
Brown, Geoff. "Hester Street." *Sight & Sound* 45, no. 1 (Winter 1975–1976): 58.
Butler, Judith. *Bodies That Matter: On the Discursive Limits of Sex*. New York: Routledge, 1993.
———. *Gender Trouble*. New York: Routledge, 1999.
Cahan, Abraham. *Yekl: A Tale of the New York Ghetto*. 1896. In *"Yekl" and "The Imported Bridegroom" and Other Stories of Yiddish New York*. Mineola, NY: Dover Publications, 1970.
Charbit, Denis. "Déclinaisons du franco-judaisme." In *Les cultures des Juifs*. Edited by David Biale et al. Paris: Editions de l'éclat, 2005. 1003–1042.
Clifford, James. *The Predicament of Culture: Twentieth Century Ethnography, Literature, and Art*. Cambridge, MA: Harvard University Press, 1988.
Cohen, Norman, and Robert Seltzer, eds. *The Americanization of the Jews: Reappraisals in Jewish Social and Intellectual History*. New York: New York University Press, 1995.
Deen, Shulem. *All Who Go Do Not Return: A Memoir*. Minneapolis: Graywolf Press, 2015.
Diner, Hasia. *The Jews of the United States: 1654–2000*. Berkeley: University of California Press, 2006.
———. *Lower East Side Memories: A Jewish Place in America*. Princeton, NJ: Princeton University Press.
———. "The Right Film at the Right Time: *Hester Street* as a Reflection of Its Era." In *The Modern Jewish Experience in World Cinema*. Edited by Lawrence Baron. Lebanon, NH: Brandeis University Press, 2011. 98–105.
Doane, Mary Ann. *The Desire to Desire: The Woman's Film of the 1940's*. Bloomington: Indiana University Press, 1987.
———. "Film and the Masquerade: Theorising the Female Spectator." *Screen* 23, nos. 3–4 (September–October 1982): 74–87.
Dundes, Alan. "The J.A.P. and the J.A.M. in American Jokelore." *Journal of American Folklore* 98, no. 390 (October–December 1985): 456–475.
Erdman, Harley. *Staging the Jew: The Performance of an American Ethnicity, 1860–1920*. Piscataway, NJ: Rutgers University Press, 1995.
Escafré-Dublet, Angéline. "L'état et la culture des immigrés, 1974–1984." *Histoire@ Politique: Politique, culture, société* 4 (January–April 2008): 15.
Feinstein, Howard. "Decade: Charlie Kaufman on *Synecdoche, New York*." *IndieWire*, December 28, 2009. http://www.indiewire.com/2009/12/decade-charlie-kaufman-on-synecdoche-new-york-246078/.
Fiedler, Leslie A. "The Demon of the Continent." In *The Pretend Indians: Images of Native Americans in the Movies*. Edited by Gretchen M. Bataille and Charles L. P. Silet. Ames: Iowa State University Press, 1980.

Finkielkraut, Alain. *Au nom de l'autre: Réflexions sur l'antisémitisme qui vient.* Paris: Gallimard, 2003.

———. *Le juif imaginaire.* Paris: Seuil, 1980. *The Imaginary Jew.* Translated by Kevin O'Neill and David Suchoff. Lincoln: University of Nebraska Press, 1994.

Freedman, Samuel. *Jew vs. Jew: The Struggle for the Soul of American Jewry.* New York: Simon and Schuster, 2000.

Freud, Sigmund. *Civilization and Its Discontents.* Translated by James Strachey. New York: W. W. Norton, 1961.

———. "Some Early Unpublished Letters." Translated by Ilse Scheier. *International Journal of Psychoanalysis* 50 (1969): 420.

Funkenstein, Amos. "The Dialectics of Assimilation." *Jewish Social Studies* 1 (Winter 1995): 1–14.

Furnish, Ben. *Nostalgia in Jewish-American Theatre and Film, 1979–2004.* New York: Peter Lang, 2005.

Gaddis, John Lewis. *The Landscape of History: How Historians Map the Past.* Oxford: Oxford University Press, 2002.

Garber, Marjorie. *Vested Interests: Cross-Dressing and Cultural Anxiety.* New York: Routledge, 1992.

Gertel, Elliot B. *Over the Top Judaism: Precedents and Trends in the Depiction of Jewish Beliefs and Observances in Film and Television.* Lanham, MD: University Press of America, 2003.

Gilbert, Sandra. "Mysteries of the Hyphen." In *Beyond the Godfather: Italian American Writers on the Real Italian American Experience.* Edited by A. Kenneth Ciongoli and Jay Parini. Hanover: University Press New England, 1997. 49–61.

Gilman, Sander. *Jewish Self-Hatred: Anti-Semitism and the Hidden Language of the Jews.* Baltimore, MD: Johns Hopkins University Press, 1990.

Goldfaden, Abraham. "Dos freilekhe Hosidl." In *Dos Yidele: Yiddishe lider af prost Yiddisher shprakh.* 1886; Warsaw: Yaakov Lidsky Book Handler, 1903. 94–100.

———. *Goldfaden-bukh.* New York: Idishn Teater Muzee, 1926.

Goldstein, Eric. *The Price of Whiteness.* Princeton, NJ: Princeton University Press, 2006.

Gordon, Mikhl. "Shtey af mayn folk." In *Shirei M. Gordon: Yidishe lider fun Mikhl Gordon.* Warsaw: NP, 1889. 29–35.

Haley, Alex. *Roots: The Saga of an American Family.* New York: Doubleday, 1976.

Hammerman, Shaina. "Reconstructing Woody: Representations of Religious Jewish Women in *Deconstructing Harry.*" In *Woody on Rye: Jewishness in the Films and Plays of Woody Allen.* Edited by Vincent Brook and Marat Grinberg. Lebanon, NH: Brandeis University Press, 2014. 171–189.

Hammerschlag, Sarah. *The Figural Jew: Politics and Identity in Postwar Jewish Thought.* Chicago: University of Chicago Press, 2010.

Heilman, Samuel, and Menachem Friedman. *The Rebbe: The Life and Afterlife of Menachem Mendel Schneerson*. Princeton, NJ: Princeton University Press, 2010.

Howe, Irving. *World of Our Fathers: The Journey of the East European Jews to America and the Life They Found and Made*. New York: New York University Press, 2005.

Hutcheon, Linda. *A Theory of Adaptation*. New York: Routledge, 2006.

Hyman, Paula. *Gender and Assimilation in Modern Jewish History: The Roles and Representations of Women*. Seattle: University of Washington Press, 1995.

Inbar, Donny. "A Closeted Jester: Abraham Goldfaden between Haskalah Ideology and Jewish Show Business." PhD dissertation, Graduate Theological Union, 2007.

Irigaray, Luce. "Women's Exile." *Ideology and Consciousness* 1 (May 1977): 62–76.

Jacobson, Matthew Frye. *Roots Too: White Ethnic Revival in Post–Civil Rights America*. Cambridge, MA: Harvard University Press, 2006.

Jay, Martin. "Taking on the Stigma of Inauthenticity: Adorno's Critique of Genuineness." *New German Critique* 97, no. 33 (2006): 15–30.

Kahn, Ava, and Marc Dollinger, eds. *California Jews*. Lebanon, NH: Brandeis University Press, 2003.

Lahr, John. "The Imperfectionist." *New Yorker*, December 9, 1996, 68–83.

Lax, Eric. *Conversations with Woody Allen*. New York: Alfred A. Knopf, 2007.

Levitt, Laura. "Impossible Assimilations, American Liberalism, and Jewish Difference: Revisiting Jewish Secularism." *American Quarterly* 59, no. 3 (2007): 807–832.

Malamud, Bernard. "Black Is My Favorite Color." In *The Stories of Bernard Malamud*. New York: Macmillan, 1983. 73–84.

Malcolm, Cheryl. "Othering the Other in Abraham Cahan's *Yekl: A Tale of the New York Ghetto*." *Amerikastudien / American Studies* 46, no. 2 (2001): 223–232.

Mazeau, Jacques, and Didier Thouart. *Les grands seconds rôles du cinéma français*. Paris: Editions PAC, 1984.

Mendelsohn, Ezra. *On Modern Jewish Politics*. Oxford: Oxford University Press, 1993.

Menegaldo, Gilles. "Woody Allen and France." In *A Companion to Woody Allen*. Edited by Peter J. Bailey and Sam B. Girgus. Malden, MA: Wiley-Blackwell, 2013. 53–72.

Michel, Sonya. "Yekl and Hester Street: Was Assimilation Really Good for the Jews?" *Literature/Film Quarterly* 5 (1977): 142–146.

Miller, Marc. *Representing the Immigrant Experience: Morris Rosenfeld and the Emergence of Yiddish Literature in America*. Syracuse, NY: Syracuse University Press, 2007.

Miron, Dan. *The Image of the Shtetl*. Syracuse, NY: Syracuse University Press, 2001.

Most, Andrea. *Making Americans: Jews and the Broadway Musical.* Cambridge, MA: Harvard University Press, 2004.

Mufti, Aamir. *Enlightenment in the Colony: The Jewish Question and the Crisis of Postcolonial Culture.* Princeton, NJ: Princeton University Press, 2007.

Mulvey, Laura. "Afterthoughts . . . Inspired by *Duel in the Sun*." *Framework* 15–17 (Summer 1981): 12–15.

———. "Visual Pleasure and Narrative Cinema." *Screen* 16, no. 3 (1975): 6–18.

Newton, Esther. *Mother Camp: Female Impersonators in America.* Chicago: University of Chicago Press, 1972.

Oury, Gérard. *Ma grande vadrouille.* Paris: Plon, 2001.

———. *Mémoires d'éléphant.* Paris: Olivier Orban, 1988.

Ozick, Cynthia. "Toward Yavneh." In *What Is Jewish Literature?* Edited by Hana Wirth-Nesher. New York: Jewish Publication Society, 1994. 20–35.

Pollitt, Katha. "Whose Culture?" In *Is Multiculturalism Bad for Women?* Edited by Susan Moller Okin. Princeton, NJ: Princeton University Press, 1999. 27–30.

Prell, Riv-Ellen. *Fighting to Become Americans: Assimilation and the Trouble between Jewish Women and Jewish Men.* Boston: Beacon Press, 1999.

Rabinovitch, Simon, ed. *Jews and Diaspora Nationalism: Writings on Jewish Peoplehood in Europe and the United States.* Lebanon, NH: Brandeis University Press, 2012.

Rapoport Albert, Ada, ed. *Hasidism Reappraised.* London: Valentine Mitchell, 1996.

Rapping, Elayne. "A Feminist's Love/Hate Relationship with Woody Allen." *Cineaste* 33, no. 3 (1998): 37–38.

Reitter, Paul. *On the Origins of Jewish Self-Hatred.* Princeton, NJ: Princeton University Press, 2012.

Ribalow, Harold. "The History of Henry Roth and *Call It Sleep*." Introduction to *Call It Sleep* by Henry Roth. Paterson: Pageant Books, 1960.

Rogin, Michael. *Blackface, White Noise: Jewish Immigrants in the Hollywood Melting Pot.* Berkeley: University of California Press, 1996.

Rollins, Peter, and John O'Connor, eds. *Hollywood's Indian: The Portrayal of Native Americans in Film.* Lexington: University Press of Kentucky, 1998.

Roskies, David. *The Search for a Useable Past.* Bloomington: Indiana University Press, 1999.

Ross, Kristin. *May '68 and Its Afterlives.* Chicago: University of Chicago Press, 2002.

Roth, Philip. *Goodbye, Columbus.* New York: Vintage Books, 1959.

Rozenblit, Marsha. *Reconstructing National Identity: The Jews of Habsburg Austria during WWI.* Oxford: Oxford University Press, 2001.

Rubel, Nora L. *Doubting the Devout: The Ultra-Orthodox in the Jewish American Imagination.* New York: Columbia University Press, 2010.

Rubinstein, Rachel. *Members of the Tribe: Native America in the Jewish Imagination.* Detroit: Wayne State University Press, 2010.

Sanders, Ronald. *Lost Tribes and Promised Lands: The Origins of American Racism.* New York: Perennial, 1992.
Sarna, Jonathan. *American Judaism.* New Haven, CT: Yale University Press, 2005.
Sartre, Jean-Paul. *Anti-Semite and Jew.* Translated by George J. Becker. New York: Schocken Books, 1948.
Schechter, Ron. *Obstinate Hebrews: Representations of Jews in France, 1715–1815.* Berkeley: University of California Press, 2003.
Schwartz, Vanessa. *It's So French: Hollywood, Paris, and the Making of Cosmopolitan Film Culture.* Chicago: University of Chicago Press, 2007.
Scott, Joan Wallach. *The Politics of the Veil.* Princeton, NJ: Princeton University Press, 2007.
Sebban, Michaël. *Lehaïm: À toutes les vies.* Paris: Hachette, 2004.
Sepinwall, Alyssa. "Sexuality, Orthodoxy and Modernity in France: North African Jewish Immigrants in Karin Albou's *La petite Jérusalem*." In *The Modern Jewish Experience in World Cinema.* Edited by Lawrence Baron. Lebanon, NH: Brandeis University Press. 340–347.
Sieg, Katrin. *Ethnic Drag: Performing Race, Nation, Sexuality in West Germany.* Ann Arbor: University of Michigan Press, 2002.
Silver, Joan Micklin, and Kenneth Turan. "A Wig, a Fence, and One White Horse." *Pakn Treger,* Fall 2003, 30–35.
Stam, Robert. "Introduction: The Theory and Practice of Adaptation." In *Literature and Film: A Guide to the Theory and Practice of Film Adaptation.* Edited by Robert Stam and Alessandra Raengo. Malden, MA: Blackwell, 2005. 1–52.
Stanislawski, Michael. *For Whom Do I Toil? Judah Leib Gordon and the Crisis of Russian Jewry.* Oxford: Oxford University Press, 1988.
Stora, Benjamin. "The Algerian War in French Memory: Vengeful Memory's Violence." In *Memory and Violence in the Middle East and North Africa.* Edited by Ussama Sadir Markdisi and Paul Silverstein. Bloomington: Indiana University Press, 2006. 151–174.
Tarr, Carrie. "French Cinema and Post-colonial Minorities." In *Post-colonial Cultures in France.* Edited by Alec Hargreaves and Marc McKinney. New York: Routledge, 1997. 59–83.
Todorov, Tzvetan. *The Fantastic: A Structural Approach to a Literary Genre.* Translated by Richard Howard. Ithaca, NY: Cornell University Press, 1975.
Turner, Frederick Jackson. *The Frontier in American History.* New York: Henry Holt and Company, 1920.
Whitfield, Stephen. "Fiddling with Sholem Aleichem: A History of *Fiddler on the Roof*." In *Key Texts in American Jewish Culture.* Edited by Jack Kugelmass. New Brunswick, NJ: Rutgers University Press, 2003. 105–125.
———. "Yentl." *Jewish Social Studies* 5, nos. 1–2 (Autumn 1998–Winter 1999): 154–176.

Whitman, Ruth. *Laughing Gas: Poems New and Selected, 1963–1990.* Detroit: Wayne State University Press, 1990.
Williams, Linda. *Hard Core: Power, Pleasure and the "Frenzy of the Visible."* Berkeley: University of California Press, 1989.
Williams, William Carlos. *Spring & All.* Paris: Contact Publishing Company, 1923.
Yezierska, Anzia. *Bread Givers.* New York: Persea Books, 2003.

INDEX

Page numbers in italics refer to figures.

Aaron, Caroline (as Doris), 63–69, 71
Abrams, Nathan, xiv
Academy Awards, 109
adaptation: as cultural process, xxvii, 105–116, 122–129; examples of, 47, 50n5, 118–120; theories of, 107–108, 116–118
Adaptation (film), 108
African-Americans. *See* blacks (racial identity and designation)
Aksenfeld, Israel, 104, 128
Albou, Karin, 86, 94–95, 113, 126
Aldrich, Robert, 42
Algeria, 45, 84, 86, 95; Oran, 98
aliyah, 96, 102
Allen, Woody, xxvii, 54–55, 62, 65, 69, 71, 127; American Apparel lawsuit, 55–58; and Hasidic imagery, 58–61, 70. *See also names of individual films*
American Apparel, 55–58, 72–73, 126, 134–135
American Tail, An, 2

Annie Hall, 22, 70; *Deconstructing Harry*, compared to, 63–66, 69–86; Easter dinner scene, 55–60, 73–74
antisemitism, 28, 34, 39–41, 91
Antler, Joyce, 105, 111
Arabs: in French history, 33, 37–38, 43, 47, 86; general representations of, xiv, xxii, xxv, 41–43, 46–47; in *Mauvaise foi*, 82, 84, 85; in *Le nom des gens*, 83–84, 85; in *La petite Jérusalem*, 91, 96–101; in *Rabbi Jacob*, 30–33, 34, 36–38, 46, 79, 89
Aramaic, 18, 116
Arkin, Kimberly, 98–99
Ashkenazic Jews, 38, 43–44, 86, 93, 99
assimilation: in America, xxi, xxiii–xxiv, 22; in France, 26, 28, 49; in *Frisco Kid*, 8, 22; in *Hester Street*, 125; in *The Jazz Singer*, 9, 22; theories of, 39, 105–106; in Woody Allen's films, 59, 70, 73, 105–106

Auschwitz, 83–84
authenticity: and adaptation, 108, 116; in *Deconstructing Harry*, 61; in *The Frisco Kid*, 4–6, 15, 20, 22–23; and gender, 59–60, 107, 124; Hasidim as authentic Jews, xiv, xxiv, 58–60, 71–72, 105, 132, 134, 136; in *Hester Street*, 113, 117–118, 120, 123; and Native Americans, 1–3, 22; in *Rabbi Jacob*, 45; representations of xiv, xxvi–xxvii, 1–6, 19; and translation, 18, 116, 127
aventures de Rabbi Jacob, Les: film, xv–xvi, xxiv, 26–50, 73; musical, 30, 47–48
"Awake, my People!," xix–xx. *See also* Gordon, Mikhl; Gordon, Yehudah Leib

ba'alei tshuvah, 65, 69
banlieue, 45, 86, 91, 94, 97, 101–102, 137. *See also* Sarcelles
bar mitzvahs, 39, 47, 66, 135
Barthes, Roland: "The Eiffel Tower," 41–42; "The Great Family of Man," 34–35, 41, 80, 92, 128; *Mythologies*, 41; "Striptease" 19–20, 22, 92
beards: as disguise, xix, 31–32, 38, 59, 68, 123; and gender, 100; Jews without beards, xii, 39, 72; as markers of religious piety, 63, 71, 123, 126, 133; and sexuality, 57–59, 68, 103n29; and shaving, 18, 109–111, 133; as signifiers of Jewishness xii, xviii–xix, xxiii, xxiv, xxviii, 33, 38, 58, 137
Berger, John, 60
Bhabha, Homi, 40–42
Bial, Henry, 46
billboards, 55–61, 68, 71, 126, 134
Bisoglio, Val, 11
black-and-white film, 113, 117, 120, 127, 129
blackface, 8–11, 21, 32–33, 36, 134–135

black hats, xiii, xxiii, 123, 136; in *The Frisco Kid*, 16; hijabs, compared to, 86; in *Rabbi Jacob*, 33; in Woody Allen's films, 59, 65, 72. *See also* hats
blacks (racial identity and designation): black Americans, xiii–xiv, xxii, xxv, 134; black French, 37, 42, 47, 86, 135; black Jews, 134–135; black liberation, 2, 118
Blauschild, Israel Mosche. *See* Dalio, Marcel
Blazing Saddles, 3
Bouzar, Dounia, 77
Brittany, 98
Broadway, xxiii, 22. *See also* musical theater
Brooklyn, 59, 72, 135
Brooks, Mel, 3. *See also* names of individual Brooks films
Butler, Judith, 32, 42, 45–46

caftans, xii, xviii–xix, xxiv, xxviii, 137
Cahan, Abraham, xxvii, 105–108, 111–117, 120–124, 127, 133
California, 4, 6; Los Angeles, xvii, 55; San Francisco, 2, 4–5, 13, 16, 23, 28. *See also* Hollywood
Canby, Vincent, 6, 8
Casablanca, 26
Catholics: Catholic habit, 133; Catholicism, 65; in France, xxii, xxvi–xxvii, 37–38, 42, 46, 137; and intermarriage, 32, 36; in *Le nom des gens*, 83–84
Cenac, Wyatt, xi–xiii, 132–135
chagrin et la pitié, Le, 55
Charlie Hebdo attack, 77–79
Charney, Dov, 56–58, 68, 72–74
Chosen, The, xv, 2
civil rights movement, 118. *See also under* blacks (racial identity and designation)

Clément, Aurore, 87–88, *93*
Clermont-Tonnerre, Count of, 82
Clifford, James, 1–3, 19–20, 22
Cohn-Bendit, Daniel, 36–37
collaboration, 39
colonialism, xxiii, 98–100; postcolonial theory, 40–41, 49
comédies communautaires. *See* ethnic comedies
communautarisme (communalism), 79, 81–82, 102
Cosma, Vladimir, 47
cowboys xxvi, 2, 6–11, 13–23, 28; "kosher cowboy," 4–6, 14, 23, 135
Cravenne, Danielle, 30, 46
Cravenne, Georges, 46
cross-dressing, 9, 46. *See also* drag
Crossing Delancey, 2
Curb Your Enthusiasm, 65–66

Daily Show, The, xi–xiv, xxiv–xxv, 132–134
Dalio, Marcel, 26–29, 42, 100; as Rabbi Jacob, 30–33, 39, 44, 48–50, 53
dance, 12–14, 21, 68, 109; Hasidic dance, 32, 34, 47, 50n5, 135–136
David, Larry, 65–66
Deconstructing Harry, xv, xxvii, 61–63, 66–67, 85, 133; *Annie Hall*, compared to, 64–65, 67–69, 72, 126; feminist reading of, 70–72; *La petite Jérusalem*, compared to, 92, 95, 107; and representations of women, 54–55, 63–64, 66–68
Deen, Shulem, 132
de France, Cecile (as Clara), 81–84, 89, 92, 95, 127
de Funès, Louis, xxvi, 26, 81; as Victor Pivert, 27–30, 33, 35, 43, 45–50
de Gaulle, Charles, 35–36
Diner, Hasia, 105, 117, 119

divorce, 109–111, 117–118, 121–122, 128
Doane, Mary Ann, 69–71
drag: ethnic, 20–21; Jewish, 32–33, 58–60; theories of, 42, 45–48, 134–135; Wild West, 9, 28. *See also* cross-dressing
Dreyfus affair, 36–37

eastern Europe, xvii, 2, 14, 44, 136; Poland, 4–5, 9, 11, 15, 19, 28, 44; Romania, xix, 10, 132, 136; Russia, xix–xx, 44, 104
Ebert, Roger, 6, 8
Ellis Island, xxii–xxiii
emancipation, xxi, 30, 41
enlightenment, xviii, 36; Jewish enlightenment (*see* Haskalah)
eruv, xvii, xxviii, 137; on *The Daily Show*, xi–xiv, xxiv, xxv, 132, 135
ethnic comedies, xvi, 79–81, 85, 88, 92, 102. *See also names of individual films*
ethnic revival; xxi, 2, 118
Everything You Always Wanted to Know About Sex, 58–59
ewige Jude, Der, xxiv

Fading Gigolo, 57
Farrow, Mia, 57, 59, 68, 72
FEMEN, 93–94
feminism, 21, 93, 125; in *Hester Street*, 111, 113, 118–120, 122, 124; second-wave feminism, 106, 117, 119; and Woody Allen, 60–61, 69–72, 127
Fiddler on the Roof, 1–2
Finkielkraut, Alain, 43–44, 47, 90, 101, 126
Ford, Harrison (as Tommy Lillard), 1, 4–22, 127
Forestier, Sara (as Baya Benmahmoud), 83–84, 89, 92, 127
France 2 (TV network), 46, 77
French revolution, xv, 28, 90

Freud, Sigmund, 26, 70
Frisco Kid, The, xv, xxvi, 1–23, 92, 95, 135; *Annie Hall*, compared to, 123; *Les aventures de Rabbi Jacob*, compared to, xxiv, xxvi, 28, 46, 48, 54, 58, 96, 107; *Hester Street*, compared to, 127–128; *The Jazz Singer*, compared to, xxiii; as object of nostalgia, xvi
Front National, 37–38
Funkenstein, Amos, 50
Furnish, Ben, 14–15

Gaddis, John Lewis, xi
Gamblin, Jacques (as Arthur Martin), 83–84, 89, 127
Garber, Marjorie, 133
gender, xv, xxiv, xxv, 79, 93; in adaptation theory, 110–112; in *The Frisco Kid*, 8–9; in *Hester Street*, 124–126; theories of, 21, 42–43, 45–46, 59–61, 69–71, 133–134; and Woody Allen, 61–69
gentiles, 23, 41, 59, 65, 112, 114; audiences, 38, 46; disguised as Jewish, xxiv, 28; Jewish-gentile romance, 7–8, 77–102; in Jewish law, 17–18; and the Jewish Question, 49–50, 59, 65, 127; and passing, xxvi, 54, 83, 112, 126; women, 114–117. *See also* Goyim
Germany xv, xvi, 6, 36, 50, 77; German Jews, 27, 36–37; Munich Olympic Games, 37
gestures: and passing, 44, 60; performance, xix, 32; as signifiers of Jewishness, xxii, 32, 58, 64. *See also* mannerisms
ghetto, xi, xxi, 113, 114, 116
ghetto girls, 120, 122. *See also* Jewish American Princess
Giraud, Claude (as Mohamed Larbi Slimane): and French relations, 37–38; and Gérard Oury, 46–47; in Hasidic disguise, 31–32; and Jewish-Arab relations, 34, 127–128; as sex symbol, 43, 89
Goldfaden, Abraham, xix–xx, xxii, xxiv
Goodman, Hazelle (as Cookie) 62, 63
Gordon, Mikhl, xx, xxii, 136
Gordon, Yehudah Leib, xix, xx, xxii, 20
Gould, Elliot, 62
Goyim, xxvi, 112, 114, 116–117, 126. *See also* gentiles
grande illusion, La, 26
Great Family of Man, The (exhibit), 34–35, 41, 80, 92. *See also* Barthes, Roland
Grodner, Israel, xix–xx, xxii, 136; compared to other performers, xxiv, xxviii, 10, 53, 132
Guybet, Henri (as Salomon), 30–31, 34, 46

habits. *See* Catholics
hair, xxvi, 54, 73, 85, 104; in *Deconstructing Harry*, 63, 65, 67–69; in *The Frisco Kid*, 11; in Hester Street, 104–117, 122, 126, 127–128, 133; in *La petite Jérusalem*, 92, 94–95, 100
Hammerschlag, Sarah, 36
hard-core pornography, 53–54, 60, 72, 95
haredim, xviii
Harper's Bazaar Indonesia, 73
Hasidic garb, 132; as costume, xix, 58, 59, 70, 136; history of, xiii, xviii; and potential sex appeal, 54, 93–95; women's attire, 72–73, 109, 111. *See also specific items of garb*
Hasidim, xiii–xxviii, 13, 31, 58, 73, 102; black Hasidim, 134–135; song, 39–40, 48–49. *See also* authenticity: Hasidim

as authentic Jews; dance: Hasidic dance; Lubavitcher Hasidim, Satmar Hasidim
Haskalah, xvii–xxiii, 137
hats, xii, 123; bandana, 16, 18, 22–23; cowboy hat, 11, 16, 19; "eruv hat," xiii–xiv, 135; feathered hat, 123–124; fedora, xviii, 123; homburg, xviii; top hat, xix; turban, 89, 100. *See also* black hats, shtreimel
headscarf ban, 90, 94, 98, 101, 110
headscarves, 77, 89–92, 100–101, 123. *See also* headscarf ban; hijab; kerchief
Hebrew, xix–xx, 18, 55, 67, 116–117
Hester Street, xvi, xxiii, xxvii, 104–129, 133
hijab, 133, 136–37. *See also* headscarves
hipsters, 135–36
History of the World: Part I, 2
Hollywood: filmic conventions, 4, 6–8, 15; France, in relation to, xv–xvi, 55; and Marcel Dalio, 26–27
Holocaust, xxiii, 44, 55, 79, 99, 136
Holy Rollers, xxiv, 126
homme est une femme comme les autres, L', xv, 48
Honeymoon Motel, 59
Howe, Irving, 118–119, 128
Hutcheon, Linda, 106, 108
Hypercacher attack, 77–78, 99

#Iam. *See* #jesuis
immigration, xxiii–xxiv, 30; and ethnic revival, 2, 118–119; to France, 45, 83, 85–86, 95; in French national discourse, 37, 81, 83, 89, 91, 98–99; in *The Frisco Kid*, 5; in *Hester Street*, xvi, xxiii, xxvii, 104–118, 120–121, 127; in *The Jazz Singer*, 8, 22
Indians. *See* Native Americans

Indonesia, 73
intermarriage, 3, 32, 34, 43, 95, 101
Islamophobia, 137
Israel, 14, 46–47; immigration to, 96, 102; war and conflict with, 33–34, 37

Jacobson, Matthew Frye, xxi–xxii, 134
Jazz Singer, The, xxiii, 8–10, 21–22
#jesuis, 77–79, 102
Jewface, 134; in *The Frisco Kid*, 9–10, 21; in *Rabbi Jacob*, 32, 36, 45
Jewish American Princess, 122. *See also* ghetto girls
Jewish Question, the, 28–30, 38, 49–50
Jewish self-hatred, xxvii, 55, 57, 65–66, 72

Kadosh, 95
Kane, Carol (as Gitl), 105, 109, 120–23
Kasmi, Baya, 83, 86
Kautman, Charlie, 108, 127
Keats, Stephen (as Jake), 104–106, 108–128, 133
kerchief, 105, 110, 125. *See also* headscarves; wigs
klezmer, 34

laïcité, 86, 90. *See also* secularism
Leclerc, Michel, 83, 86
Lehaïm: A toutes les vies, 96–99
Le Pen, Jean-Marie, 37. *See also* Front National
Levitt, Laura, xxiii–xxiv, 39
Libération, 77, 92
Los Angeles, xvii, 55
Love and Death, 59
Lower East Side, xxiii, 39, 53, 113, 118
Lubavitcher Hasidim, 48–49, 55. *See also* Schneerson, Rebbe Menachem Mendel

Malamud, Bernard, 112
Malcolm, Cheryl, 112
Manhattan, 39, 55
mannerisms, 14, 41, 44, 69. *See also* gestures
"Ma Normandie" (song), 39–40, 49
"Marseillaise, La," 48
masculinity, 7–8, 59–60, 70, 75n22
Mauvaise foi, 80–85, 88, 95–96
May 1968, 35–38, 43, 77–79, 101
MC Solaar, 47–48, 50n5
Mendelssohn, Moses, xix–xx
mezuzahs, 39, 82
mikvah, 87–88, 92–93, 93
modesty, xxvii, 54, 87, 90–93
Montebello, Fabrice, 80
Moore, Demi (as Helen), 66–70, 67
Mosaïque, 98–99
mothers, 43, 81–87, 90–91, 96, 119; Jewish American Mother, 122
Mufti, Aamir, xxv, xxvii, 13
multiculturalism, xiii, xvi, xxiv, 127, 137; in America xxi–xxii, 20, 106, 119, 125, 132–133; in France xxi–xxii, 30, 32–43, 49, 101
musical theater, xvi, 30, 47, 106. *See also* Broadway
Muslims: attire, 126, 133, 136–137; as identity category, xiv, xxv, 110; Jewish-Muslim relations, xvi, xxvii, 77–102; population in France, 38, 45

national identity, viii, xvii, xxi, xxvi; American national identity, 133–134; French national identity, 34, 37–38, 42, 46–49, 80–82, 90
nationalism: American, xxii; Arab, 37–38; black, 118; French, 34, 35, 38, 95
Native Americans, xiv, xxv, 3–4, 10; Wampanoag trial in Mashpee, 1–4, 20, 22–23; in western film, 3, 9–14
Nativeface, 10, 11

Nazism, xxiii, 26–28, 34, 39, 44, 49; propaganda xxiv, 100, 132
New Testament, 116–117
Newton, Esther, 59–60, 134–35
New York, 104, 109, 113. *See also* Brooklyn; Lower East Side; Manhattan
New York Magazine, 134–35
niggunim. *See* Hasidim: song
nom des gens, Le, 80, 83–85, 88, 96. *See also* names of individual actors and screenwriters from the film
Normandy, 30, 39–40, 49. *See also* "Ma Normandie" (song)
North Africa, 41, 43, 45, 81–86, 89, 98–99; immigrants, 81, 83, 84. *See also* names of specific countries
nostalgia, xiv–xviii, 2, 14–15, 28, 44
"Nous sommes tous . . . ," 36, 77, 79. *See also* #jesuis
Nouvelle Vague, 30
November 2015 Paris attacks, 78–79

OPEC (Organization of the Petroleum Exporting Countries), 33–34
Oury, Gérard, 26–27, 33–34, 38, 42–50, 53
Ozick, Cynthia, 41

Palestinian liberation, 37–38, 46–47, 82
Pan-Arabism. *See under* nationalism
Paris: Hollywood, compared to, xv–xvi, xxi; and Jewish imagery, xvii, 26–27, 33, 36–39, 47–49; and *La petite Jérusalem*, 86, 96, 98, 101–102; and *Rabbi Jacob*, 30–33, 34, 39–41, 45–46, 49; responses to terrorism, 77–80, 102
passing, 22, 49, 54, 83, 85, 101
patch. *See* wigs
petite Jérusalem, La, xxvii, 85–102, 107, 113, 125–126, 137
peyos, xviii, 72; as costume, xxiii, xxiv, 48, 136; in *Hester Street*, 110, 123; in

Rabbi Jacob, 31–33, 47–48, 52n43; as visual shorthand for Jewishness, xii, xix, xxiii, xxviii, 38, 58, 132–133; in Woody Allen's films, 59, 68
phylacteries. *See* tefilin
piety: and authenticity, 71, 85, 136; Hasidic dress as symbol of, xxiii, 133, 135–136; and modesty, 92–94, 110; and sexuality, 53, 57, 68, 73, 85, 110, 126; and wigs, 110, 114–115, 117, 126
police: in French history, 37, 43, 46, 78; in *Le nom des gens*, 84; in *La petite Jérusalem*, 91; and *Rabbi Jacob*, 30–31, 47, 78
Pollitt, Katha, 119
Pompidou, Georges, 35
posters, 26–28, 33, 49–50, 100
prayer, 22, 48, 67; Ashkenazic, 87, 93–95, 101; Indian, 12–13
prayer shawl. *See* tallis
Prell, Riv Ellen, 111–113, 120, 127
Previn, Soon Yi, 57, 62, 68, 72, 75n13
Price Above Rubies, A, 126
pride movements, xvi, 2, 112, 118, 136
Protestants, xxi, xxiii, 25n24, 111; WASPs, 59, 137
Protests: anti-gay, 136; FEMEN, 93–94; May 1968, 36–37; and multiculturalism, xxi; and Palestinian cause, 30, 34, 46, 77, 101; and Twitter, 78

Qu'est-ce qu'on a fait au bon Dieu? xvi, 80

rabbis, 135–137; in *The Frisco Kid*, 2–24, 127–128; in *Hester Street*, 111; in *Rabbi Jacob*, 26–50; in Woody Allen's films, 58–59, 68. *See also* Schneerson, Rebbe Menachem Mendel
race, xxv, 98, 132, 134–135; and antisemitism, xxiv, 28; white race, xxi–xxii, xxiv, 2–3, 8–14, 37–38, 118. *See also* blackface; racism; *and specific racial designations (Arab, black, Native American, etc.)*
racism, xxiii, 11, 35; in *Rabbi Jacob*, 30, 41–43; racist Jews, 99. *See also* antisemitism; blackface
Ramadan, 82
rap, 30, 47–48
règle du jeu, La, 26, 27
Renoir, Jean, 26
republicanism (French), 28, 79–81, 90, 92, 96–101
retroversion, 116–118, 124, 127. *See also* translation (theory)
Riviere, Joan, 70
Roberts, Doris (as Mrs. Kavarsky), 110, 114–115, 115, 121–123
Rogin, Michael, 8–10, 134. *See also* blackface
Romania, xix, 10, 132, 136
Roncin, Joachim, 78
Roots (novel and miniseries), 118
Ross, Kristin, 35–37
Roth, Henry, 118
Roth, Philip, 123–24
Rubinstein, Rachel, 3–4
rue des Rosiers, 34, 38, 42, 44–45, 100, 135, 137

Sabbath xi, 16–18, 30, 96
Sarcelles, 86, 91, 96, 98, 100
Satmar Hasidim, 73
Schneerson, Rebbe Menachem Mendel, 48–49, 55
Schwartz, Vanessa, xv–xvi
Scott, Joan Wallach, 77, 89–90
Sebban, Michaël, 96–97, 99
secularism, xxi, 85–86; secular Jews xvii–xix, xxii–xxvi, 10, 13, 21, 23, 43–44, 48–49, 60, 65–69, 73, 105, 133–137; secular Muslims, 89–90, 97, 100. *See also* laïcité

Seidman, Naomi, 116–17
Sephardic Jews, 48, 81, 99
September 11th attacks, 77
Serious Man, A, xxiv, 135
Shakespeare, William, 1, 3–4, 41
shtreimel, 104, 123; as costume, xviii, xix; as fashion, 73; in *Rabbi Jacob*, 32, 99. *See also* black hats; hats
sidelocks. *See* peyos
Silver, Joan Micklin, 104–129, 130n19
slogans, 36–38, 77–78, 98, 101. *See also* #jesuis; "Nous sommes tous . . ."
Some Like It Hot, 45
Stam, Robert, 106–108, 110, 124–25
Stewart, Jon, xi–xiii, 134
Stranger Among Us, A, 2, 126
Streisand, Barbra, 106
Striptease (movie), 68
sweatshops, 109, 114
synagogues, xii, xxiii, 5, 15–16, 44, 96, 135; Holy Temple, 44

Take the Money and Run, 58
tallis, 93
Talmud, 17–19, 126, 135
Tarr, Carrie, 80–81
tefilin, 52n42, 93
terrorism, 30, 46–47, 77–79, 100. *See also* names *of individual terrorist attacks*
Thompson, Danièle, 38, 47, 49–50
Tillete de Clermont Tonnerre, Hédi (as Djamel), 87–89, 91–92, 94–96, 98–101
Todeschini, Bruno (as Ariel), 86–87, 91–93, 96, 98, 101
Todorov, Tzvetan, 132
Tootsie, 45
Torah, xvii, 15, 101; scroll, 5–6, 11–12, 15–18, 21, 23
translation (theory), xxvii, 18, 10–106, 114–117, 126, 129
Transparent, 53

trials, 1–4, 22–23, 57. *See also* Allen, Woody: American Apparel lawsuit; Native Americans: Wampanoag trial in Mashpee
Trigano, Shmuel, 78–79
Tucci, Stanley (as Epstein), 66–69, *67*
Tumblr, 135
Tunisia, 86, 90–91, 95–96
Turner, Frederick Jackson, 9–10
Turturro, John, 59
Twitter, 78, 102n2
tzitzit, 16, 20, 136

Valette, Fanny (as Laura), 86–102, *87*
Valls, Manuel, 77, 99
veil. *See* headscarves; hijab
vérité si je mens, La, 48
Vichy regime, 36–39, 43
Vishniac, Roman, 113, 130n19

weddings: in *The Frisco Kid*, 5, *5*, 21, 96, 128; in *Rabbi Jacob*, 30–31, 34, 96. *See also* intermarriage
Weisshaus, Yoel, 72–74
western (film genre), 3, 8–11, 14–15, 23, 28; revisionist western, 10–11, 13
wigs, xxvii, 11, 54, 65, 85, 133; in *Hester Street*, 104–129
Wilder, Gene, 3; as Rabbi Avram Belinski, 4–23, 28, 46, 123, 127–128, 135
Wild West, 2–3, 6–7, 9, 12, 14–17, 127. *See also* western (film genre)
Williams, Linda, 53–54, 72
Williams, William Carlos, 128
World War II, 35. *See also* Holocaust

yarmulke: as costume, 19–20, 23, 123, 126; as way to differentiate Jewish types, 63, 73, 111
Yekl, 105, 108–109, 112–114, 119, 126–127
Yentl, 2, 53, 106

Yezierska, Anzia, 119
Yiddish, 18; accent, 3, 15–16, 32, 39–40, 42, 59; in *Hester Street*, 105, 113–117, 120–121, 124, 127–129; as signifier of Jewish authenticity, 10–11, 37, 55–56, 62; theater, xx, xix, xxiv, 136
Yom Kippur War, 38, 46

Zelig, 58, 68
Zem, Roschdy, 81, 86; as Ismael, 81–84, 89, 128
Zionism, 14, 30, 37, 63
Zylberstein, Elsa (as Mathilde), 87–93, 101–102

SHAINA HAMMERMAN is a cultural historian and media critic who writes about representations of race, religion, ethnicity, and nationality on screens big and small. She holds a PhD in Jewish history and culture from the Graduate Theological Union. She writes and teaches in the San Francisco Bay Area.

www.ingramcontent.com/pod-product-compliance
Lightning Source LLC
Chambersburg PA
CBHW050110170426
43198CB00014B/2521